# Perspectives

## on

## Public Bureaucracy

# Perspectives
# on
# Public Bureaucracy

## A Reader on Organization

THIRD EDITION

♦

Edited with Introductions by
*Fred A. Kramer*
University of Massachusetts, Amherst

Winthrop Publishers, Inc.
*Cambridge, Massachusetts*

Library of Congress Cataloging in Publication Data

Kramer, Fred A    1941–    comp.
  Perspectives on public bureaucracy.

  Includes bibliographical references.
  1. Public administration—Addresses, essays,
lectures.    2. Organizations—Addresses, essays,
lectures.    3. Bureaucracy—Addresses, essays, lectures.
I. Title.
JF1351.K7    1981        350        80–26393
ISBN 0–87626–659–6

*Cover design by Janis Capone*

*Copyright © 1981, 1977, 1973 by Winthrop Publishers, Inc.*
17 Dunster Street, Cambridge, Massachusetts 02138

10   9   8   7   6   5   4   3   2   1

*For Matilda Hider*

# Contents

◆

# Preface

I HAVE ALWAYS BEEN fascinated by large organizations. Organization and decision theories, managerial styles, and the behavior of people in organizations affect an organization's ability to deal with its environment. There is no "one best way" to treat these aspects of an organization; what is "best" depends on the situation confronting the organization at a particular time.

This collection of articles and explanatory essays presents several perspectives on how public bureaucracies might deal with these issues. If the student or practitioner has been exposed to various perspectives, he or she will be more able to understand the motives and actions of the people with whom he or she works. Hopefully, such an understanding will suggest means for coping with the situation at hand and will reduce the frustration of trying to change large-scale organizations.

I have chosen these selections from a variety of sources because, in my experience in federal, state, and local governments, they reflect the way some managers deal with organizational problems in public bureaucracies. The theoretical orientation of the readings is by design. Mason Haire has suggested that "all managerial policies have a theory behind them," although the theory is generally implicit.[1] Managers generally use practical techniques to solve problems that confront them. They often do not recognize the theoretical foundation that governs most of their behavior. It

---

[1] *Psychology in Management* (New York: McGraw-Hill, 1964), p. 19.

*ix*

is my hope that these articles will bring the theoretical perspectives into the open.

In commenting on the first edition of *Perspectives*, the late Wallace Sayre suggested that I add articles that emphasize the political dimension more. Sayre used to say that "public and private management are similar in all the unimportant ways."[2] My orientation is to see political implications in virtually everything, so I did not explicitly emphasize power and politics in the selections for the earlier editions. In this edition, however, I have finally taken Sayre's advice by adding the Eugene Lewis selection.

There are, however, political implications for the reader to discover in all the articles. Private sector experience cannot be transplanted to the public sector without pruning and grafting. The purpose of these selections is to encourage the reader to think of the possibilities of improving public management. Which managerial theories and techniques work in the public sector? Which ones can be made to work?

I wish to thank Jim Murray and John Covell of Winthrop Publishers and Raeia Maes for their help at various stages in this project and with the companion volume, *Dynamics of Public Bureaucracy*, which is coming out in a new edition. I also want to express my deep gratitude to the authors of these selections.

I welcome hearing from students, teachers, and practicing public administrators about suggestions for future editions.

*F. A. K.*

---

[2] Quoted in Joseph L. Bower, "Effective Public Management," *Harvard Business Review* 55: 132 (March-April 1977).

# Perspectives
## on
# Public Bureaucracy

# Bureaucracy
## and
## Environmental Change

◆

WE DO NOT HAVE to look far to find areas in which governmental action has not been very successful. Discrimination in housing, poverty, crime, and racism are just a few issues that have resisted governmental efforts to solve them. Many public programs have not lived up to the reasonable expectations of their designers. The reasons for these policy failures are complex, but part of the explanation lies in failures of public management to mobilize both internal resources of government and the external resources of politics. Usually public management is concerned with techniques of internal management, but, as Norton Long has pointed out, public management is doomed to failure unless it can gain the support needed to do the job from the larger political system.[1]

This volume presents several perspectives on public management. By understanding the nature of bureaucratic organization and its relationship to the political environment, persons working in the public sector might be better able to accomplish the public's business. And such knowledge might make those outside the public sector more effective in dealing with public bureaucracies.

Warren Bennis, who has been in the forefront of managerial change for over two decades as a researcher, consultant, and university president, is a strong believer in participative management. Indeed, Bennis has claimed that *"democracy becomes a functional necessity whenever a social system is competing for survival under conditions of chronic change."*[2] To Bennis, democracy is a system of beliefs that governs behavior, and one of the main values of this belief system is a search for truth. Under conditions of change, people in organizations must make

*1*

decisions based on information that reflects reality. Many rigid bureaucratic organizations distort information. These organizations might make decisions that appear to conform to the information they have, but if the information has been systematically distorted in some way, the decision will be incorrect. If an organization makes too many incorrect decisions, it will not survive.

Although Bennis deals with the private sector in the article that follows, he is concerned with the internal and external processes, both of which affect public bureaucracies. His term *reciprocity* deals with the conflicts between individuals and the organizations for which they work—the internal aspects. Some of the organization theories he refers to in his overview will be dealt with in detail in this volume. *Adaptability* refers to the organization's ability to deal with its external environment. It used to be assumed that the external environment of private-sector organizations was quite stable. Now it appears that "environmental turbulence" caused by many factors, including increased governmental involvement, may threaten the ability of firms to achieve their stated objectives. The politically charged environments of public bureaucracies have often been subject to changes that challenge their survival.

Using the Bennis article as a preview of organizational theories, which you will be able to study in more depth later, what kind of additional information might you want to assess his contention that "we will all witness and participate in the end of bureaucracy"? Is he talking about all levels of organization? Or just the top levels? Where do the top levels stop? If public bureaucracies adopted the structural reforms advocated by Bennis to resolve the reciprocity problem, how might that affect citizens?

## PERSPECTIVES

Observers of public bureaucracies have long been concerned with adaptability to the environment. John Gaus, writing in the thirties and forties, saw public organizations tied to their physical and social surroundings. Gaus sought to explain the actions of public bureaucracies with reference to "people, place, physical technology, social technology, wishes and ideas, catastrophe, and personality." He thought these referents would explain "why particular activities are undertaken through government and the problems of policy, organization and management generally that result" from governmental action or inaction.[3]

Key aspects of the environment of a public agency are the special relationships that develop between the agency and its clientele, the agency and the legislative committees that control its programs and budget, and the clientele and the legislative committees. These relationships, which are depicted in figure 1, tend to be mutually beneficial for the participants. To use a biological metaphor, they are *symbiotic.* These symbiotic relationships have been called "policy whirlpools," "policy subsystems," and "interest group liberalism" by a generation of political scientists.[4]

These symbiotic triangles develop because power in a complex modern society tends to be decentralized. Central executives, the top of the governmental executive hierarchy, cannot be expected to be knowledgeable and concerned with all aspects of policy that are theoretically under their control. Because of the lack of support from the upper levels of the hierarchy, the agencies generally do not have enough power to carry out their mandates. They often must rely on the clientele to help them develop and enforce regulations or mobilize support. This reliance on clientele tends to make the agencies be "reasonable" in regulating the clientele and expansive in providing services to them.

Because the agencies are beholden to the legislature for money and program authorization, they want to help those legislators who are in positions to help or harm them. These people are generally those in leadership positions or on the committees and subcommittees that directly affect the work of the agencies. The agencies can see that favored legislators get certain programs for their districts—a practice that helps legislators get reelected. The clientele is also in a position to help legislators get reelected. Clientele can deliver campaign contributions—and in some cases votes—to key legislators who support favored agency programs.

But the policy triangle does not explain why some interests are effective in influencing policy and others are not. More important, it tends to deal with groups, not citizens. In a government of the people, by the people, and for the people, the role of citizens in dealing with their government is important. Eugene Lewis presents a more sophisticated

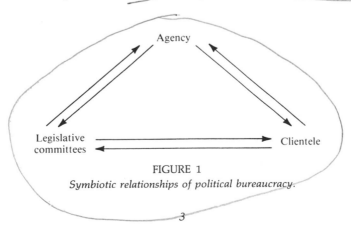

FIGURE 1
*Symbiotic relationships of political bureaucracy.*

version of the symbiotic triangle by dividing what we have called clientele into three categories—constituents, clients, and victims.

As you read the Lewis article assess the worth of these categories. Do they significantly add to the understanding of the environment in which agencies operate? Do agency relations concerned primarily with treating citizens in one of these three ways contribute to the stability of the environment or radically alter stability? Do these categories help explain changes in agency policies?

## NOTES

1. Norton Long, "Power and Administration," *Public Administration Review* 9: 257–64 (Autumn 1949).

2. Warren G. Bennis and Philip E. Slater, *The Temporary Society*, vol. 4 (New York: Harper & Row, 1968), p. 4. Emphasis in the original.

3. John Gaus, *Reflections on Public Administration* (University, Alabama: University of Alabama Press, 1947), p. 9.

4. One of the best books on this relationship is Grant McConnell, *Private Power and American Democracy* (New York: Alfred A. Knopf, 1966). Also see A. Lee Fritschler, *Smoking and Politics*, 2nd. ed. (Englewood Cliffs, N.J.: Prentice-Hall, 1975) and Theodore Lowi, *The End of Liberalism*, 2nd. ed. (New York: W. W. Norton & Company, 1979).

# 1

# Organizational Developments and the Fate of Bureaucracy

♦

*Warren G. Bennis*

ORGANIZATIONS ARE COMPLEX, GOAL-SEEKING social units. In addition to the penultimate task of realizing goals, they must undertake two related tasks if they are to survive: 1) they must maintain the internal system and coordinate the "human side," and 2) they must adapt to and shape the external environment.

The means employed for the first task is a complicated system of social processes which somehow or other gets organizations and their participants to accommodate to their respective goals. This process of mutual compliance, where the two parties conform to and accommodate one another, is called *reciprocity*. The means for the second task has to do with the way the organization transacts and exchanges with its environment; this is called *adaptability*.

The social arrangement developed to accomplish the tasks of reciprocity and adaptability in contemporary society is called bureaucracy. I use that term descriptively, not as an epithet or as a metaphor *à la* Kafka's *Castle*, which conjures up an image of red tape, faceless masses standing in endless lines, and despair. Bureaucracy, as I use it, is a social invention, perfected during the Industrial Revolution to organize and direct the activities of the firm and later (at the turn of the century) conceptualized by the great German sociologist, Max Weber.

*Reprinted from "Organizational Developments and the Fate of Bureaucracy," by Warren G. Bennis,* Sloan Management Review, *Vol. 7, No. 2, pp. 41–55, by permission of the publisher. Copyright © 1966 by the Sloan Management Review Association. All rights reserved.*

Ironically, though Weber worked heroically to create a value-free science, the term bureaucracy has taken on such negative connotations that even dictionaries use the term in the vernacular. For example, the *Oxford Dictionary* quotes Carlyle as saying: "The Continental nuisance called 'Bureaucracy'." It also defines a bureaucrat as "one who endeavors to concentrate power in his bureau." However empirically valid these descriptions may be, bureaucracy in a more technical sense, revered in theory by sociologists and in practice by most businessmen, has become the most successful and popular device for achieving the major tasks of organization. To paraphrase Churchill's ironic remark about democracy, we can say of bureaucracy that it is the worst possible theory of organization, apart from all others that have so far been tried.

Now is the time to challenge the conceptual and empirical foundations of bureaucracy. To jump to my conclusion first, I will argue that bureaucracy which has served us so well in the past, both as an "ideal type" and a practical form of organization, will not survive as the dominant form of human organization in the future. Social organizations behave like other organisms: they transform themselves through selective adaptation, and new shapes, patterns, models—currently recessive—are emerging which promise basic changes. This argument is based on the assertion that the methods and social processes employed by bureaucracy to cope with its internal environment (reciprocity) and its external (adaptability) are hopelessly out of joint with contemporary realities. So within the next 25 to 50 years we will all witness and participate in the end of bureaucracy.[1]

The remainder of this paper elaborates this viewpoint. First, I shall take up the problem of linkage one: how organizations get men to comply, the problem of reciprocity. In this section I shall discuss how contemporary psychologists and students of organizational behavior attempt to resolve this issue. Then I shall discuss the second crucial linkage: adaptability, and then present current thinking about this. Finally, I shall sketch the conditions and structure for organizations of the future.

## 1. LINKAGE ONE:
### THE PROBLEM OF RECIPROCITY

The problem of reciprocity, like most human problems, has a long and venerable past. The modern version of this one goes back at least 160 years and was precipitated by an historical paradox: the twin births of modern individualism and modern industrialism. The one brought about a deep concern for the constitutional guarantees of personal rights and a passionate interest in individual emotions and growth. The other brought about increased rationalization and mechanization of organized activity.

*Individualism & industrialization*

By coinciding, the growth of technology and enterprise tended to subvert the newly won individual freedoms and to subordinate them to the impersonal dictates of the workplace. . . .

In its crudest form, the controversy is a conflict over priorities of criteria: the individual's needs, motives, goals, and growth *versus* the organization's goals and rights. . . .

## Enter Bureaucracy

Bureaucracy is a unique solution in that it links man s needs to organizational goals. It achieves this linkage through an influence structure based on *legal-rational* grounds instead of on the vagaries of personal power. The governed agree to obey through the rights of office and the power of reason: superiors rule because of their role incumbency and their technical (rational) competence. In short, bureaucracy is a machine of social influence which relies exclusively on reason and law. Weber once likened the bureaucratic mechanism to a judge *qua* computer:

> Bureaucracy is like a modern judge who is a vending machine into which the pleadings are inserted together with the fee and which then disgorges the judgement together with its reasons mechanically derived from the code.[2]

The bureaucratic machine model was developed as a reaction against the personal subjugation, nepotism, cruelty, emotional vicissitudes and subjective judgments which passed for managerial practices in the early days of the Industrial Revolution. For Weber, the true hope for man lay in his ability to rationalize, calculate, to use his head, as well as his hands and heart. Roles, institutionalized and reinforced by legal tradition, rather than personalities; rationality and predictability, rather than irrationality and unanticipated consequences; impersonality, rather than close personal relations; technical competence rather than arbitrary rule or iron whims—these are the main characteristics of bureaucracy.

This is bureaucracy: the pyramidal organization which dominates so much of our thinking and planning related to organizational behavior, and which mediates the organization-individual dilemma through a rational system of role constraints.

## Critiquing Bureaucracy

It does not take a great critical imagination to detect the flaws and problems in the bureaucratic model. We have all *experienced* them: bosses with less technical competence than their underlings; arbitrary and zany rules; an informal organization which subverts or replaces the formal apparatus; confusion and conflict among roles; and cruel treatment of subordinates based not on rational grounds but on quasi-legal, or worse, inhumane grounds. . . .

Almost everybody . . . approaches bureaucracy with a chip on his shoulder. It has been attacked for many different reasons: for theoretical confusion and contradictions, for moral and ethical reasons, on practical grounds or for inefficiency, for methodological weaknesses, for containing too many implicit values and for containing too few. . . . The criticisms can be categorized as the following:

a. Bureaucracy does not adequately allow for the personal growth and the development of mature personalities.

b. It develops conformity and "group-think."

c. It does not take into account the "informal organization" and the emergent and unanticipated problems.

d. Its systems of control and authority are hopelessly outdated.

e. It has no adequate juridicial process.

f. It does not possess adequate means for resolving differences and conflicts between ranks, and most particularly, between functional groups.

g. Communication (and innovative ideas) are thwarted or distorted due to hierarchical divisions.

h. The full human resources of bureaucracy are not utilized due to mistrust, fear of reprisals, etc.

i. It cannot assimilate the influx of new technology or scientists entering the organization.

j. It modifies the personality structure such that man becomes and reflects the dull, gray, conditioned "organization man."

Weber himself came around to condemn the apparatus he helped immortalize. While he felt that bureaucracy was inescapable, he also thought it might strangle the spirit of capitalism or the entrepreneurial attitude, a theme which Schumpeter later developed. And in a debate on bureaucracy Weber once said, more in sorrow than in anger:

It is horrible to think that the world could one day be filled with nothing but those little cogs, little men clinging to little jobs and striving towards bigger ones—a state of affairs which is to be seen once more, as in the Egyptian records, playing an ever increasing part in the spirit of our present administrative system and especially of its offspring, the students. This passion for bureaucracy . . . is enough to drive one to despair. It is as if in politics . . . we were deliberately to become men who need "order" and nothing but order, who become nervous and cowardly if for one moment this order wavers, and helpless if they are torn away from their total incorporation in it. That the world should know no men but these: it is such an evolution that we are already caught up in, and the great question is therefore not how we can promote and hasten it, but what can we oppose to this machinery in order to keep a portion of mankind free from this parcelling-out of the soul, from this supreme mastery of the bureaucratic way of life.[3]

I think it would be fair to say that a good deal of the work on organizational behavior over the past two decades has been a footnote to the bureaucratic "backlash" which aroused Weber's passion: saving mankind's soul "from the supreme master of bureaucracy." Very few of us have been indifferent to the fact that the bureaucratic mechanism is a social instrument in the service of repression, that it treats man's ego and social needs as a constant, or as non-existent or as inert, that these confined and constricted needs insinuate themselves into the social processes of organizations in strange, unintended ways, that those very matters which Weber claimed escaped calculation—love, power, hate—are not only calculable and powerful in their effects, but must be reckoned with.

## Resolutions of Linkage One: The Reciprocity Dilemma

Of the three resolutions to the discrepancy between individual and organizational needs, only the last truly holds our interest now. The first resolution minimizes or denies the problem; it asserts that there is no basic conflict. The second is more interesting than this. It allows for conflict, but resolves it through an absolute capitulation on the side of the organization or the individual; one or the other, total victory or unconditional surrender. Essentially it is a way out of the conflict; for it seems to exclude ambiguity or conflict or the mutual adaption that provides chronic tension.

It might be useful to say more about the second resolution, for it is far from unpopular. Too often, it is chosen by those who view organization solely as a system of impersonal forces or solely as a function of individual personalities. Daniel Levinson[4] calls this split vision the "mirage and sponge" theories of organization. The former view, implied in most psychoanalytic literature and held by most romantics, asserts that all role behaviors are functions of personality or mere byproducts of unconscious motivations and fantasy. The "sponge" theorists, seen most commonly in sociological circles, hold that man is infinitely plastic and will yield to or be shaped by role demands. If, for example, you view Eichmann solely as an unwitting instrument of the system, of the German bureaucracy, and see the "banality of evil," then the sponge theory seems to dominate. If, on the other hand, you tend to focus exclusively on Eichmann himself as evil, and as a victim of aggressive instincts, then the mirage theory seems to hold. . . .

9

Mirage theories are equally popular and undoubtedly less dull, partly because they oversimplify and partly because they tend to glamorize events through personalization. It is gossip-column analysis: Cuba went Communist because Fidel's brother Raul was jilted by a capitalistic girl. It is the Homeric prose of *Time* magazine and it tends to reinforce our narcissism more than the eunuchism of the sponge theories.

Resolutions one and two interest us only a little because they tend to conceal the predicament: the first, by pretending it doesn't exist and the second, by camouflaging it through imputing false victories. But the problem cannot be disguised or suppressed, and the "give-away," it seems to me, is the proliferation of paired-opposite terms mutually antagonistic in nature, which flaunt the basic nature of this duality. I refer to the following: individual-organization, personality-pyramid, democratic-autocratic, participative-hierarchical, national-natural, formal-informal, mechanic-organic, task-maintenance, rational-illogical, human relations-scientific management, external-internal, hard-soft, achievement-socialization, theory X-theory Y, concern for people-concern for production, etc.

These paired dualities—ancient relics, as it were, from a distant, Manichaean world—reflect the two distinct traditions in the study of organizational behavior: the orderly, rational, predictable, Apollonian world of human strivings. Over the past several decades, a number of students of organizations, mindful of this dilemma, have been proposing a number of interesting, theoretical, and practical resolutions which go a long way in revising, if not transforming, the very nature of the bureaucratic mechanism. Let us now sample some of those resolutions.

### Ten Approaches to the Problem

By way of introduction, I should say a few words about the ten approaches I will present and how I came to choose them. First of all, they are a diverse lot, with only one trait in common: an explicit recognition of the inescapable tension between individual and organizational goals. Aside from that, they approach the problem in a variety of ways using different value systems, theoretical and research traditions, and assigning divergent priorities to the centrality of the problem. Second of all, I have not—nor could I [have]—include[d] all the possible solutions or suggestions that are available. I have ignored, as well, those ubiquitous and important mechanisms of socialization which operate spontaneously and naturally in human organizations, such as reward systems, identification, etc. Nor have I cited the work of personnel psychology or human engineering, both of which are concerned with reducing the discrepancy between individual and organizational goals. Strictly speaking, I have selected for inclusion a number of recent, moderately well-known ideas associated with a particular author.

The ten approaches can be grouped under five categories:

*Exchange theories*

1. Barnard-Simon: inducement-contribution exchange
2. H. Levinson: psychological contract

*Group theories*

3. Mayo: the managerial elite
4. Likert: the key role of the primary group and "linking pins" between groups

*Value theories*

5. Argyris: interpersonal competence
6. Blake and Mouton: the managerial grid

*Structural theory*

7. Shepard: organic systems

*Situational theories*

8. McGregor: management by objective
9. Leavitt: management by task
10. Thompson and Tuden: management by decision

*Exchange Theories*

1. The Barnard-Simon theory of exchange is an equilibrium model, very similar to an economic transaction, which specifies the conditions under which an organization can induce participation. On the one hand, there are inducements offered to the participants by the organization. These usually are wages, income, services. For each inducement there is a corresponding utility value. On the other hand, there are contribution utilities: these are the payments the participant makes to the organization, usually specified as work.

From this abstract generalization, predictions can be made concerning the participants' services by estimating the inducement-contributions balance. The greater the difference between inducements and contributions, the more satisfied—and the more compliant—the participant. In addition, a zero point on the utility scale can be derived which shows the point at which the individual is indifferent to leaving the organization as well as a point at which the participants' dissatisfactions cause search behavior and withdrawal from the organization.

2. The Levinson[5] model of reciprocity is also an equilibrium model, but the terms of the inducement-contribution ratio are converted into motivational units, usually of an unconscious kind. These units of exchange represent the psychological contract. According to Levinson, reciprocity is established by the participants and the organization through fulfilling the terms of the contract. The employees' contributions to the organization are energy, work, and commitment. The organization, for its part, provides a psychological anchor in times of rapid social change and a hedge against personal losses. In addition, the organization, through transference phenomena, provides the employees with defense mechanisms through social structure, an opportunity for growth and mastery, and a focal point for cathexis.

### Group Theories

3. Elton Mayo challenged the fundamental basis of a society which was organized around archaic, economic hypotheses which grew out of an eighteenth century, purely competitive model of society. Mayo referred to these as the Rabble Hypothesis: society consists of unorganized individuals, every individual acts in a manner calculated to secure his own self-interest, and man is logical. Mayo believed that management was blinded by the economic facts of life to the importance of association and human affiliation as a motivating force. Mayo and his associates were really among the first to view industrial organization as a social system as well as an economic-technical system.

With this profound (now seemingly mundane) insight, Mayo saw the possibilities in using *cooperation* as an instrument to mediate the reciprocity dilemma. But in order to realize the norm of cooperation, a managerial elite, trained in the facts of social life, must take the responsibility. He wrote:

The administrator of the future must be able to understand the human-social facts for what they are, unfettered by his own emotions or prejudice. He cannot achieve this ability except by careful training—a training that must include knowledge of relevant technical skills of the systematic order of operations, and of the organization of cooperation.[6]

Thus, success of the organization was based on the manager's ability to develop the effective organization of sustained cooperation.

4. The Likert[7] theory of management also depends heavily on the importance of the cohesive, primary work group as a motivator: to this extent it resembles the Mayo orientation. Yet, there are important differences at the *strategic* level. For Mayo, a managerial elite was a necessity, while for Likert, cooperation between groups could be maintained through points of articulation which Likert refers to as

"linking pins." Furthermore, in Likert's theory, decisions should be made at that point of the organizational social space where they are most relevant and where the data are available. Thus, the Likert solution entails a key role performing the linking pin solution—rather than a managerial elite—and the use of the group to mediate the reciprocity dilemma.

## Value Theories

5. Argyris starts from the position that the value system of bureaucracy itself has to be modified before individual growth and productivity can be attained.[8] He argues that bureaucratic values, which dominate organizational life, are basically impersonal values. These bureaucratic values lead to poor, shallow, and mistrustful relationships between members of the organization or what Argyris calls, "non-authentic" relationships. These, in turn, reduce interpersonal competence, which leads to mistrust, intergroup conflict, rigidity, lowered problem-solving capacity, and eventually to a decrease in whatever criteria the organization uses to measure over-all effectiveness. Managers brought up under this system of values are badly cast to play the intricate human roles now required of them. Their ineptitude and anxieties lead to systems of discord and defense which interfere with the effectiveness of the system.

Argyris' solution is to develop the interpersonal competence of the management group such that they can accept and install new values, values which permit and reinforce the expression of feeling, of experimentalism and the norms of individuality, trust, and concern.

6. Blake and Mouton[9] have developed a solution for the reciprocity dilemma which is referred to as the managerial grid. They conceptualize the organization-individual dilemma by dimensionalizing the problem along two axes. On the basis of this twofold analytic framework, it is possible to locate eight types of managerial styles. One dimension is "concern for people" and the other dimenson is "concern for production." Management, according to Blake and Mouton, has to maximize both of these concerns, rather than one or the other. They call this desired state "team management." To arrive at this state, an elaborate system of *organizational training and development* is developed which encompasses both the linking pin function and development of interpersonal competence.

## Structural Theory

7. Shepard,[10] Burns and Stalker,[11] and others have attempted to replace the mechanical structure of bureaucracy with what they call an "organic" structure. Their structural approach presents a strong reaction against the idea of organizations as *mechanisms* which, they

13

claim, has given rise to false conceptions (such as static equilibria, frictional concepts like "resistance to change," etc.) and worse, false notions of social engineering and change such as "pushing social buttons," thinking of the organization *à la* Weber as a machine, etc. Organic systems are proposed as the natural alternative to mechanical systems. They emerge and adapt spontaneously to the needs of the internal and external systems rather than operate through programmed codes of behavior which are contained in formal role specifications of the mechanical structure. As in the Likert group theory, decisions are made at the point of greatest relevance, and roles and jobs devolve to the "natural" incumbent. Shepard claims that the bureaucratic (or mechanical) systems differ from the organic systems in the ways shown in Table 1.

## Situational Theories

A number of resolutions have been worked out which stress situational demands as a mediating factor. Three of the most significant of these are:

8. Management by Objective, first noted by Drucker and further developed by McGregor,[12] attempts to link organizational goals to individual needs through the principle of "integration." It is a complicated process which entails a "working through" of the conflicts between individual objectives and organizational goals (almost in the psychotherapeutic sense) by the manager and his subordinates. The working through depends, to some extent, on the self-control and maturity of the individuals concerned and on a norm of collaboration between superiors and subordinates. Thus integration can be realized only if attention is kept both on the objectives of management and on the human processes which develop collaborative relationships between ranks.

9. Leavitt[13] stresses the task constraints of the organization and the

TABLE 1. *Mechanical Versus Organic Systems*

| Mechanical Systems | Organic Systems |
| --- | --- |
| Individual skills | Relationships between and within groups |
| Authority-obedience relationships | Mutual confidence and trust |
| Delegated and divided responsibility rigidly adhered to | Interdependence and shared responsibility |
| Strict division of labor and hierarchical supervision | Multigroup membership and responsibility |
| Centralized decision making | Wide sharing of control and responsibility |
| Conflict resolution through suppression, arbitration or warfare | Conflict resolution through bargaining or problem-solving |

development of managerial practices which are appropriate to the task. Thus he views the organization as a differentiated set of sub-systems, rather than as a unified whole, which leads to the recognition that the organization must fit the task, rather than the other way around. In this way, he seriously challenges some of the other theories proposed above by asserting that in some parts of the system, highly authoritative (sponge theory) systems of management will have to be employed which under-stress participative norms and which resolve the organization-individual tension in favor of the system. At the same time, other parts of the system will apparently operate with close to minimum discrepancy between organizational goals and individual needs.

In a provocative article with Whisler,[14] Leavitt suggests, keeping an eye on the computerized organizations of the future, that organizations will resemble not the pyramid, but a football (top management) which represents a ruling group very like Coleridge's idea of clerisy, a scholarly elite (trained in the arts of computers, mathematics, and statistics) balanced on the point of a churchbell. "Within the football," they write, "problems of coordination, individual autonomy, and group decision making, and so [on] should arise more intensely than ever. We expect they will be dealt with quite independently of the bell portion of the company, with distinctly different methods of remuneration, control, and communication."

Thus, management-according-to-task will lead to a number of divergent forms of organization within the over-all system. In the football and the churchbell resolution, for example, we can envision an organic head and a mechanical bottom.

10. Thompson and Tuden[15] have developed a typology of organizational processes based on the types of decision issues called for. They derive four types of organizational structures which appear appropriate to a particular decision issue. Along one dimension are beliefs about causation of decision and agreement *versus* non-agreement. Table 2 shows the relationships among the fourfold classification.

From this analytic classification, Thompson and Tuden derive four strategies: computation, compromise, judgment, and inspiration:

TABLE 2. *Thompson and Tuden's Typology*

| Beliefs About Causation | Preference About Possible Outcomes | |
| --- | --- | --- |
| | *Agreement* | *Non-agreement* |
| *Agreement* | Computation in *bureaucratic* structure | Bargaining in *representative* structure |
| *Non-agreement* | Majority judgment in *collegial* structure | Inspiration in *"anomic"* structure |

and four organizational *structures* appropriate to the particular strategy. Where decisions are clearcut, beliefs about causation and agreement about consequences are present, the bureaucratic structure is appropriate for the strategy of computation. Where there is agreement about outcomes but disagreement about causality, then majority judgment is required. Thompson and Tuden argue that a collegial structure, typical of the university and some voluntary organizations, would be appropriate. Where there is agreement about causation but disagreement about causality, then majority judgment is required. Where there is agreement about causation but disagreement about outcomes of decision, then compromise through representative government—typical of government operations—would be appropriate.

## Summary

Table 3 summarizes the major resolutions presented and the strategies implied to resolve the reciprocity issue:

TABLE 3. *Ten Major Approaches to Resolving the Reciprocity Dilemma*

| Author | Resolution | Strategy |
|---|---|---|
| 1. Barnard-Simon | Inducement-contribution | Economic incentives |
| 2. Levinson | Psychological contract | Psychological reciprocity |
| 3. Elton Mayo | Organization of cooperation | Managerial elite |
| 4. Likert | Group involvement | Linking pin and group development |
| 5. Argyris | Value change | Interpersonal competence |
| 6. Blake | Team management | Group and organization development |
| 7. Shepard | Organic structures | Group and organization development |
| 8. McGregor | Management by objective | Integration through collaboration and self-control |
| 9. Leavitt | Management by task | Task determines organizational arrangements |
| 10. Thompson and Tuden | Organization by decision | Decision determines organizational arrangements |

These ten resolutions provide a perspective on revisions to the theory of bureaucracy. Some, like the Barnard-Simon model, are conservative, basically neo-Weberian in tone. Others, like the proposals of Argyris and Shepard, call for radical alterations in the value system or structure of bureaucracy. Still others, more moderate in tone, suggest a flexible arrangement based on situational demands. In all cases, they raise serious questions about the viability and future of the bureaucratic mechanism.

. . .[All these revisions are] reactions for or against certain humanistic and democratic values and the author's desire to optimize—certainly assert—these values. The argument is based on the idea that the effectiveness of bureaucracy should be evaluated on human and economic criteria. To this extent, they represent normative resolutions in that they aim to supplement a restrictive view of organizational effectiveness criteria by including not only some variant of efficiency (productivity, profit, etc.), but also human gains, such as satisfaction or personal growth. Furthermore, their revisions tend to be "inner-directed," if I can use that term in this context. That is, they tend to concentrate on the internal system and its human components rather than the external relations and problems of the environmental transactions.

The emphasis on the normative side and the accompanying inner-directedness has been off target, I believe, and ironically so. For though it appears on the surface that the case against bureaucracy has to do with its ethical-moral posture and its social fabric, the real *coup de grace* to bureaucracy has come from a totally unexpected direction, from the environment. While various proponents of "good human relations" have been fighting bureaucracy on humanistic grounds and for Christian values, bureaucracy seems most likely to founder on its inability to adapt to rapid changes in the environment.

## 2. LINKAGE TWO:
### THE PROBLEM OF ADAPTABILITY

The capability of bureaucracy to succeed in its transactions and exchanges with its external environments has, until recently, gone unchallenged. For good reason: it was an ideal weapon to harness and routinize the human and mechanical energy which fueled the Industrial Revolution. It could also function in a highly competitive, fairly undifferentiated and stable environment. The pyramidal structure of bureaucracy, where power was concentrated at the top—perhaps by one person or a group that had the knowledge and resources to control the entire enterprise—seemed perfect to "run a railroad." And undoubtedly for tasks like building railroads, for the routinized tasks of the nineteenth and early twentieth centuries, bureaucracy was and is an eminently suitable social arrangement.

Now three new elements, already visible, promise to give new shape to American society and its organizational environments. They are: (1) the exponential growth of science, (2) the growth of intellectual technology, and (3) the growth of research and development activities.[16]. . .

Science and technology have profoundly changed the shape and texture of the organizational environment in the following ways:

*The rate of change is accelerating at an increasing rate.* As Ellis Johnson said:

> . . . in those large and complex organizations where the once-reliable constants have now become "galloping variables" because of the impact of increasing complexity, trial and error must give way to an organized search for opportunities to make major shifts in the means of achieving organizational objectives.[17]

*The boundary position of the firm is changing.* As A. T. M. Wilson[18] has pointed out, the number and pattern of relations between the manager and eight areas of relevant social activity have become more active and complicated. The eight areas are: government, distributors and consumers, shareholders, competitors, raw material and power suppliers, sources of employees (particularly managers), trade unions, and groups within the firms. Over the last twenty-five years, the rate of transactions with these eight social institutions has increased and their importance in conducting the enterprise has grown.

*The causal texture of the environment has become turbulent.* Emery and Trist,[19] in an important paper, have conceptualized the field of forces surrounding the firm as a turbulent environment which contains the following characteristics:

> 1. The environment is a field of forces which contains *causal* mechanisms and pose[s] important choices for the firm.
>
> 2. The field is dynamic, with increasing interdependencies among and between the eight social institutions specified above.
>
> 3. There is, among the institutions relating to the firm, a deepening interdependence between the economic and other facets of society. This means that economic organizations are increasingly enmeshed in legislation and public regulation.
>
> 4. There is increasing reliance on research and development to achieve competitive advantage and a concomitant change gradient which is continuously felt in the environmental field.
>
> 5. Finally, maximizing cooperation rather than competition between firms appears desirable because their fates may become basically positively correlated.

The upshot of all this is that the environmental texture of the firm, shaped by the growth of science and technology, has changed in just those ways which make the bureaucratic mechanism most problematical. Bureaucracy thrives under conditions of competition and certainty, where the environment is stable and, above all, predictable. The texture of the environment now holds in its turbulent and emerging field of forces causal mechanisms so rapidly changing and unpredictable that it poses insuperable problems for—and implies the end of—bureaucracy.

My argument so far can be summarized quickly. The first assault on bureaucracy arose from its incapacity to resolve the tension between individual and organizational goals. A number of resolutions emerged to mediate this conflict by supplementing the ethic of productivity with the ethic of personal growth and/or satisfaction. The second and more major shock to bureaucracy is caused by the scientific and technological revolution. It is the requirement of adaptability to the environment which leads to the predicted demise of bureaucracy as we know it.

Now, some students of organization have attempted to resolve this current dilemma, though not nearly in the same number or with the same vigor as they have the reciprocity issue. It is noteworthy that those who have made the attempt, like Burns, Stalker, Shepard, Leavitt, Argyris, and Simon, have been particularly attentive to—and have derived many of their ideas from—research and development organizations or professional associations, such as hospitals, universities, and the like. For the organizations of the future will undoubtedly resemble these, and will inherit their problems and attributes.

## A Forecast for Organizations of the Future

A forecast falls somewhere between a prediction and a prophecy. It lacks the divine guidance of the latter and the empirical foundation of the former. But somewhere between inspiration and scientific certainty is a vision of the future of organizational life, which can be pieced together by detecting certain trends of the past and certain changes in the present that are on top of us. On this thin empirical ice, I want to set forth some of the conditions of organizational life in the next 25 to 50 years.

*The environment.* As I mentioned before, the environment will be shifting and hold relative uncertainty due to the increase of research and development activities. The external environment will become increasingly differentiated, interdependent, and more salient to the firm. There will be greater interpenetration of the legal policy and economic factors, leading more and more to imperfect competition and other features of an oligopolistic and government-business controlled economy. (Telstar and similar operations, partnerships between industry and government, will become typical.) And because of the immensity and expense of the projects, there will be fewer identical units competing for the same buyers or sellers. In short, three main features of the environment will be: interdependence rather than competition, turbulent rather than steady competition, and large rather than small enterprises.

19

*Aggregate population characteristics.* We are living in what Peter Drucker calls the "educated society," and I think this feature is the most distinctive characteristic of our times. Within fifteen years, two-thirds of our population (living in metropolitan areas) will attend college. Adult education programs, not the least of which are the management development courses of such universities as M.I.T., Harvard, and Stanford, are expanding and adding intellectual breadth. All this, of course, is not just "nice" but necessary. . . . [C]omputers can do the work of most high school graduates—more cheaply and effectively. Fifty years ago education used to be called nonwork and intellectuals on the payroll (and many staff) were considered "overhead." Today, the survival of the firm depends, more than ever before, on the proper exploitation of brain power.

One other characteristic of the population which will aid our understanding of organizations of the future is increasing job mobility. The lowered expense and ease of transportation, coupled with the very real needs of a dynamic environment, will change drastically the idea of "owning" a job—or "roots," for that matter. Participants will be shifted and will change from job to job and employer to employer with much less fuss than we are accustomed to.

*Work-relevant values.* The increased level of education and rate of mobility will bring about certain changes in the values the population will hold regarding work. People will tend to: 1) be more rational, be intellectually committed, and rely more heavily on forms of social influence which correspond to their value system; 2) be more "other directed," and will rely on their temporary neighbors and work-mates for companionships; and 3) require more involvement, participation and autonomy in their pattern of work.

The first value stems from the effects of education and professionalization. The second is the best empirical guess I can make based on Riesman's ideas[20] and McClelland's data[21] that as industrialization increases, other-directedness increases. My own experience also leads me to think that "having relatives" and "having relationships" are negatively correlated. So we will tend to rely more heavily than we do now on temporary social arrangements, on our immediate and constantly changing colleagues. The third prediction is based on the idea that jobs of the future will require more responsibility and discretion, and that education and need-for-autonomy are positively correlated.

*Tasks and goals of the firm.* The tasks of the firm will be more technical, complicated, and unprogrammed. They will rely far more on intellectual power and the higher cognitive processes than on muscle power. They will be far too complicated for one man to comprehend, not to say control;

they will call for the collaboration of professionals in a project organization.

Similarly, goals will become more differentiated and complicated, and oversimplified clichés, like "increasing profits" and "raising productivity," will be heard less than goals having to do with adaptive-innovative-creative capabilities. For one thing (as is true in universities and laboratories today), productivity cannot easily be quantified with the number of budgets produced, articles published, or number of patents. And hospitals have long ago given up the idea of using the number of patients discharged as an index of efficiency. For another thing, meta-goals will have to be articulated and developed: that is, supra-goals which shape and provide the foundation for the goal structure. For example, one meta-goal might be the system for detecting new and changing goals of the firm, or methods for deciding priorities among goals.

Finally, there will be an increase in goal conflict, more and more divergency and contradictoriness between and among effectiveness criteria. Just as in hospitals or universities today, there is a conflict between the goal of teaching and the goal of research, so there will be increased conflict among goals in organizations of the future. Part of the reason for this is implied in the fact that there will be more professionals in the organization. Professionals tend to identify as much with their professional organizations as with their employers. In fact, if universities can be used as a case in point, more and more of their income stems from outside professional sources, such as private or public foundations. Professionals tend not to make good "company men" and are divided in their loyalty between professional values and organizational demands.[22] This role conflict and ambiguity are both cause and consequence of the goal conflict.

*Organizational structure.* Given the task structure, population characteristics, and features of environmental turbulence, the social structure in organizations of the future will take on some unique characteristics. First of all, the key word will be temporary: Organizations will become adaptive, rapidly changing *temporary systems.*[23] Second, they will be organized around *problems-to-be-solved.* Third, these problems will be solved by groups of relative *strangers* who represent a diverse set of professional skills. Fourth, given the requirements of coordinating the various projects, *articulating points* or "linking pin" personnel will be necessary who can speak the diverse languages of research and who can relay and mediate between various project groups. Fifth, the groups will be conducted on *organic* rather than on mechanical lines; they will emerge and adapt to the problems, and leadership and influence will fall to those who seem most able to solve the problems rather than to programmed role expectations. People will be differentiated, not according to rank or roles, but according to skills and training.

Adaptive, temporary systems of diverse specialists solving problems, coordinated organically via articulating points will gradually replace the theory and practice of bureaucracy. Though no catchy phrase comes to mind, it might be called an *organic-adaptive* structure.

(As an aside: what will happen to the rest of society, to the manual laborers, to the poorly educated, to those who desire to work in conditions of dependency, and so forth? Many such jobs will disappear; automatic jobs will be automated. However, there will be a corresponding growth in the service-type of occupation, such as organizations like the Peace Corps and AID. There will also be jobs, now being seeded, to aid in the enormous challenge of coordinating activities between groups and organizations. For certainly, consortia of various kinds are growing in number and scope and they will require careful attention. In times of change, where there is a wide discrepancy between cultures and generations, an increase in industrialization, and especially urbanization, society becomes the client for skills in human resources. Let us hypothesize that approximately 40% of the population would be involved in jobs of this nature, 40% in technological jobs, making an organic-adaptive majority with, say, a 20% bureaucratic minority.)

*Motivation in organic-adaptive structures.* The way organizations tie people into their systems so that they become effective units is the motivational basis of organizational behavior and its most pressing problem.[24] In fact, the first part of this paper on reciprocity explains how the theory and practice of bureaucracy fail to solve this problem. In the organic-adaptive structure, the reciprocity problem will be eased somewhat because individual and organizational goals should coincide more. This is made possible because organizations will provide more meaningful and satisfactory tasks. In short, the motivational problem will rely heavily on the satisfaction intrinsic to the task and to the participants' identification with his profession. . . .

There is another consequence which I find inescapable but which many will deplore. There will be a reduced commitment to work groups. These groups, as I have already mentioned, will be transient and changing. While skills in human interaction will become more important due to the necessity of collaboration in complex tasks, there will be a concomitant reduction in group cohesiveness. I would predict that in the organic-adaptive system people will have to learn to develop quick and intense relationships on the job, and learn how to endure their loss. . . .

Jobs in the next century should become *more*, rather than less, involving; man is a problem-solving animal and the tasks of the future guarantee a full agenda of problems. In addition, the adaptive process itself may become captivating to many.

At the same time, I think the future I describe is far from a Utopian or necessarily a "happy" one. Coping with rapid change, living in temporary systems, setting up (in quick-step time) meaningful relations—then breaking them all augur strains and tensions. Learning how to live with ambiguity and to be self-directing will be the task of education and the goal of maturity.

## Structures of Freedom

I should mention now one last consequence of the new adaptive-organic structure which has a profound interaction with the reciprocity issue which concerned us earlier. In these new organizations, participants will be called on to utilize their minds and imagination[s] more than any society previously has allowed. New standards will be sought for the development of creative and imaginative cognitive processes. In other words, fantasy and imagination will be legitimized in ways that today seem strange. And if we think of our social structures as instruments of repression with the necessity of repression and suffering derived from it, as Marcuse[25] says, varying with the maturity of the civilization, then perhaps we are approaching an age where organizations can sanction the play and freedom which imagination and thought involve. The need for instinctual renunciation decreases as man achieves rational mastery over nature. In short, organizations of the future will require fewer restrictions and repressive techniques because of the legitimization of play and fantasy, accelerated through the rise of science and intellectual achievements.

Not only will the problem of adaptability be overcome through the organic-adaptive structure, but the problem we started with, reciprocity, will be resolved. Bureaucracy, with its "surplus repression," was a monumental discovery for harnessing muscle power *via* guilt and instinctual renunciation. In today's world it is a prosthetic device, no longer useful. For we now require organic-adaptive systems as structures of freedom to permit the expression of play and imagination and to exploit the new pleasure of work.

### NOTES

1. . . .[G]enerally speaking, I am talking about the so-called advanced, not the under semi, or partially advanced countries.

2. R. Bendix, *Max Weber: An Intellectual Portrait* (New York: Doubleday, 1960), p. 421.

3. Ibid., pp. 455–56.

4. D. Levinson, "Role, Personality and Sub-structure in the Organizational Setting," *The Journal of Abnormal and Social Psychology* 58 (1959), 170–80.

5. H. Levinson, "Reciprocation: The Relationship between Man and Organization," invited address at the Division of Industrial and Business Psychology, American Psychological Association, September 3, 1963.

6. E. Mayo, *The Social Problems of an Industrial Civilization* (Cambridge, Mass.: Harvard University Press, 1945), p. 122.

7. R. Likert, *New Patterns of Management* (New York: McGraw-Hill, 1961).

8. C. Argyris, *Integrating the Individual and the Organization* (New York: John Wiley, 1964); C. Argyris, *Interpersonal Competence and Organizational Effectiveness* (Homewood, Ill.: Irwin-Dorsey Press, 1962); C. Argyris, *Personality and Organization* (New York: Harper, 1957).

9. R. R. Blake and J. S. Mouton, *The Managerial Grid* (Houston, Texas: Gulf Publishing, 1964).

10. H. A. Shepard, "Changing Interpersonal and Intergroup Relationships in Organizations," in J. March, ed., *Handbook of Organizations* (New York: Rand McNally, 1965), pp. 1115–1143.

11. T. Burns and G. M. Stalker, *The Management of Innovation* (Chicago: Quadrangle Books, 1961).

12. D. McGregor, *The Human Side of Enterprise* (New York: McGraw-Hill, 1960).

13. H. J. Leavitt, "Unhuman Organizations," in Leavitt and L. Pondy, eds., *Readings in Managerial Psychology* (Chicago: University of Chicago Press, 1964).

14. Leavitt and T. L. Whisler, "Management in the 1980's," in Leavitt and Pondy, eds., *Readings in Managerial Psychology* (Chicago: University of Chicago Press, 1964).

15. J. D. Thompson and A. Tuden, "Strategies and Processes of Organizational Decision," in Thompson, P. B. Hammond, R. W. Hawkes, B. H. Junker, and A. Tuden, eds., *Comparative Studies in Administration* (Pittsburgh: University of Pittsburgh Press, 1959), pp. 195–216.

16. D. Bell, "The Post Industrial Society," in E. Ginzberg, ed., *Technology and Social Change* (New York: Columbia University Press, 1964), p. 44.

17. E. A. Johnson, "Introduction," in McClosky and Trefethen, eds., *Operations Research for Management* (Baltimore: Johns Hopkins University Press, 1954), p. xii.

18. A. T. M. Wilson, "The Manager and His World," *Industrial Management Review*, 1961, fall.

19. F. E. Emery and E. L. Trist, "The Causal Texture of Organizational Environments." Paper read at the International Congress of Psychology, Washington, D.C., September, 1964. [Also available in *Human Relations* 18 (February 1965), pp. 21–32.]

20. D. Riesman, with N. Glazer and R. Denny, *The Lonely Crowd* (New Haven, Conn.: Yale University Press, 1950).

21. D. McClelland, *The Achieving Society* (Princeton, N.J.: Van Nostrand, 1961).

22. A. W. Gouldner, "Cosmopolitans and Locals: Toward an Analysis of Latent Social Roles, I," *Administrative Science Quarterly* 2 (1957), 281–306.

23. M. B. Miles, "On Temporary Systems," in Miles, ed., *Innovation in Education* (New York: Bureau of Publications, Teachers College, Columbia University, 1964), pp. 437–90.

24. D. Katz, "The Motivational Basis of Organizational Behavior," *Behavioral Science 4* (1964), 131–46.

25. H. Marcuse, *Eros and Civilization* (Boston: Beacon Press, 1955).

# 2

## Public Bureaucracy in Everyday Life

♦

*Eugene Lewis*

### INTRODUCTION

I WAS BROUGHT UP to believe that in America the people determined what the government is and does. Teachers, history books, friends, and the mass media led me to believe in the truth of certain propositions. I believed that through the electoral process, leaders gained high office in order to convert the will of the people into laws which were then faithfully executed by administrators. I was taught that candidacy equaled issue advocacy and that elected officials had the power, knowledge, and mandate to give the people the results they wanted. I believed that the government of the United States acted on the desires of the people through a set of historically sacred institutions and laws that guaranteed not only responsiveness, but also fairness, equity, and tolerance. Above all, I had an abiding faith in the heroic capacity of American governmental power to deal with any condition or crisis, domestic or foreign.

As I grew older, I became aware of "exceptions"[1] to these propositions and accounted for them in two ways. At first, I simply thought them aberrations—mistakes by honest men or the evil doings of evil men. Questions of right and wrong in politics could readily be resolved domestically by resort to political heroes and pronouncements. Foreign policy was easy:

*From Eugene Lewis, American Politics in a Bureaucratic Age: Citizens, Constituents, Clients, and Victims. © 1977, Winthrop Publishers, Inc., Cambridge Massachusetts, Reprinted by permission.*

either "they" were on "our" side, or they were not. When this first kind of explanation wore thin, I moved on to a second, more developmental rationale for the exceptions. I thought that they could be conceived of as "stumbling blocks" on the path toward realization of the propositions of my childhood that I had now come to believe were "ideals" rather than descriptive truth.

As my knowledge of the variety and magnitude of the exceptions grew, I began to suspect that they were not exceptions at all. The *expectations* of childhood belief mixed with the *exceptions* of emerging adult political knowledge led to inevitable clashes between myths and realities. There seemed to be forces in the world over which no one, apparently, had political control. I began to rethink my notions of politics and of the state itself. The symbols of sovereignty, of an heroic past and leadership, were no longer of much comfort. That common article of faith so present in my youth called "Americanism" or "believing in America" had little to do with my experience of America. The discrepancies between descriptions of politics and my observation of politics in a variety of settings left me with two very common feelings: moral outrage about the hypocrisy of it all and utter confusion about how things really worked. By the time I was twenty, I understood that the myths, symbols, and rituals of American democracy were, at least partially, devices to reassure and comfort the confused and uncertain. . . .

Intellectual traditions that dealt with political power, organizational phenomena, and values as interrelated and vital aspects of an evolving American political system were difficult to find. But important statements about each were discoverable within the intellectual values of several disciplines.

My objective was to develop some concepts that would relate the behaviors of individuals and groups to a formulation of the ancient notion of the state. Consistent with this, I wished to explain some important aspects of political behavior in an historical and organizational context. The possibility of achieving so grand a goal was dim. It still is. But a realization of that goal seemed to me to lie in a work of integration that would attempt to tie together some of the thought possessed by the several disciplines.

## Homo Bureaucratus

Most of us were born in hospitals at least parts of which were built and equipped by public funds administered by some public agency. The medical personnel who attended our births undoubtedly were educated from kindergarten through graduate school in institutions either wholly or partially supported and regulated by public agencies. Any medications were used only after they had received government approval as had the physician who prescribed them and the pharmacist who prepared them. Conditions of the delivery room and the certification that one has indeed been born are matters of direct governmental concern and regulation.

From birth to elementary school, the absence or presence of parents, their economic well-being, and indeed much of the simple surroundings of young children are affected in varying degrees by government involvement. The economic conditions which either enhance or detract from our parents' ability to support us are a function of governmental interventions through fiscal and monetary policies. Even the air we breathe and the water and food we consume are matters of direct state concern. Our lives are protected against violent biblical contingencies like fire, flood, and famine by public agencies.

For most of us education is a matter of the end products of public policy and management. What we learn, from whom we may learn it, and when we are supposed to learn are the legal responsibility of a set of public agencies. Within the public primary and secondary school, governmental agencies provide meals, dental services, eye examinations, and social service counseling for our families and ourselves should the need arise. Some services must be received on threat of legal sanction and others must be complied with under the duress of informal social sanction. American colleges and universities are increasingly dependent upon government funding and regulation, whether they are public institutions or not. Most of us attend public institutions of higher learning that are variously supported, regulated, and/or directed by some national, state, or local agency of government.

An enormous number of us enter a labor market dominated by public policy decisions and providing employment opportunities either in public bureaucracies themselves or in private firms whose economic well-being is directly related to the actions of government agencies. It is difficult to imagine many categories of employers unaffected by government policy as interpreted and implemented by public bureaucracies. Our personal income from employment is likely to be reduced by one-quarter to one-third as a result of taxation in one form or another. Our marriages, our home purchases, the threads of our adulthood from the liberation of the driver's license to the insurance of our burial . . . all of these major events in our individual biographies are regulated, limited, stimulated, or directly authorized by public agencies. Too often during the past thirty-five years millions of us have become actual or potential involuntary public employees of the armed forces.

As the beginning of our lives occurs under a variety of interventions from public agencies, so too are our later years likely to be heavily involved with such agencies. Once again we are probably hospital-bound.

But this time we will undoubtedly have to stay a bit longer. The regulation, licensing, and whatnot of the services provided, while important, probably will not be paramount in our thoughts. Few of us can afford to pay for prolonged hospitalization and medical care if we are already dependent on government agencies to assist us in providing the necessities of everyday life. As our government-regulated pension plans are supplemented by the mandatory pension plan for which government has taxed us, we may begin to comprehend our growing dependence upon public bureaucracies for what is left of our lives.

Our biographies are molded by the actions of public organizations in an enormous and complex variety of circumstances. In nearly every instance mentioned above, *public organizations* intervene to expand or contract the possible courses of action open to us. An important series of questions seem to flow from these commonplace observations. How do we as citizens of a democratic society relate to these institutions of public control? In what ways are the policies, regulations, and "outcomes" of public organizations created? What have the traditional values of democracy like representation, accountability, and liberty itself to do with the operations of these organizations that are so crucial to the conduct of our everyday lives?

The view taken here is that rather than the *homo politicus*[2] archetype of Athens, our vision might be more accurately served by identifying the American public in terms of a *homo bureaucratus*, for in the important matters of our public lives we are more involved with public bureaucracy than we are with parties, elections, and legislatures. That element of American government and politics which consists of public organizations is an increasingly significant institutional and political force. In the course of illustrating its power over most of the vital aspects of society and economy, I will attempt to describe and analyze those characteristics of public bureaucracy which have brought it to the eminence which I claim for it. First, however, I will make an attempt to describe how *homo bureaucratus* interacts with public organizations.

## MODES OF INTERACTION

### Citizen

The most generalized and venerable notion of interaction between a person and his government is the concept of citizenship. The idea of citizenship has enjoyed a powerful position in American political ideology. Citizenship, one learns early on, entails certain rights and privileges, among which are the election of representatives, payment of taxes, and obedience to the law of the land. Citizenship is a global notion encompassing a kind of continuing interaction between rulers and ruled which assumes knowledgeability and interest in things governmental on the part of the ruled and a healthy respect for the rule of law and election returns on the part of the rulers. The scope of citizen interest is supposed to be broad, and those who legislate on its behalf are to be aware of the conflict between the representation of the public interest and the representation of special interests. Mechanisms devised by the Founding Fathers and later architects of constitutionalism were meant to deal with such conflicts. In case mechanisms for the insurance of the representation of the public interest faltered, the doctrine of judicial review was created to make certain that the public interest under the rule of law as provided by the Constitution was in fact adhered to. These structural devices and others were created to insure an interactive process which was so lacking in the eighteenth-century European monarchies.

Today, citizenship as an interactive means for insuring that the will of the people is translated into policies and laws has lost much of its meaning. The contemporary status of citizenship seems most significant in symbolic terms. People vote, pay taxes, and comply with rules and laws for a variety of reasons, many of which are justified by belief in the conception of citizenship as outlined above. The symbolic aspects of citizenship provide psychological gratification by giving people feelings of efficacy, patriotism, and the general illusion of participation.

But as an active element in the formation of public policy, the concept leaves much to be desired. Except in the smallest electoral units, the sequence that begins with a vote for a candidate and ends with a policy change is seldom discoverable. The voice of the citizenry can rarely be directly heard on any given issue. Occasionally, policy outcomes are influenced by politicians and bureaucrats who fear the possible reaction of the entire citizenry. But as a whole, the attention and concern of the citizenry are either highly segmented or too diffuse to translate into policies.

One finds that the modern idea of citizenship is associated more with loyalty to country and willingness to comply with laws and rules than with participation. If citizenship is too diffuse a notion to explain the way people interact with their government, how then might one conceive of the idea? A central contention of this [selection] is that citizenship is most significantly experienced by people as bureaucratic constituents, clients, and victims. I identify these as interaction modes; "mode" is taken to mean both the form of interaction and the frequency of its occurrence.

*Constituent*

The representation of a geographically defined group of people is the usual sense in which the term "constituency" is used. One recalls the Burkean legislator's problem of choosing between that which will benefit all and that which will benefit only the legislator's constituency. Hanna Pitkin summarizes the range of positions on this matter:[3]

> A number of positions have at one time or another been defended between the two poles of mandate and independence. A highly restrictive mandate theorist might maintain that true representation occurs only when the representative acts on explicit instructions from his constituents, that any exercise of discretion is a deviation from this ideal. A more moderate position might be that the representative may exercise some discretion, but must consult his constituents before doing anything new or controversial, and then do as they wish or resign. A still less extreme position might be that the representative may act as he thinks his constituents would want, unless or until he receives instructions from them, and then he must obey. Very close to the independence position would be the argument that the representative must do as he thinks best, except insofar as he is bound by campaign promises or an election platform. At the other end is the idea of complete independence, that constituents have no right even to extract campaign promises; once a man is elected he must be completely free to use his own judgment.

If one applies Pitkin's description to groups constituted in a number of ways and arraying themselves among a variety of pertinent issue constellations, then how and to whom are interests likely to be represented? The politics of *intra*organizational representation are likely to be guided by a set of norms very different from those characteristic of elected constituency representatives.

Such voluntary associations as clubs, veterans groups, some professional societies, "public" interest groups, conservationists, manufacturers' organizations, and some unions represent the interests of their membership according to a variety of loose and tangentially "democratic" procedures. Often the mechanisms of such organizationally "democratic" voluntary organizations include polls of opinion and election of officers. The trappings of democracy, however, are often its fullest realization; the common situation is domination by elites of the internal workings of the organization as well as of its representation to the external environment.[4] Such elites often consist of the most interested members of the organization. Their interest is fueled by (among other things) needs to enhance their personal social status, wealth, or potential for influence inside and outside the organizational framework. Representation of interests, which tend toward maximal inclusivity according to elite perception, occurs when the threat of elite displacement is substantial or when there is a significant value consensus between leaders and followers.

The benefits of labor union membership and membership in other economic associations that represent their members' interests do not necessarily include every member; and of those who are beneficiaries, not all share equally as a result of membership. Mancur Olson has dealt with the question of collective and noncollective goods and service provision in the context of economic groups like labor unions and trade associations.[5] At this point it seems sufficient to say that membership in an organization which actively seeks to promote organizational interests as well as those of its individual members does not necessarily maximize individual benefits.

Group membership of a voluntary (and quasi-voluntary) nature is a central concern for many scholars who deal with the nature of representation in American politics.[6] Lobbying, pressure through advertising, campaign contributions, letter writing campaigns, and a variety of other techniques characterize the actions of such voluntary and quasi-voluntary groups. This distinction is arbitrarily drawn to distinguish between, say, the NAACP and a teamster local; membership in the NAACP is usually a matter of preference, but membership in the teamster local is a condition of employment.

As government became involved in new and different aspects of economic and social life during the twentieth century, the locus and character of constituency representation changed. While legislative constituencies remained significant, a new kind of relationship began to evolve at the administrative level. Indeed, the continued well-being and growth of some cabinet-level agencies became linked more to servicing their constituents than to anything else.

The most obvious example of this phenomenon is the Department of Agriculture. Its organizational history and development in many ways epitomize the creation of that most significant evolving constituency-government relationship: the bureaucratic one. Grant McConnell[7] has written most eloquently on the subject. He argues that farmers had little expectation of exercising much "voice" (to borrow Albert Hirschman's term)[8] in either political party at the end of the last century. That is not to say that the farm vote was not a potent factor in the calculations of politicians at the national level, but rather that the farm voice was one of many, often conflicting, voices. A narrowing of the focus of voice in national policy and a change in the institutional setting for its exercise occurred which had serious consequences for the representation of agricultural interests.

The Department of Agriculture reached into the vast geography of the nation in the form of thousands of county agents. The most powerful agricultural interest group was the Farm Bureau which was not a "general farm group," but rather a highly skilled lobby which had organized a "farm bloc" in Congress. McConnell's description of bureaucratic constituency organization and representation through county agents provides one with an almost classic map of the reformulated idea of constituency.[9]

Most agents were publicly paid organizers and functionaries of the Farm Bureaus; at the same time they were the Department of Agriculture's only field service across the nation. In theory public and private servants concurrently, the county agents were effectively immune from Department orders and domination. The substantial national support given to the extension system was funneled through grants-in-aid to the states. Only trivial federal restrictions went with these gifts. The agencies for state supervision of the agents were the land-grant colleges of agriculture, which maintained their own independence from political direction. Even within the colleges, the extension system tended to be rather autonomous. In effect, then, the agents were most closely tied to the local counties in which they worked, where they were beholden to county government and even more to the Farm Bureaus they had organized and which they served as partial employees. Officially, their status was more ambiguous: they were national, state, and local officials; they were also privately employed. Informally, however, there was little doubt where their effective political responsibility lay—to the locally influential farmers. And these were well-knit into the Farm Bureaus.

Several important themes of bureaucratic constituency are tied together here. Clearly, the representation of the interests of the Farm Bureaus is paramount both for the Department of Agriculture and for the farm bloc in Congress. The role of representative is that of a nonelected public official known as a county agent and who is beholden to private interests in a relationship sanctioned by law. McConnell clearly contends, furthermore, that local Farm Bureaus were dominated by the most powerful farmers.

The confusion of jurisdictional authorities, which is a property of federalism, and the "nonpolitical" character of colleges were perfect ground for the development of a system that thoroughly obliterates the public-private distinction and that permits the domination of national policy by those who are most likely to be affected by it. Not only can one readily observe the possibilities of conflict of interest being elevated to a status of institutional legitimacy, but one can also perceive the idea of constituency being reduced to a system of representation of the powerful in the name of the many.

McConnell's description exemplifies the point that the meaning of bureaucratic constituency tends to have an aspect of classical corporatism. In other words, the organizational form which is the primary constituent of the agency has the common characteristic of private formal organization in which members receive the benefits of membership without being able to specify or alter significantly the nature of those benefits. Indeed, the assumption is that what is good for the powerful farmer is good for all farmers. Furthermore, one can infer that what is good for Farm Bureau elites is good for the Department of Agriculture and for the general public. The constituency of the Department of Agriculture is issue-specific; that is, it tends to concern itself with matters salient to agricultural policy and those policies which affect agriculture, and it tends to be a self-governing entity operating with the full blessings of law and custom.

What of the nonpowerful member of the Farm Bureau and the farmer, who doesn't even belong to the organization? McConnell draws some strong conclusions about this in his general statement about private power. He argues that the cost of such private aggregations of public power is great in terms of the ideal of representation of constituency interests.[10]

> The recognition of a right of autonomy, self-determination, or self-regulation may be expedient, given the group's power. But it does not eliminate the power over its members which the leadership of the group may have; indeed, it is more likely than not to enhance that power. When, under the guise of serving an ideal of democracy as the self-government of small units, the coercive power of public authority is given to these groups, their internal government becomes a matter of serious concern.

What we know of the internal government of such groups substantiates McConnell's argument for the most part. Hierarchies that provide little or no opportunity for effective bottom-up representation or accountability seem to characterize most large private organizations linked in a constituency relationship to public agencies.

As a general proposition, then, a bureaucratic constituent is usually a formal organization that is interdependent with a public bureaucracy. Interdependence in this sense means the surrender of power for mutual benefit.[11] Thus, the ability of the public bureaucracy to act depends in large measure upon the agreement of its constituencies. Constituents of public agencies are similarly constrained in their actions. Bureaucratic constituents in general are policy-specific and possess resources that give them the potential to threaten incumbent bureaucrats.

Agriculture constituents, for example, concern themselves with issues and policies that directly affect them; they are unlikely to dissipate their attention and energies in nonagricultural areas. The resources they have which may be used to threaten the Agriculture Department include influence over certain congressmen, senators, and governors through campaign contributions, propaganda, and bloc voting. The USDA has an arsenal of its own (e.g., administrative rule making, professionalized expertise, budgetary initiative).

In an important sense, institutions within the formal boundaries of the state can themselves be understood to be bureaucratic constituents. When congressmen and senators find themselves dependent upon bureaucracies for perfectly legal discretionary administrative actions, they become in effect bureaucratic constituents. For instance, those who trade votes with bureaucrats in exchange for favorable treatment in their districts in order to enhance their reelection chances are interdependent with public bureaucracies. In the realms of political economy and national defense, I will illustrate how bureaucracies can build constituency relationships inside as well as outside the formal boundaries of government.

## Client

The term "client" as used here refers to a person or group of people who are dependent upon a patron, in this case a governmental patron. A client differs from a constituent individual or group primarily because the client is not significantly able to alter the behavior of his (or its) bureaucratic patron, but the constituent individual or group may indeed be able to influence outcomes of the policy process. Collectively organized constituents (like labor unions) may be called a *descriptive group insofar as group actions in the political arena in some ways characterize the manifest wishes of some or all members of the constituency. The ascriptive character of clientele groups (like the poor) arises out of their identification by bureaucrats and politicians in terms of a set of attributes which individuals possess but which do not constitute a basis upon which they organize themselves for collective action.* Indeed, clients tend not to organize for the representation of interests. A clientele is an aggregation of individuals and groups that interacts in a dependent fashion with one or more government agencies. Clients do not normally represent even a potential threat to public bureaucracy, but constituent groups do.

The needs and wants of a clientele are likely to be effectively made by public officials rather than by privately organized claimants. The needs and wants of clientele are most often articulated in the professionalized social welfare and control structures of public organizations. Although this may also be true of a constituency, the bureaucratic advocate's articulation of interest is unlikely to be a response to demand external to the public agency. Intra-agency professionals decide what client "demand" is according to some combination of professional and agency standards.

My reformulation of constituency involves an incomplete transfer of a traditional legislative–electoral concept to a new institutional focus. In some ways the idea of clientele in the bureaucratic context resembles the doctor–patient relationship. A patient is dependent upon the rituals and practices of the medical profession which render him almost powerless before the physician. One may find another doctor, even a quack, but one cannot usually find an organization that competes with government. If doctors had constituents, they would have to give serious attention to the possibility of their being removed or their decisions being overridden by others. Patients can (sometimes) go elsewhere if they are displeased with the physician. Bureaucratic clients have no such market possibilities except under conditions of interbureaucratic competition. In that situation, the clientele of the loser may be attached to the winner without any expectation that the clientele as here defined would raise objection.

Although I have stipulated that one can think of clients both as groups and as individuals, it is the latter form in which one can most easily discover clientele relationships. Welfare recipients tend to be the clients of social workers in the employ of some large public organization or another. AFDC mothers may have demands, requests, needs, and wants, but they are defined (and thus either recognized or ignored) by public employees who act under a set of rules not created or even influenced by the recipient. Indeed, the public employee who actually administers the rules may have had as little to do with their creation as the client. Farm organizations sit down with legislators and administrators and carefully assist them in the formulation of rules governing a variety of interactions which may affect the lives of the farmers represented. Not all farmers and not all farmers' interests are represented, but some are. In regard to public welfare, one may describe many influences on the history of welfare legislation without ever describing the group constituency process or the role of citizenship.[12]

Those groups which tend to be identified as collectivities by virtue of sharing a common ascriptive characteristic, such as being poor, are a crucial part of the "environment" of that vast element of government activity called "social welfare." The poor, the young, and the infirm are the most obvious clientele groups dependent upon government. Since they are either completely unorganized or ineffectively organized, they have no direct influence on policy making.

Perhaps less easily identified are those clients who are neither old, young, poor, nor sick. Postal patrons, auto licensees and registrants, and those who pay taxes are also clients, but episodically so. At one time or another during our lives each of us becomes a client. The agencies connected with these relationships are under most conditions correctly perceived as "purposive machines"[13] which process the paper necessary to continue our lives. Failure to conform to the rules of such processors or a mistake on the part of the agency itself brings penalties upon the client. Like taxation, one's ability to obtain redress or correction varies according to one's resources. If one has little time and money, one makes a more costly expenditure of those resources than a wealthy person does to retrieve an important letter, straighten out a problem with the IRS, or transfer title to an automobile. If one has one's secretary or lawyer "handle" these matters, one is not likely to notice the costs. If, however, one is unfortunate enough to become a permanent or semipermanent member of a public agency clientele network, then the matter of costs and potential costs is more serious.

Few clients have sufficient resources to consider attempting to transform a clientele into a constituency. The public agency often has the resources necessary for life itself or its continued maintenance at a "reasonable" level. Clients are resources of the agency which serves them, as are constituents, but they are passive resources which public agencies normally cannot or will not mobilize even for the greater power and glory of the organization.

A clientele is represented in the policy process by the agency responsible for it. The professionalization of social service personnel, educators, and medical people explains much about the idea of clientele. These professions are involved in discretionary classification routines which permit only a limited amount and scope of interaction between the client and the patron bureaucracy. Instead of citizens or constituents, people are defined and responded to in terms of the initial category typification most readily dealt with by the professional. "Student," "patient," "AFDC mother," "indigent," and "vagrant" are labels that are useful in defining and acting upon individuals who have (or are) problems.

These individuals surrender to discretionary classification when they define themselves or are defined by others as being in need of help. Discretionary classification routines are those rules followed by individual practitioners of any profession to determine, diagnose, or judge an aspect of another whose "problem" is perceived by the practitioner as coming within the purview of his profession and the administrative rules which constrain it. Once such routines are fixed in the mind and eye of the beholder through education, training, and peer reinforcement, the possibility of the beholden's altering them is difficult to imagine outside of fiction. Clients thus defined by one who is backed by the power of profession and the legitimacy of the state are likely to act and be acted upon in a manner consistent with the "doctor knows best" stereotype.

These routines begin processes that set formal and informal limits on interactions which are appropriate to the client's needs and to the expectations of the professional. One interesting aspect of the client–professional relationship is that it is conceived by both actors as being outside the political process. In other words, the large group of citizens who meet at the vague boundaries of public organizations as professionals and as clients manage a definitional exercise that appears to remove their behaviors from politics.

There is much popular political belief that protects us from describing client–professional relationships as being political. Without going into the variety of ways one can conceive of the political, one can suggest that public agencies involved in allocative decisions within the framework of agency-generated rules are engaged in a political process. The public character seems to not matter in client-centered situations as described above. Yet one might be remiss in failing to identify as political those aspects of rule making, enforcement, and adjudication which directly affect both the client who receives the service and the aggregate which provides the resources. It should be stressed that the ancient administration/politics dichotomy is not being suggested, but rather a newer phenomenon. Clients have their lives influenced in important ways by professionals who act with the authority of expertise and the legitimacy of the state. The same situation does not pertain to constituency relationships. The AFL–CIO hires economists from the same outstanding graduate institutions that the Treasury and Department of Labor customarily patronize. Such "balancing of experts" is not part of the client–professional relationship.

The debate over public/private and policy/administration distinctions perhaps becomes more useful at the level of the descriptive client organization. Client organizations are here defined as those collective entities whose existence is predicated wholly or in great part on the patronage of a government agency. For example, one might point to the hundreds of firms that engage in no other activity but supplying the Department of Defense with some specialized good or service. The number of specialized firms that are agency dominated because of spatial or locational factors is difficult to estimate. But one need only visit a large government installation in an isolated area to see the web of motel owners, food franchisers, and so on, totally dependent upon trade created by the agency. They have little if any voice in the conduct of agency affairs appropriate to them. Indeed, like the saloon owner who fears being declared off-limits to military personnel, such spatially relevant private firms may be understood as extensions or satellites of the agency which enforce agency norms and conform to whatever extraterritorial rules the agency lays down.

Functionally defined client organizations exist in nonmarket situations to the extent that they have little or no private sector interactions. Manufacturers of hardware for defense, space exploration, and avionic purposes are ready examples of client organizations. Usually, these are small-scale manufacturers who are separated from the patron agency, in part because of ideological rigidities that normally forbid government agencies from manufacturing goods. The distinction between a patron agency and its client organization is meaningful in terms of costs and legalities, not in terms of organizational power or policy. Such client organizations are creatures of the patron. When the patron is healthy, they flourish; when the patron suffers reverses (as NASA did in the late 1960s and early 1970s), they either die or they develop other kinds of businesses.

Client organizations and people who are clients are at least beneficiaries of organizational outputs. In the case of an economic client organization, accumulated benefits over time could put the firm in a position to diversify sufficiently to reduce or negate the potential effects of the withdrawal of agency patronage. Even individual cliental relationships create the possibility of alternate sources of support, although such possibilities may be dim indeed. The modal client of public agencies probably can expect a dependency of substantial duration. One can conceive of clientele networks, which consist of unorganized individuals, mobilizing into some sort of constituency-like group. Patients in veterans' hospitals could conceivably enlist the support of the American Legion and VFW in order to improve services and conditions in VA hospitals. Such things are imaginable, but they are not likely to endure beyond the resolution of the issue (or issues). The final interaction mode admits of no such potentiality for representation of interest.

## Victim

Millions of Americans live a daily struggle to obtain the necessities for minimal existence. Hunger and the other deprivations of poverty define one class of victims. The very bottom of the egg-shaped structure of American society exerts absolutely no direct influence over the actions of public organizations. The policies of such organizations not only define the conditions of existence and the possible modes of interaction for this population, but they also decide vital personal matters without ever having interacted with those affected. These people have their lives altered as a function of the "aggregate" effect of policy or policies. They are the "unanticipated consequences" of urban renewal policies, food stamp administration, drug control programs, and regulatory acts in general.

Victims are not clients. They are a nameless mass whose destiny is subject to forces created by policy implementation. Victims, unlike those of us whose lives are episodically bounded by policy outcomes and public agency regulation, live existences highly dependent upon public policy decisions which take place beyond their consciousnesses. Those in our midst who cannot obtain minimal education, employment, food, or shelter are essentially bereft of resources, and their inability to obtain these resources is to some greater or lesser extent a result of governmental activity.

Whether government has a responsibility to provide the minima of existence is not a question germane to this particular argument. Victims, as I am defining them, are relevant to policy outcomes simply because of the pervasiveness of the governmental presence in post-industrial society. Insofar as government creates positive or negative externalities which have impact on the minima of existence, it creates victims as mindlessly as it may create beneficiaries. (Externalities are the unintended economic and social effects of government action.) Victimization is more than a simple extension of the idea of the relatively powerless client. One might reasonably argue that the extension of negative externalities to clients may end in victimization. The argument presented here is that part of the population identified as victims of aggregate policy outcomes are totally passive actors whose identity is more readily described statistically than in interactive terms. Indeed, it may even be inappropriate to discuss these victims interactively at all.

Victims of aggregate policy outcomes are acted upon by changes in the economic and social environment which occur as a partial result of government activity. The existence of the group itself is an ascriptive exercise, since one cannot easily locate such a residual category of humanity in the literature of public policy. By residual category, I mean to suggest that aggregate policy victims are most easily defined as those who receive little or no food on a daily basis, whose children receive little or no education, who live in conditions of minimal shelter and sanitation, and who do not interact with government, except as objects.

Those who are the objects of government policy seldom know that they are the objects of governmental policy. The "poor," as conceived of by politicians and bureaucrats of the 1960s, were usually anonymous. Indeed, the "discovery" of the poor by the War on Poverty Programs was in many ways an exercise in defining an ascriptive class, followed by an attempt to mobilize members of that class into clients, and perhaps even constituents.[14] While the program may have failed, at the very least it did highlight one segment of the forgotten millions directly affected by policy outcomes who are here identified as victims. To be sure, not all the poor are victims. Many are clients and some are constituents. Those who are neither are simply passive recipients of environmental changes which are in part determined by the actions of public agencies.

There are victims of public agency outputs who are all too aware of the rules, regulations, and demands of government. Those who are defined as insane, mentally retarded, or alcoholic are not likely to enjoy even a cliental relationship, if they are inmates of public institutions. Mental institutions, public hospitals, juvenile prisons, and other caretaker agencies are often not much different from maximum security institutions or cemeteries for the living. One simple way to dispose of such persons intellectually is to define them as something less than human and therefore not the proper subject for a discussion of the ways in which members of society interact with the most visible parts of the government they supposedly control. What a distance from citizen to mental patient! If one simply argues that citizenship is minimally defined in terms of individual rights of freedom to speak, move about, own property and the like, subject to the codes of civil and criminal law, then the status of mental patients who have violated no law and who are not incarcerated voluntarily becomes rather a nice intellectual question.[15]

The presence of total institutions in a democratic society has long been an analytical anomaly.[16] The removal of some members of society from the possibility of exercising minimal rights of citizenship is normally justified and understood in terms of the urgent need being met by the organization of which the citizen is a member (i.e., crew member of a ship in wartime) or because of the potential danger to society, should members of the institution be allowed public freedom (i.e., mental patients, convicted felons). Perhaps there is something worth the note of political scientists in understanding the popularity of two novels of the 1960s which describe two public agencies attempting to exercise total control over their non-voluntary membership. Many students have perceived the protagonists of *Catch-22* and *One Flew Over the Cuckoo's Nest* as being metaphorical equivalents of post-industrial man confronting society itself as if it were a total institution. Certainly part of that construction of reality can be understood to describe the category which we have identified as victims.

Victimization in the second sense (i.e., the direct action of public agencies upon persons as objects) is normally a function of the police power (i.e., health, safety, and welfare) of government. In America, orphans, the physically and mentally handicapped, the poor, some of the aged, the criminal, and the indigent have historically been the responsibility of the states and municipalities. The federal government has entered the field only lately. At the local level the most common discoverer and creator of victims (of crimes and of government) are the police. Policemen deal with the widest range of human behavior normally confronted by any representative of public bureaucracy. The discretionary classification routines they follow and their ability to enforce them differentially have been the subject of much study in the past ten years.[17] It is not news that the poor, the black, the young, the indigent, and the ignorant are treated differently by the police. They are also victims, as we have defined them, because for all practical purposes, when they are arrested or have their homes or persons searched, they have little practical recourse for redress of grievance.

Police occupy a unique position as agents of public authority in regard to the question of individual interaction with government. The criminal justice system in general tends to create organizational victims by virtue of the differential enforcement of the law, the bail system, and the arrest of social deviants and "criminals without victims." Drug users, prostitutes, alcoholics, homosexuals, and other social deviants become victims, not only by the laws that make them criminal, but also by the differential possibilities of arrest. White, wealthy, and middle-aged homosexuals, alcoholics, or drug users seldom suffer the stigma of arrest and conviction. The capacity to arrest and stigmatize is basic to the coercive power of the state to create victims. Such victim creation is almost always an act of administrative discretion by a public agent, the policeman. Thus, within the ancient and honorable obligation of the state to maintain public order and to arrest criminals fall those discretionary possibilities for creating the role of victim, as I have restrictively used the term.

Two kinds of victims have been generally identified: (1) those who are indirectly victimized by macroscopic negative externalities (like inflation) generated by the action of public agencies and (2) those who are directly confronted by a public agency that exercises the power to effectively deny them their basic constitutional rights. Representation of these victims is held to be strictly an internal bureaucratic matter, the concern of the press, or political officials. In no circumstance short of open rebellion is it to be expected that victims ever represent their own wishes, wants, or needs.

## RECAPITULATION AND SYNTHESIS

What might one reasonably infer to be the dimensions underlying these distinctions (citizen, constituent, client, victim)? Efficacy and the sense of efficacy have been matters of direct or implied concern in discussion of each interaction mode. *Efficacy is the power to produce intended results. The sense of efficacy implies a belief about one's ability to so produce.* It has been argued thus far that efficacy is improbable on the part of citizens, is probable for the elites who govern most constituencies, is highly unlikely for clients, and is absent for victims.

I have discussed the *sense of efficacy* in terms of representation. Representation takes place in public bureaucracy in a way most appropriate to the narrowly defined descriptive interests or ascriptive characteristics of constituents, clients, and victims. The notion of the citizenry aggregated for representational purposes seems a wistful artifact of a probably nonexistent past. Constituent organizations tend to have control over those who represent them within public organizations. Members of constituent organizations, however, tend to have their interests represented by generally unresponsive, dominant intraorganizational elites. Clients have their interests represented for them but their interests are authoritatively reinterpreted by the mediating symbols of the professionalized agencies that dominate them. Occasionally, clients can look like constituents or be made to look like constituents, but the normal case is official reinterpretation of client interest. The interests of victims are defined totally by those given the mandate for their control.

Finally, an effort has been made to assess the dependency of each of the classes of interaction upon the agency or agencies to which it is most appropriate. Citizenship continues to be a notion so diffuse as to make it meaningless to this analysis. Except in the aggregate, where all agencies are interdependent with the entire citizenry, and in rare cases of citizen attentiveness to a single issue, the idea of citizen as a mode of interaction has little meaning. The category must not be excluded from the discussion, however; the idea of citizenship is not a straw man of intellectual pretension; it is a powerful symbolic typification, common to the culture and to the literature of politics and public administration. There are those who believe that the citizenry's sense of political efficacy underpins the political order to a substantial degree. Further, while citizenship appears not terribly useful as an interaction mode, the concept of citizenship may be a significant and general received value of those who dominate the policy process.

Constituents are interdependent with their ruling organizational or institutional elites. The definition of the term "constituent" at the macroscopic level implies mutuality of benefit, although the relationship between agency and constituency may not always be equal in benefit and power. Normally, the client is a supplicant whose needs and/or wants can be satisfied only by agency action. The client's dependency is mitigated at a general level by the absolute need of professionalized agencies to have clientele in order to justify their existences. Usually, however, the client, unlike the constituent, has few resources with which to create a truly interdependent relationship with the agency. The client is likely to have ascribed characteristics (like being poor) appropriate to the discretionary classification (he qualifies for aid or he does not) routines of the professionalized bureaucrats who interact with him.

Victims occupy two logically obvious categories: they are either intentional victims or they are unintentional victims. For instance, at the moment this is being written, the bottom one-fifth of the socioeconomic structure of America (an ascriptive group) seems to be suffering the unintended, unfortunate consequences of macroeconomic policy decisions made several years ago by various high-level federal officials. The social world that this bottom one-fifth confronts is bounded and shaped by government action over time. As government agencies identify more conditions in the social order in need of governmental intervention, it becomes easier to substantiate the claim that large numbers of people who do not directly interact with any agency on a long-term basis are nevertheless profoundly affected by the complex environmental impact of agency policies. This is particularly so of that group of interactions characteristic of victims.

One might read these pages and conclude that he has at one time or another experienced some or all of the interactive modes. This is not an unreasonable conclusion. It suggests that our relationship with government is dependent upon a set of contingencies set in time and space rather than upon some transcendent and enduring form of interaction. This is so for many of us. For millions of others, however, the distinctions drawn here do indeed constitute modal points of enduring interaction with the political system. Indeed, for many these typifications may be the labels most ap-

TABLE 1. *Citizenry—Bureaucracy Relationships*

| Dimensions of Interaction | Interaction Modes Constituent | Client | Victim |
|---|---|---|---|
| Character of interest representation | Highly focused; locationally, functionally specific | Highly focused; authoritatively reinterpreted | Disembodied |
| Efficacy: power to alter policy outcomes | Great | Little | None |
| Dependence: upon a public agency for viability | Interdependence | Nearly complete | Total |

propriate for understanding the relationships between the rulers and the ruled.

Thus an hypothesis: Citizenship is most accurately described by the behaviors of public bureaucracies and the constituent, client, and victim networks with which they interact. This hypothesis may be elaborated by a more careful summary of some key dimensions that separate the modes of interaction. These are sketched below and are summarized in Table 1.

1. *The character of interest representation.* The assumption is that the interests of persons appropriate to a particular public agency are represented and that the specificity and location of that representation are politically significant and empirically discoverable.

2. *Efficacy: the power to alter outcomes.* The question here is does the population described have the (legal, political, or economic) power to (a) initiate or prevent the appearance of a serious item on the agency agenda and/or (b) initiate or prevent successful implementation once a policy decision has been reached?

3. *Dependence upon a public agency for viability.* If dependency connotes the obverse of power and interdependence connotes the surrender of power for mutual benefit, then a reasonable question about the modes of interaction entails a consideration of whether the bureaucratic dog wags the public tail or vice versa. Our analysis suggests that the question seems as inappropriate for the "citizen" category as it seems self-evident for the "victim" category. The difficulty is not so much with the dimension as it is with the general theoretical premises available to deal with the relationships between the polity and public organizations. In any case, the viability dimension attempts to answer the empirical question: can those most

closely identified with the mode of interaction survive (literally and figuratively) if the public agency upon which they depend either ceases to exist or radically alters its relevant outputs?

Major questions arise out of the claims made thus far. If it is true that America is a nation of bureaucratic constituents, clients, and victims, then what sort of general conceptual framework might help one account for this situation? If the conceptual framework is descriptive, then how does it operate and how has it come into existence? . . .

## NOTES

1. This term comes from Murray Edelman, *The Symbolic Uses of Politics* (Urbana: University of Illinois Press, 1970). My introductory discussion parallels many of Edelman's analyses.

2. See Robert A. Dahl, *Who Governs?* (New Haven: Yale University Press, 1961), pp. 224–27, for a characterization of political man and his apolitical counterpart, *Homo civicus*.

3. Hanna Pitkin, *The Concept of Representation* (Berkeley: University of California Press, 1967), p. 146.

4. The literature on the oligarchic nature of private government leadership is extensive and goes back well into the last century in the writing of Michels, for instance. The general question is addressed in Sanford Lakoff and Daniel Rich, eds., *Private Government* (Glenview, Ill.: Scott, Foresman, 1973). For a famous exception to the general proposition proffered here, see Lipset, Trow, and Coleman's *Union Democracy* (Glencoe, Ill.: Free Press, 1956). Lipset takes a more general look at the question of the political process in unions and arrives at conclusions which are not significantly different from the ones presented here in his *Political Man* (New York: Doubleday, 1960), chapter 12.

5. Mancur Olson, *The Logic of Collective Action* (Cambridge, Mass.: Harvard University Press, 1971).

6. Robert A. Dahl, *A Preface to Democratic Theory* (Chicago: University of Chicago Press, 1956); Theodore J. Lowi, *The End of Liberalism* (New York: W. W. Norton, 1969); E. E. Schattschneider, *The Semi-Sovereign People* (New York: Holt, 1960); Arthur F. Bentley, *The Process of Government* (Bloomington: Principia, 1949); David Truman, *The Governmental Process* (New York: Knopf, 1951); and Pitkin, *The Concept of Representation*.

7. Grant McConnell, *Private Power and American Democracy* (New York: Knopf, 1967).

8. Albert O. Hirschman, *Exit, Voice and Loyalty* (Cambridge, Mass.: Harvard University Press, 1970).

9. McConnell, *Private Power and American Democracy*, pp. 232–33.

10. Ibid., pp. 341–42.

11. James D. Thompson in *Organizations in Action* (New York: McGraw-Hill, 1967) reformulates the notion of interdependence suggested by Richard M. Emerson, "Power-Dependence Relations," *American Sociological Review* (February 1962), 31–40.

12. The work of Frances Fox Piven and Richard A. Cloward is very interesting to me as an illumination of the constituency-client distinction drawn here. In their *Regulating the Poor* (New York: Random House, 1971), they trace public welfare history in functional and economic terms. I read them to affirm what I describe as a cliental relationship and find poignant confirmation of this view in their "crisis" solution to the "welfare mess." Briefly, they suggest that organizing all the eligible poor for purposes of flooding the welfare agencies with clients would bring the system to a halt and compel an alteration in present policies. They argue (see p. 321 of *Regulating the Poor*) that this strategy would result in a minimum income program financed nationally. The strategy is essentially an attempt at mobilizing clients rather than attempting to convert clients to constituents. They (correctly, I think) saw the rules of the bureaucracy as the only lever or means for representation of interests of the poor.

13. J. D. Thompson, *Organizations in Action*, pp. 16–17, identifies such organizations as having "mediating" core technologies. He says: ". . . mediating technology requires operating in standardized ways and extensively; e.g., with multiple clients or customers distributed in time and space."

14. For a more complete argument on the subject, see Eugene Lewis, *The Urban Political System* (Hinsdale, Ill.: Dryden, 1973), pp. 256–266.

15. Thomas S. Szasz, *The Myth of Mental Illness* (New York: Delta, 1961).

16. David J. Rothman, *The Discovery of the Asylum* (Boston: Little, Brown, 1971). This is a very important historical work that deals with a variety of total institutions created in the zeal of early-nineteenth-century reform. He discusses the creation and development of almshouses, workhouses, lunatic asylums, and penitentiaries. In this day of "psychiatric justice" and crimes without victims, such historical analysis is very helpful to the political scientist who would try to place nondemocratic public institutions in contemporary settings.

17. James Q. Wilson, *Varieties of Police Behavior* (Cambridge: Harvard University Press, 1968) and Jerome H. Skolnick, *Justice Without Trial* (New York: Wiley, 1966). These two studies, among hundreds of others, make the point in different ways, I believe.

# Mechanistic Monocratic Organization

◆

CHANGE THAT IS FORCED upon public organizations through technological or political factors does not affect all bureaucratic units to the same extent. Even in times of violent change some elements of government will still be operating on a "business as usual" basis. Max Weber's development of an "ideal type" bureaucracy and Luther Gulick's account of the "principles of administration" influence the attitudes of many administrators toward change in public bureaucracies.

Although Weber did not coin the term *bureaucracy*,[1] his name is intimately associated with the concept because he sought to neutralize the perjorative connotation of the term through the development of an antiseptic, "ideal type" model. An ideal type is a methodological construct that attempts to conceptualize a pure or idealized form of the phenomena about which one wants to generalize. Although one can conceive of various characteristics that would describe the idealized picture of a phenomenon—say, bureaucracy—he would not find all of those characteristics, in their pure form, present in any particular bureaucratic structure he might study. An ideal type corresponds to a pole at one end of a continuum; reality lies along the continuum, but not at the pole position that represents the idealized form. Whereas ideal types are not subject to proof or disproof by empirical verification, they do provide standards against which specific cases can be compared. Therefore, the pure bureaucratic structure described by Weber does not occur in the real world, but is a grouping of the characteristics that Weber thought contributed to a hypothetically rational and effective organization.

Although Weber's most lasting contribution in social science is the stress he placed on bureaucracy, he was more generally concerned with the state and the sources of its legitimation or authority. Weber's view of authority involved three ideal type relationships: traditional; charismatic; and legal-rational.[2] Traditional authority claimed legitimacy on the basis of the sanctity of the powers of control that had been handed down from the past and that have presumably always existed. Persons exercising authority in a traditional system do so according to traditionally transmitted rules. In the ideal type traditional authority system postulated by Weber, change is inhibited by precedent. Those exercising authority are afraid to stretch the traditional ways of doing things because the ensuing change might undercut their own sources of legitimacy. One of the attributes of traditional authority, however, is that there is an area of control open to the whims of the people who occupy places of authority in the system. This creates intensely personal relations between the rulers and the ruled. Caprice is an accepted form of dealing with people who resort to the traditional authorities to resolve conflicts. If the traditional ruler oversteps even these loose traditional bounds of arbitrariness, he personally may be deposed but a successor would be chosen by traditional means and the system of authority would continue.

Charismatic authority is intensely personal, too, but the sources of that authority are quite different. The charismatic individual has authority by virtue of innate personal qualities through which he is able to inspire devotion from his followers. The position a charismatic leader occupies in society is not sanctified by traditional criteria. The charismatic person is not bound by the traditional rules and is capable of sparking revolutionary changes. Charismatic authority does not accept any system of rules for organizing society. There is no law, no hierarchy, no formalism except the basic demand of devotion to the charismatic figure. His followers are duty-bound to help him in his effort to accomplish his mission. They follow not because of rules but because of personal devotion. The leader intervenes whenever and wherever he feels like it, unbound by tradition or law. This makes charismatic authority an anathema to regularized routines.

Weber claimed that before the industrial revolution, the traditional and charismatic authorities were responsible for just about all of the orientation for action. The early modern period brought in the need to establish social organization on a stable basis, but a stable basis that would still be open to change. The legal-rational system of authority, to Weber, was such a system. The intensely personal nature of authority in the change-oriented charismatic situation and the whimsical use of personal power in the change-negating traditional system gave way to a more impersonal kind of authority based on rules. Such rules could be rationally changed to cope with changes in the environment in a systematic, more highly predictable way than could be accounted for by either of the other ideal types of authority. The quintessence of legal-rational authority was to be found in the ideal type bureaucracy.

In reading Weber's view of bureaucracy, the student should ask himself the following questions: What functions does the hierarchy perform? Is Weber describing an efficient machine? Under what conditions might his bureaucracy work best? What is the role of the individual in the organization? How do bureaucracies cope with change? Is an ideal type construct helpful in understanding the way bureaucrats behave?

Whereas Weber's seminal work in bureaucracy has long been respected, Gulick's "Notes on the Theory of Organization" has not had so venerable a history. Academic public administrators know the work primarily because of Herbert Simon's trenchant criticism of Gulick's principles of public administration as being merely proverbs.[3] "Look before you leap," and "He who hesitates is lost" are two proverbs that purport to give guidance under similar conditions. Which does one follow? Similarly, Simon viewed most of the principles of public administration as being antithetical and therefore not useful as guides to organizational behavior. Simon was looking for concepts upon which to build a science of administrative behavior, and he felt that the proverbs did not provide an adequate basis for science.

Practitioners with little administrative background, however, have often found the principles useful. The simplicity of the Gulick formulations lend themselves readily to use. The common sense embodied in the principles does provide, as even Simon admitted, "criteria for describing and diagnosing administrative situations."[4] Gulick's formulation of the principles, when taken as codified common sense rather than rigorous theory, gives the administrator a ready-made, albeit rough, framework that can be used to sort out his values. The sorting out of values, when combined with a study of the conditions under which various principles may be applicable, can be of great use. Much of the empirical organization research has focused on the consequences of formal organizational forms under varying environmental conditions.[5]

Harold Seidman, a leading student of governmental reorganization, has noted the usefulness of Gulick's writings. "Flawed and imperfect as they may be, the orthodox 'principles' remain the only simple, readily understood, and comprehensive set of guidelines available to the president and the Congress for resolving problems of executive branch structure."[6] Every federal government reorganization effort since the Brownlow Committee of 1937 has incorporated the organizational views presented in the selection reprinted here. Unfortunately for Gulick's reputation, most of his followers—and certainly virtually all of his critics—failed to heed his caveats as well as his claims.

Some of the principles have fared far better than others. POSDCORB, an acronym for Planning, Organizing, Staffing, Directing, Co-ordinating, Reporting, and Budgeting, is an example of Gulick's thought that is widely accepted today by practitioners and even some academics. After years of wandering in the wilderness, POSDCORB had been heralded as an extremely useful summary statement of what administrators do, with the recommendation that an *E*, for Evaluation, be added to the formulation. Such a suggestion came from a distinguished academician who ended his guest editorial in the *Public Administration Review*, the leading journal in the field, with the plea: "Let's give evaluation its due—let's put an E in POSDECORB."[7]

Although many of the principles appear to have validity, the student should apply his analytic powers to them. Are they really proverbs? What might be alternative principles that seem equally valid but have different consequences if acted upon? Does Gulick qualify his remarks so that the modern reader would not regard them as principles? Do the principles adequately reflect reality? Are these principles consistent with views of public bureaucracy in a democratic society? What is the role of professionals in the organization? Can politics be divorced from administration? How does Gulick propose to deal with change? Gulick has been criticized as being overly mechanistic. Is he?

### NOTES

1. Martin Albrow attributes the term to Vincent de Gournay, a French physiocrat who first used "bureaucracy" to describe Prussian government in 1745. See Albrow, *Bureaucracy* (New York: Frederick A. Praeger, Inc., 1970), p. 3.

2. See Max Weber, *The Theory of Social and Economic Organization*, Talcott Parsons, tr. (New York: The Free Press, 1947), pp. 341–342, 358–363.

3. Herbert A. Simon, *Administrative Behavior: A Study of Decision-Making Processes in Administrative Organizations* (New York: The Macmillan Company, 1957), pp. 20–44.

4. Ibid., p. 36.

5. For an example of such research, see John J. Morse and Jay W. Lorsch, "Beyond Theory Y," *Harvard Business Review* 48, no. 3 (May/June 1970): 61–68. Also see Jay Galbraith, *Designing Complex Organizations* (Reading, Mass.: Addison-Wesley Publishing Company, 1973).

6. Harold Seidman, *Politics, Position, and Power*, third edition (New York: Oxford University Press, 1980), pp. 8–9.

7. Orville F. Poland, "Why Does Public Administration Ignore Evaluation," *Public Administration Review* 31, no. 2 (March/April 1971): 202. In a similar vein, S. Kenneth Howard argues that "besides the POSDCORB functions, modern developments have charged administrators with two other noteworthy responsibilities . . . : intergovernmental relations and innovation." S. Kenneth Howard, *Changing State Budgeting* (Lexington: Council of State Governments, 1973), p. 25.

# 3

# Bureaucracy

♦

*Max Weber*

MODERN OFFICIALDOM FUNCTIONS IN the following specific manner:

I. There is the principle of fixed and official jurisdictional areas, which are generally ordered by rules, that is, by laws or administrative regulations.

1. The regular activities required for the purposes of the bureaucratically governed structure are distributed in a fixed way as official duties.

2. The authority to give the commands required for the discharge of these duties is distributed in a stable way and is strictly delimited by rules concerning the coercive means, physical, sacerdotal, or otherwise, which may be placed at the disposal of officials.

3. Methodical provision is made for the regular and continuous fulfilment of these duties and for the execution of the corresponding rights; only persons who have the generally regulated qualifications to serve are employed.

In public and lawful government these three elements constitute "bureaucratic authority." In private economic domination, they constitute bureaucratic "management." Bureaucracy, thus understood, is fully de-

---

From Max Weber: Essays in Sociology, *edited and translated by H. H. Gerth and C. Wright Mills. Copyright 1946 by Oxford University Press, Inc.; renewed 1973 by Hans H. Gerth. Reprinted by permission of the publisher. Footnotes deleted.*

veloped in political and ecclesiastical communities only in the modern state, and, in the private economy, only in the most advanced institutions of capitalism. Permanent and public office authority, with fixed jurisdiction, is not the historical rule but rather the exception. This is so even large political structures such as those of the ancient Orient, the Germanic and Mongolian empires of conquest, or of many feudal structures of state. In all these cases, the ruler executes the most important measures through personal trustees, table companions, or court servants. Their commissions and authority are not precisely delimited and are temporarily called into being for each case.

II. The principles of office hierarchy and of levels of graded authority mean a firmly ordered system of super- and subordination in which there is a supervision of the lower offices by the higher ones. Such a system offers the governed the possibility of appealing the decision of a lower office to its higher authority, in a definitely regulated manner. With the full development of the bureaucratic type, the office hierarchy is monocratically organized. The principle of hierarchical office authority is found in all bureaucratic structures: in state and ecclesiastical structures as well as in large party organizations and private enterprises. It does not matter for the character of bureaucracy whether its authority is called "private" or "public."

When the principle of jurisdictional "competency" is fully carried through, hierarchical subordination—at least in public office—does not mean that the "higher" authority is simply authorized to take over the business of the "lower." Indeed, the opposite is the rule. Once established and having fulfilled its task, an office tends to continue in existence and be held by another incumbent.

III. The management of the modern office is based upon written documents ("the files"), which are preserved in their original or draft form. There is, therefore, a staff of subaltern officials and scribes of all sorts. The body of officials actively engaged in a "public" office, along with the respective apparatus of material implements and the files, make up a "bureau." In private enterprise, "the bureau" is often called "the office."

In principle, the modern organization of the civil service separates the bureau from the private domicile of the official, and, in general, bureaucracy segregates official activity as something distinct from the sphere of private life. Public monies and equipment are divorced from the private property of the official. This condition is everywhere the product of a long development. Nowadays, it is found in public as well as in private enterprises; in the latter, the principle extends even to the leading entrepreneur. In principle, the executive office is separated from the household, business from private correspondence, and business assets from private fortunes. The more consistently the modern type of business management has been carried through, the more are these separations the case. The beginnings of this process are to be found as early as the Middle Ages.

It is the peculiarity of the modern entrepreneur that he conducts himself as the "first official" of his enterprise, in the very same way in which the ruler of a specifically modern bureaucratic state spoke of himself as "the first servant" of the state. The idea that the bureau activities of the state are intrinsically different in character from the management of private economic offices is a continental European notion and, by way of contrast, is totally foreign to the American way.

IV. Office management, at least all specialized office management—and such management is distinctly modern—usually presupposes thorough and expert training. This increasingly holds for the modern executive and employee of private enterprises, in the same manner as it holds for the state official.

V. When the office is fully developed, official activity demands the full working capacity of the official, irrespective of the fact that his obligatory time in the bureau may be firmly delimited. In the normal case, this is only the product of a long development, in the public as well as in the private office. Formerly, in all cases, the normal state of affairs was reversed: official business was discharged as a secondary activity.

VI. The management of the office follows general rules, which are more or less stable, more or less exhaustive, and which can be learned. Knowledge of these rules represents a special technical learning which the officials possess. It involves jurisprudence, or administrative or business management.

The reduction of modern office management to rules is deeply embedded in its very nature. The theory of modern public administration, for instance, assumes that the authority to order certain matters by decree— which has been legally granted to public authorities—does not entitle the bureau to regulate the matter by commands given for each case, but only to regulate the matter abstractly. This stands in extreme contrast to the regulation of all relationships through individual privileges and bestowals of favor, which is absolutely dominant in patrimonialism, at least in so far as such relationships are not fixed by sacred tradition.

## THE POSITION OF THE OFFICIAL

All this results in the following for the internal and external position of the official:

I. Office holding is a "vocation." This is shown, first, in the requirement of a firmly prescribed course of training, which demands the entire capacity for work for a long period of time, and in the generally prescribed and special examinations which are prerequisites of employment. Furthermore, the position of the official is in the nature of a duty. This determines the internal structure of his relations, in the following manner: Legally and actually, office holding is not considered a source to be exploited for rents or emoluments, as was normally the case during the Middle Ages and frequently up to the threshold of recent times. Nor is office holding considered a usual exchange of services for equivalents, as is the case with free labor contracts. Entrance into an office, including one in the private economy, is considered an acceptance of a specific obligation of faithful management in return for a secure existence. It is decisive for the specific nature of modern loyalty to an office that, in the pure type, it does not establish a relationship to a *person,* like the vassal's or disciple's faith in feudal or in patrimonial relations of authority. Modern loyalty is devoted to impersonal and functional purposes. Behind the functional purposes, of course, "ideas of culture-values" usually stand. These are *ersatz* for the earthly or supra-mundane personal master: ideas such as "state," "church," "community," "party," or "enterprise" are thought of as being realizd in a community; they provide an ideological halo for the master.

The political official—at least in the fully developed modern state—is not considered the personal servant of a ruler. Today, the bishop, the priest, and the preacher are in fact no longer, as in early Christian times, holders of purely personal charisma. The supra-mundane and sacred values which they offer are given to everybody who seems to be worthy of them and who asks for them. In former times, such leaders acted upon the personal command of their master; in principle, they were responsible only to him. Nowadays, in spite of the partial survival of the old theory, such religious leaders are officials in the service of a functional purpose, which in the present-day "church" has become routinized and, in turn, ideologically hallowed.

II. The personal position of the official is patterned in the following way:

1. Whether he is in a private office or a public bureau, the modern official always strives and usually enjoys a distinct *social esteem* as compared with the governed. His social position is guaranteed by the prescriptive rules of rank order and, for the political official, by special definitions of the criminal code against "insults of officials" and "contempt" of state and church authorities.

The actual social position of the official is normally highest where, as in old civilized countries, the following conditions prevail: a strong demand for administration by trained experts; a strong and stable social differentiation, where the official predominantly derives from socially and economically privileged strata because of the social distribution of power; or where the costliness of the required training and status conventions are binding upon him. The possession of educational certificates . . . are [sic] usually linked with qualification for office. Naturally, such certificates or patents enhance the "status element" in the social position of the official. For the rest, this status factor in individual cases is explicitly and impassively acknowledged; for example, in the prescription that the acceptance or rejection of an aspirant to an official career depends upon the consent ("election") of the members of the official body. This is the case in the German army with the officer corps. Similar phenomena, which promote this guild-like closure of officialdom, are typically found in patrimonial and, particularly, in prebendal officialdoms of the past. The desire to resurrect such phenomena in changed forms is by no means infrequent among modern bureaucrats. For instance, they have played a role among the demands of the quite proletarian and expert officials (the *tretyj* element) during the Russian revolution.

Usually the social esteem of the officials as such is especially low where the demand for expert administration and the dominance of status conventions are weak. This is especially the case in the United States; it is often the case in new settlements by virtue of their wide fields for profit-making and the great instability of their social stratification.

2. The pure type of bureaucratic official is *appointed* by a superior authority. An official elected by the governed is not a purely bureaucratic figure. Of course, the formal existence of an election does not by itself mean that no appointment hides behind the election—in the state, especially, appointment by party chiefs. Whether or not this is the case does not depend upon legal statutes but upon the way in which the party mechanism functions. Once firmly organized, the parties can turn a formally free election into the mere acclamation of a candidate designated by the party chief. As a rule, however, a formally free election is turned into a fight, conducted according to definite rules, for votes in favor of one of two designated candidates.

In all circumstances, the designation of officials by means of an election among the governed modifies the strictness of hierarchical subordination. In principle, an official who is so elected has an autonomous position opposite the superordinate official. The elected official does not derive his position "from above" but "from below," or at least not from a superior authority of the official hierarchy but from powerful party men ("bosses"), who also determine his further career. The career of the elected official is not, or at least not primarily, dependent upon his chief in the administration. The official who is not elected but appointed by a chief normally functions more exactly, from a technical point of view, because, all other circumstances being equal, it is more likely that purely functional points of consideration and qualities will determine his selection and career. As laymen, the governed can become acquainted with the extent to which a candidate is expertly qualified for office only in terms of experience, and hence only after his service. . . .

3. Normally, the position of the official is held for life, at least in public bureaucracies; and this is increasingly the case for all similar structures. As a factual rule, *tenure for life* is presupposed, even where the giving of notice or periodic reappointment occurs. In contrast to the worker in a private enterprise, the official normally holds tenure. Legal or actual life-tenure, however, is not recognized as the official's right to the possession of office, as was the case with many structures of authority in the past. Where legal guarantees against arbitrary dismissal or transfer are developed, they merely serve to guarantee a strictly objective discharge of specific office duties free from all personal considerations. In Germany, this is the case for all juridical and, increasingly, for all administrative officials.

Within the bureaucracy, therefore, the measure of "independence," legally guaranteed by tenure, is not always a source of increased status for the official whose position is thus secured. Indeed, often the reverse holds, especially in old cultures and communities that are highly differentiated. In such communities, the stricter the subordination under the arbitrary rule of the master, the more it guarantees the maintenance of the conventional seigneurial style of living for the official. Because of the very absence of these legal guarantees of tenure, the conventional esteem for the official may rise in the same way as, during the Middle Ages, the esteem of the nobility of office rose at the expense of esteem for the freemen, and as the king's judge surpassed that of the people's judge. In Germany, the military officer or the administrative official can be removed from office at any time, or at least far more readily than the "independent judge," who never pays with loss of his office for even the grossest offense against the "code of honor" or against social conventions of the salon. For this very reason, if other things are equal, in the eyes of the master stratum the judge is considered less qualified for social intercourse than are officers and administrative officials, whose greater dependence on the master is a greater guarantee of their conformity with status conventions. Of course, the average official strives for a civil-service law, which would materially secure his old age and provide increased guarantees against his arbitrary removal from office. This striving, however, has its limits. A very strong development of the "right to the office" naturally makes it more difficult to staff them with regard to technical efficiency, for such a development decreases the career-opportunities of ambitious candidates for office. This makes for the fact that officials, on the whole, do not feel their dependency upon those at the top. This lack of a feeling of dependency, however, rests primarily upon the inclination to depend upon one's equals rather than upon the socially inferior and governed strata. The present conservative movement among the Badenia clergy, occasioned by the anxiety of a presumably threatening separation of church and state, has been expressly determined by the desire not to be turned "from a master into a servant of the parish."

4. The official receives the regular *pecuniary* compensation of a normally fixed *salary* and the old age security provided by a pension. The salary is not measured like a wage in terms of work done, but according to "status," that is, according to the kind of function (the "rank") and, in addition, possibly, according to the length of service. The relatively great security of the official's income, as well as the rewards of social esteem, make the office a sought-after position, especially in countries which no longer provide opportunities for colonial profits. In such countries, this situation permits relatively low salaries for officials.

5. The official is set for a "career" within the hierarchical order of the public service. He moves from the lower, less important, and lower paid to the higher positions. The average official naturally desires a mechanical fixing of the conditions of promotion: if not of the offices, at least of the salary levels. He wants these conditions fixed in terms of "seniority," or possibly according to grades achieved in a developed system of expert examinations. Here and there, such examinations actually form a character *indelebilis* of the official and have lifelong effects on his career. To this is joined the desire to qualify the right to office and the increasing tendency toward status group closure and economic security. All of this makes for a tendency to consider the offices as "prebends" of those who are qualified by educational certificates. The necessity of taking general personal and intellectual qualifications into consideration, irrespective of the often subaltern character of the educational certificate, has led to a condition in which the highest political offices, especially the positions of "ministers," are principally filled without reference to such certificates.

* * *

### TECHNICAL ADVANTAGES
### OF BUREAUCRATIC ORGANIZATION

The decisive reason for the advance of bureaucratic organization has always been its purely technical superiority over any other form of organization. The fully developed bureaucratic mechanism compares with other organizations exactly as does the machine with the nonmechanical modes of production.

Precision, speed, unambiguity, knowledge of the files, continuity, discretion, unity, strict subordination, reduction of friction and of material and personal costs—these are raised to the optimum point in the strictly bureaucratic administration, and especially in its monocratic form. As compared with all collegiate, honorific, and avocational forms of administration, trained bureaucracy is superior on all these points. And as far as complicated tasks are concerned, paid bureaucratic work is not only more precise but, in the last analysis, it is often cheaper than even formally unremunerated honorific service.

Honorific arrangements make administrative work an avocation and, for this reason alone, honorific service normally functions more slowly, being less bound to schemata and being more formless. Hence it is less precise and less unified than bureaucratic work because it is less dependent upon superiors and because the establishment and exploitation of the apparatus of subordinate officials and filing services are almost unavoidably less economical. Honorific service is less continuous than bureaucratic and frequently quite expensive. This is especially the case if one thinks not only of the money costs to the public treasury—costs which bureaucratic administration, in comparison with administration by notables, usually substantially increases—but also of the frequent economic losses of the governed caused by delays and lack of precision. The possibility of administration by notables normally and permanently exists only where official management can be satisfactorily discharged as an avocation. With the qualitative increase of tasks the administration has to face, administration by notables reaches its limits—today, even in England. Work organized by collegiate bodies causes friction and delay and requires compromises between colliding interests and views. The administration, therefore, runs less precisely and is more independent of superiors; hence, it is less unified and slower. All advances of the Prussian administrative organization have been and will in the future be advances of the bureaucratic, and especially of the monocratic, principle.

Today, it is primarily the capitalist market economy which demands that the official business of the administration be discharged precisely, unambiguously, continuously, and with as much speed as possible. Normally, the very large, modern capitalist enterprises are themselves unequalled models of strict bureaucratic organization. Business management throughout rests on increasing precision, steadiness, and, above all, the speed of operations. This, in turn, is determined by the peculiar nature of the modern means of communication, including, among other things, the news service of the press. The extraordinary increase in the speed by which public announcements, as well as economic and political facts, are transmitted exerts a steady and sharp pressure in the direction of speeding up the tempo of administrative reaction towards various situations. The optimum of such reaction time is normally attained only by a strictly bureaucratic organization.

Bureaucratization offers above all the optimum possibility for carrying through the principle of specializing administrative functions according to purely objective considerations. Individual performances are allocated to functionaries who have specialized training and who by constant practice learn more and more. The "objective" discharge of business primarily means a discharge of business according to *calculable rules* and "without regard for persons."

"Without regard for persons" is also the watchword of the "market" and, in general, of all pursuits of naked economic interests. A consistent execution of bureaucratic domination means the leveling of status "honor." Hence, if the principle of the free market is not at the same time restricted, it means the universal domination of the "class situation." That this consequence of bureaucratic domination has not set in everywhere, parallel to the extent of bureaucratization, is due to the differences among possible principles by which polities may meet their demands.

The second element mentioned, "calculable rules," also is of paramount importance for modern bureaucracy. The peculiarity of modern culture, and specifically of its technical and economic basis, demands this very "calculability" of results. When fully developed, bureaucracy also stands, in a specific sense, under the principle of *sine ira ac studio* [without wrath or affection]. Its specific nature, which is welcomed by capitalism, develops the more perfectly the more the bureaucracy is "dehumanized," the more completely it succeeds in eliminating from official business love, hatred, and all purely personal, irrational, and emotional elements which escape calculation. This is the specific nature of bureaucracy and it is appraised as its special virtue.

The more complicated and specialized modern culture becomes, the more its external supporting apparatus demands the personally detached and strictly "objective" *expert*, in lieu of the master of older social structures, who was moved by personal sympathy and favor, by grace and gratitude. Bureaucracy offers the attitudes demanded by the external apparatus of modern culture in the most favorable combination. As a rule, only bureaucracy has established the foundation for the administration of a rational law conceptually systematized on the basis of such enactments as the latter Roman imperial period first created with a high degree of technical perfection. During the Middle Ages, this law was received along with the bureaucratization of legal administration, that is to say, with the displacement of the old trial procedure, which was bound to tradition or to irrational presuppositions, by the rationally trained and specialized expert.

\* \* \*

## THE PERMANENT CHARACTER
## OF THE BUREAUCRATIC MACHINE

Once it is fully established, bureaucracy is among those social structures which are the hardest to destroy. Bureaucracy is *the* means of carrying "community action" over into rationally ordered "societal action." Therefore, as an instrument of "societalizing" relations of power, bureaucracy has been and is a power instrument of the first order—for the one who controls the bureaucratic apparatus.

Under otherwise equal conditions, a "societal action," which is methodically ordered and led, is superior to every resistance of "mass" or even of "communal action." And where the bureaucratization of administration has been completely carried through, a form of power relation is established that is practically unshatterable.

The individual bureaucrat cannot squirm out of the apparatus in which he is harnessed. In contrast to the honorific or avocational "notable," the professional bureaucrat is chained to his activity by his entire material and ideal existence. In the great majority of cases, he is only a single cog in an ever-moving mechanism which prescribes to him an essentially fixed route of march. The official is entrusted with specialized tasks, and normally the mechanism cannot be put into motion or arrested by him, but only from the very top. The individual bureaucrat is thus forged to the community of all the functionaries who are integrated into the mechanism. They have a common interest in seeing that the mechanism continues its functions and that the societally exercised authority carries on.

The ruled, for their part, cannot dispense with or replace the bureaucratic apparatus of authority once it exists. For this bureaucracy rests upon expert training, a functional specialization of work, and an attitude set for habitual and virtuoso-like mastery of single yet methodically integrated functions. If the official stops working, or if his work is forcefully interrupted, chaos results, and it is difficult to improvise replacements from among the governed who are fit to master such chaos. This holds for public administration as well as for private economic management. More and more the material fate of the masses depends upon the steady and correct functioning of the increasingly bureaucratic organizations of private capitalism. The idea of eliminating these organizations becomes more and more utopian.

The discipline of officialdom refers to the attitude-set of the official for precise obedience within his *habitual* activity, in public as well as in private organizations. This discipline increasingly becomes the basis of all order; however great the practical importance of administration on the basis of the filed documents may be. The naive idea of Bakuninism of destroying the basis of "acquired rights" and "domination" by destroying public documents overlooks the settled orientation of *man* for keeping to the habitual rules and regulations that continue to exist independently of the documents. Every reorganization of beaten or dissolved troops, as well as the restoration of administrative orders destroyed by revolt, panic, or other catastrophes, is realized by appealing to the trained orientation of obedient compliance to such orders. Such compliance has been conditioned into the officials, on the one hand, and, on the other hand, into the governed. If such an appeal is successful it brings, as it were, the disturbed mechanism into gear again.

The objective indispensability of the once-existing apparatus, with its peculiar, "impersonal" character, means that the mechanism—in contrast to feudal orders based upon personal piety—is easily made to work for anybody who knows how to gain control over it. A rationally ordered system of officials continues to function smoothly after the enemy has occupied the area; he merely needs to change the top officials. This body of officials continues to operate because it is to the vital interest of everyone concerned, including above all the enemy.

\* \* \*

### THE POWER POSITION OF BUREAUCRACY

Everywhere the modern state is undergoing bureaucratization. But whether the *power* of bureaucracy within the polity is universally increasing must here remain an open question.

The fact that bureaucratic organization is technically the most highly developed means of power in the hands of the man who controls it does not determine the weight that bureaucracy as such is capable of having in a particular social structure. The ever-increasing "indispensability" of the officialdom, swollen to millions, is no more decisive for this question than is the view of some representatives of the proletarian movement that the economic indispensability of the proletarians is decisive for the measure of their social and political power position. If "indispensability" were decisive, then where slave labor prevailed and where freemen usually abhor work as a dishonor, the "indispensable" slaves ought to have held the positions of power, for they were at least as indispensable as officials and proletarians are today. Whether the power of bureaucracy as such increases cannot be decided *a priori* from such reasons. The drawing in of economic interest groups or other non-official experts, or the drawing in of non-expert lay representatives, the establishment of local, inter-local, or central parliamentary or other representative bodies, or of occupational associations—these *seem* to run directly against the bureaucratic tendency. How far this appearance is the truth must be discussed in another chapter rather than in this purely formal and typological discussion. In general, only the following can be said here:

Under normal conditions, the power position of a fully developed bureaucracy is always overtowering. The "political master" finds himself in the position of the "dilettante" who stands opposite the "expert," facing the trained official who stands within the management of administration. This holds whether the "master" whom the bureaucracy serves is a "people," equipped with the weapons of "legislative initiative," the "referendum," and the right to remove officials, or a parliament, elected on a more aristocratic or more "democratic" basis and equipped with the right to vote a lack of confidence, or with the actual authority to vote it. It holds whether the master is an aristocratic, collegiate body, legally or actually based on self-recruitment, or whether he is a popularly elected president, a hereditary and "absolute" or a "constitutional" monarch.

Every bureaucracy seeks to increase the superiority of the professionally informed by keeping their knowledge and intentions secret. Bureaucratic administration always tends to be an administration of "secret sessions": in so far as it can, it hides its knowledge and action from criticism. Prussian church authorities now threaten to use disciplinary measures against pastors who make reprimands or other admonitory measures in any way accessible to third parties. They do this because the pastor, in making such criticism available, is "guilty" of facilitating a possible criticism of the church authorities. The treasury officials of the Persian shah have made a secret doctrine of their budgetary art and even use secret script. The official statistics of Prussia, in general, make public only what cannot do any harm to the intentions of the power-wielding bureaucracy. The tendency toward secrecy in certain administrative fields follows their material nature: everywhere that the power interests of the domination structure toward *the outside* are at stake, whether it is an economic competitor of a private enterprise, or a foreign, potentially hostile polity, we find secrecy. If it is to be successful, the management of diplomacy can only be publicly controlled to a very limited extent. The military administration must insist on the concealment of its most important measures; with the increasing significance of purely technical aspects, this is all the more the case. Political parties do not proceed differently, in spite of all the ostensible publicity of Catholic congresses and party conventions. With the increasing bureaucratization of party organizations, this secrecy will prevail even more. Commercial policy, in Germany for instance, brings about a concealment of production statistics. Every fighting posture of a social structure toward the outside tends to buttress the position of the group in power.

The pure interest of the bureaucracy in power, however, is efficacious far beyond those areas where purely functional interests make for secrecy. The concept of the "official secret" is the specific invention of bureaucracy, and nothing is so fanatically defended by the bureaucracy as this attitude, which cannot be substantially justified beyond these specifically qualified areas. In facing a parliament, the bureaucracy, out of a sure power instinct, fights every attempt of the parliament to gain knowledge by means of its own experts or from interest groups. The so-called right of parliamentary investigation is one of the means by which parliament seeks such knowledge. Bureaucracy naturally welcomes a poorly informed and hence a powerless parliament—at least in so far as ignorance somehow agrees with the bureaucracy's interests. . . .

Only the expert knowledge of private economic interest groups in the field of "business" is superior to the expert knowledge of the bureaucracy. This is so because the exact knowledge of facts in their field is vital to the economic existence of businessmen. Errors in official statistics do not have direct economic consequences for the guilty official, but errors in the calculation of a capitalist enterprise are paid for by losses, perhaps by its existence. The "secret," as a means of power, is, after all, more safely hidden in the books of an enterpriser than it is in the files of public authorities. For this reason alone authorities are held within narrow barriers when they seek to influence economic life in the capitalist epoch. Very frequently the measures of the state in the field of capitalism take unforeseen and unintended courses, or they are made illusory by the superior expert knowledge of interest groups. . . .

# 4

# Notes
# on the
# Theory of Organization

◆

*Luther H. Gulick*

EVERY LARGE-SCALE OR COMPLICATED enterprise requires many men to carry it
forward. Wherever many men are thus working together the best results
are secured when there is a division of work among these men. The theory
of organization, therefore, has to do with the structure of coordination imposed upon the work-division units of an enterprise. Hence it is not possible to determine how an activity is to be organized without, at the same
time, considering how the work in question is to be divided. Work division
is the foundation of organization; indeed, the reason for organization.

## 1. THE DIVISION OF WORK

It is appropriate at the outset of this discussion to consider the reasons for
and the effect of the division of work. It is sufficient for our purpose to note
the following factors.

### Why Divide Work?

Because men differ in nature, capacity and skill, and gain greatly in
dexterity by specialization;

Because the same man cannot be at two places at the same time;

---

From Papers on the Science of Administration, *edited by Luther H. Gulick and Lyn-
dall Urwick, Copyright 1937 by the Institute of Public Administration, New York.
Reprinted by permission. Footnotes have been abridged and renumbered.*

Because one man cannot do two things at the same time;

Because the range of knowledge and skill is so great that a man cannot within his life-span know more than a small fraction of it.

In other words, it is a question of human nature, time, and space. . . .

The introduction of machinery accentuates the division of work. Even such a simple thing as a saw, a typewriter, or a transit requires increased specialization and serves to divide workers into those who can and those who cannot use the particular instrument effectively. Division of work on the basis of the tools and machines used in work rests no doubt in part on aptitude, but primarily upon the development and maintenance of skill through continued manipulation. . . .

The nature of these subdivisions is essentially pragmatic, in spite of the fact that there is an element of logic underlying them. They are therefore subject to a gradual evolution with the advance of science, the invention of new machines, the progress of technology, and the change of the social system. In the last analysis, however, they appear to be based upon differences in individual human beings. But it is not to be concluded that the apparent stability of "human nature," whatever that may be, limits the probable development of specialization. The situation is quite the reverse. As each field of knowledge and work is advanced, constituting a continually larger and more complicated nexus of related principles, practices and skills, any individual will be less and less able to encompass it and maintain intimate knowledge and facility over the entire area, and there will thus arise a more minute specialization because knowledge and skill advance while man stands still. Division of work and integrated organization are the bootstraps by which mankind lifts itself in the process of civilization.

### The Limits of Division

There are three clear limitations beyond which the division of work cannot to advantage go. The first is practical and arises from the volume of work involved in man-hours. Nothing is gained by subdividing work if that further subdivision results in setting up a task which requires less than the full time of one man. . . .

The second limitation arises from technology and custom at a given time and place. In some areas nothing would be gained by separating undertaking from the custody and cleaning of churches, because by custom the sexton is the undertaker; in building construction it is extraordinarily difficult to redivide certain aspects of electrical and plumbing work and to combine them in a more effective way, because of the jurisdictional conflicts of craft unions; and it is clearly impracticable to establish a division of cost accounting in a field in which no technique of costing has yet been developed.

This second limitation is obviously elastic. It may be changed by invention and by education. If this were not the fact, we should face a static division of labor. It should be noted, however, that a marked change has two dangers. It greatly restricts the labor market from which workers may be drawn and greatly lessens the opportunities open to those who are trained for the particular specialization.

The third limitation is that the subdivision of work must not pass beyond physical division into organic division. It might seem far more efficient to have the front half of the cow in the pasture grazing and the rear half in the barn being milked all the the time, but this organic division would fail. Similarly there is no gain from splitting a single movement or gesture like licking an envelope, or tearing apart a series of intimately and intricately related activities.

It may be said that there is in this an element of reasoning in a circle; that the test here applied as to whether an activity is organic or not is whether it is divisible or not—which is what we set out to define. This change is true. It must be a pragmatic test. Does the division work out? Is something vital destroyed and lost? Does it bleed? . . .

## 2. THE COORDINATION OF WORK

If subdivision of work is inescapable, coordination becomes mandatory. There is, however, no one way to coordination. Experience shows that it may be achieved in two primary ways. These are:

1. By organization, that is, by interrelating the subdivisions of work by allotting them to men who are placed in a structure of authority, so that the work may be coordinated by orders of superiors to subordinates, reaching from the top to the bottom of the entire enterprise.

2. By the dominance of an idea, that is, the development of intelligent singleness of purpose in the minds and wills of those who are working together as a group, so that each worker will of his own accord fit his task into the whole with skill and enthusiasm.

These two principles of coordination are not mutually exclusive; in fact, no enterprise is really effective without the extensive utilization of both.

Size and time are the great limiting factors in the development of coordination. In a small project, the problem is not difficult; the structure of authority is simple, and the central purpose is real to every worker. In a large, complicated enterprise, the organization becomes involved, the lines of authority tangled, and there is danger that the workers will forget that there is any central purpose, and so devote their best energies only to their own individual advancement and advantage.

The interrelated elements of time and habit are extraordinarily important in coordination. Man is a creature of habit. When an enterprise is built up gradually from small beginnings, the staff can be "broken in" step by step. And when difficulties develop, they can be ironed out, and the new method followed from that point on as a matter of habit, with the knowledge that that particular difficulty will not develop again. Routines may even be mastered by drill as they are in the army. When, however, a large new enterprise must be set up or altered overnight, then the real difficulties of coordination make their appearance. The factor of habit, which is thus an important foundation of coordination when time is available, becomes a serious handicap when time is not available, that is, when change rules. The question of coordination therefore must be approached with different emphasis in small and in large enterprises; in simple and in complex situations; in stable and in new or changing organizations.

## Coordination Through Organization

Organization as a way of coordination requires the establishment of a system of authority whereby the central purpose or objective of an enterprise is translated into reality through the combined efforts of many specialists, each working in his own field at a particular time and place.

It is clear from long experience in human affairs that such a structure of authority requires not only many men at work in many places at selected times, but also a single directing executive authority.[1] The problem of organization thus becomes the problem of building up between the executive at the center and the subdivisions of work on the periphery an effective network of communication and control.

The following outline may serve futher to define the problem:

I. First Step: Define the job to be done, such as the furnishing of pure water to all of the people and industries within a given area at the lowest possible cost;

II. Second Step: Provide a director to see that the objective is realized;

III. Third Step: Determine the nature and number of individualized and specialized work units into which the job will have to be divided. As has been seen above, this subdivision depends partly upon the size of the job (no ultimate subdivision can generally be so small as to require less than the full time of one worker) and upon the status of technological and social development at a given time;

IV. Fourth Step: Establish and perfect the structure of authority between the director and the ultimate work subdivisions.

It is this fourth step which is the central concern of the theory of organization. It is the function of this organization (IV) to enable the director (II) to coordinate and energize all of the subdivisions of work (III) so that the major objective (I) may be achieved efficiently.

## The Span of Control

In this undertaking, we are confronted at the start by the inexorable limits of human nature. Just as the hand of man can span only a limited number of notes on the piano, so the mind and will of man can span but a limited number of immediate managerial contacts. . . . The limit of control is partly a matter of the limits of knowledge, but even more is it a matter of the limits of time and energy. As a result, the executive of any enterprise can personally direct only a few persons. He must depend upon these to direct others, and upon them in turn to direct still others, until the last man in the organization is reached.

This condition placed upon all human organization by the limits of the span of control obviously differs in different kinds of work and in organizations of different sizes. Where the work is of a routine, repetitive, measurable and homogeneous character, one man can perhaps direct several score workers. This is particularly true when the workers are all in a single room. Where the work is diversified, qualitative, and particularly when the workers are scattered, one man can supervise only a few. This diversification, dispersion, and non-measurability is of course most evident at the very top of any organization. It follows that the limitations imposed by the span of control are most evident at the top of an organization, directly under the executive himself.

But when we seek to determine how many immediate subordinates the director of an enterprise can effectively supervise, we enter a realm of experience which has not been brought under sufficient scientific study to furnish a final answer. . . .

It is not difficult to understand why there is . . . divergence of statement among authorities who are agreed on the fundamentals. It arises in part from the differences in the capacities and work habits of individual executives observed, and in part from the non-comparable character of the work covered. It would seem that insufficient attention has been devoted to three factors: first, the element of diversification of function; second, the element of time; and third, the element of space. A chief of public works can deal effectively with more direct subordinates than can the general of the army, because all of his immediate subordinates in the department of public works will be in the general field of engineering, while in the army there will be many different elements, such as communications, chemistry, aviation, ordnance, motorized service, engineering supply, transportation, etc., each with its own technology. The element of time is also of great significance as has been indicated above. In a stable organization the chief executive can deal with more immediate subordinates than in a new or changing organization. Similarly, space influences the span of control. An organization located in one building can be supervised through more immediate subordinates than can the same organization if scattered in several cities. When scattered there is not only need for more supervision, and therefore more supervisory personnel, but also for a fewer number of contacts with the chief executive because of the increased difficulty faced by the chief executive in learning sufficient details about a far-flung organization to do an intelligent job. The failure to attach sufficient importance to these variables has served to limit the scientific validity of the statements which have been made that one man can supervise but three, or five, or eight, or twelve immediate subordinates.

These considerations do not, however, dispose of the problem. They indicate rather the need for further research. But without further research we may conclude that the chief executive of an organization can deal with only a few immediate subordinates; that this number is determined not only by the nature of the work, but also by the nature of the executive; and that the number of immediate subordinates in a large, diversified, and dispersed organization must be even less than in a homogeneous and unified organization to achieve the same measure of coordination.

## One Master

From the earliest times it has been recognized that nothing but confusion arises under multiple command. "A man cannot serve two masters" was adduced as a theological argument because it was already accepted as a principle of human relation[s] in everyday life. In administration this is known as the principle of "unity of command."[2] The principle may be stated as follows: A workman subject to orders from several superiors will be confused, inefficient, and irresponsible; a workman subject to orders from but one superior may be methodical, efficient, and responsible. Unity of command thus refers to those who are commanded, not to those who issue the commands.[3]

The significance of this principle in the process of coordination and organization must not be lost sight of. In building a structure of coordination, it is often tempting to set up more than one boss for a man who is doing work which has more than one relationship. Even as great a philosopher of management as Taylor fell into this error in setting up separate foremen to deal with machinery, with materials, with speed, etc., each with the power of giving orders directly to the individual workman.[4] The rigid adherence to the principle of unity of command may have its absurdities; these are, however, unimportant in comparison with the certainty of confusion, inefficiency, and irresponsibility which arise from the violation of the principle.

## Technical Efficiency

. . . It has been observed by authorities in many fields that the efficiency of a group working together is directly related to the homogeneity of the work they are performing, of the processes they are utilizing, and of the purposes which actuate them. From top to bottom, the group must be unified. It must work together.

It follows from this (1) that any organizational structure which brings together in a single unit work divisions which are non-homogeneous in work, in technology, or in purpose will encounter the danger of friction and inefficiency; and (2) that a unit based on a given specialization cannot be given technical direction by a layman.

In the realm of government it is not difficult to find many illustrations of the unsatisfactory results of non-homogeneous administrative combinations. It is generally agreed that agricultural development and education cannot be administered by the same men who enforce pest and disease control, because the success of the former rests upon friendly cooperation and trust of the farmers, while the latter engenders resentment and suspicion. Similarly, activities like drug control established in protection of the consumer do not find appropriate homes in departments dominated by the interests of the producer. In the larger cities and in states it has been found that hospitals cannot be so well administered by the health department directly as they can be when set up independently in a separate department, or at least in a bureau with extensive autonomy, and it is generally agreed that public welfare administration and police administration require separation, as do public health administration and welfare administration, though both of these combinations may be found in successful operation under special conditions. No one would think of combining water supply and public education, or tax administration and public recreation. In every one of these cases, it will be seen that there is some element either of work to be done, or of the technology used, or of the end sought which is non-homogeneous.

Another phase of the combination of incompatible functions in the same office may be found in the common American practice of appointing unqualified laymen and politicians to technical positions or to give technical direction to highly specialized services. As Dr. Frank J. Goodnow pointed out a generation ago, we are faced here by two heterogeneous functions, "politics" and "administration," the combination of which cannot be undertaken within the structure of the administration without producing inefficiency.

## Caveamus Expertum

At this point a word of caution is necessary. The application of the principle of homogeneity has its pitfalls. Every highly trained technician, particularly in the learned professions, has a profound sense of omniscience and a great desire for complete independence in the service of society. When employed by government he knows how to render this service. He tends to be utterly oblivious of all other needs, because, after all, is not his particular technology the road to salvation? Any restraint applied to him is "limitation of freedom," and any criticism "springs from ignorance and jealousy." Every budget increase he secures is "in the public interest," while every increase secured elsewhere is "a sheer waste." His efforts and maneuvers to expand are "public education" and "civic organization," while similar efforts by others are "propaganda" and "politics."

Another trait of the expert is his tendency to assume knowledge and authority in fields in which he has no competence. In this particular, educators, lawyers, priests, admirals, doctors, scientists, engineers, accountants, merchants, and bankers are all the same—having achieved technical competence or "success" in one field, they come to think this competence is a general quality detachable from the field and inherent in themselves. They step without embarrassment into other areas. They do not remember that the robes of authority of one kingdom confer no sovereignty in another; but that there they are merely a masquerade.

The expert knows his "stuff." Society needs him, and must have him more and more as man's technical knowledge becomes more and more extensive. But history shows us that the common man is a better judge of his own needs in the long run than any cult of experts. Kings and ruling classes, priests and prophets, soldiers and lawyers, when permitted to rule rather than serve mankind, have in the end done more to check the advance of human welfare than they have to advance it. The true place of the expert is, as A. E. [Buck] said so well, "on tap, not on top." The essential validity of democracy rests upon this philosophy, for democracy is a way of government in which the common man is the final judge of what is good for him.

Efficiency is one of the things that is good for him because it makes life richer and safer. That efficiency is to be secured more and more through the use of technical specialists. These specialists have no right to ask for, and must not be given, freedom from supervisory control, but in establishing that control, a government which ignores the conditions of efficiency cannot expect to achieve efficiency.

## 3. ORGANIZATIONAL PATTERNS

*Organization Up or Down?*

One of the great sources of confusion in the discussion of the theory of organization is that some authorities work and think primarily from the top down, while others work and think from the bottom up. This is perfectly natural, because some authorities are interested primarily in the executive and in the problems of central management, while others are interested primarily in individual services and activities. Those who work from the top down regard the organization as a system of subdividing the enterprise under the chief executive, while those who work from the bottom up look upon organization as a system of combining the individual units of work into aggregates which are in turn subordinated to the chief executive. It may be argued that either approach leads to a consideration of the entire problem, so that it is of no great significance which way the organization is viewed. Certainly it makes this very important practical difference: those who work from the top down must guard themselves from the danger of sacrificing the effectiveness of the individual services in their zeal to achieve a model structure at the top, while those who start from the bottom must guard themselves from the danger of thwarting coordination in their eagerness to develop effective individual services. . . .

*Organizing the Executive*

. . . What is the work of the chief executive? What does he do? The answer is POSDCORB.

POSDCORB is, of course, a made-up word designed to call attention to the various functional elements of the work of a chief executive because "administration" and "management" have lost all specific content. POSDCORB is made up of the initials and stands for the following activities:

Planning, that is working out in broad outline the things that need to be done and the methods for doing them to accomplish the purpose set for the enterprise;

Organizing, that is the establishment of the formal structure of authority through which work subdivisions are arranged, defined, and coordinated for the defined objective;

Staffing, that is the whole personnel function of bringing in and training the staff and maintaining favorable conditions of work;

Directing, that is the continuous task of making decisions and embodying them in specific and general orders and instructions and serving as the leader of the enterprise;

Coordinating, that is the all important duty of interrelating the various parts of the work;

72

Reporting, that is keeping those to whom the executive is responsible informed as to what is going on, which thus includes keeping himself and his subordinates informed through records, research, and inspection;

Budgeting, with all that goes with budgeting in the form of fiscal planning, accounting and control.

This statement of the work of a chief executive is adapted from the functional analysis elaborated by Henri Fayol in his "Industrial and General Administration." It is believed that those who know administration intimately will find in this analysis a valid and helpful pattern, into which can be fitted each of the major activities and duties of any chief executive.

If these seven elements may be accepted as the major duties of the chief executive, it follows that they *may* be separately organized as subdivisions of the executive. The need for such subdivision depends entirely on the size and complexity of the enterprise. In the largest enterprises, particularly where the chief executive is as a matter of fact unable to do the work that is thrown upon him, it may be presumed that one or more parts of POSDCORB should be suborganized. . . .

## Aggregating the Work Units

In building the organization from the bottom up we are confronted by the task of analyzing everything that has to be done and determining in what grouping it can be placed without violating the principle of homogeneity. This is not a simple matter, either practically or theoretically. It will be found that each worker in each position must be characterized by:

1. The major *purpose* he is serving, such as furnishing water, controlling crime, or conducting education;

2. The *process* he is using, such as engineering, medicine, carpentry, stenography, statistics, accounting;

3. The *persons or things* dealt with or served, such as immigrants, veterans, Indians, forests, mines, parks, orphans, farmers, automobiles, or the poor;

4. The *place* where he renders his service, such as Hawaii, Boston, Washington, the Dust Bowl, Alabama, or Central High School.

Where two men are doing exactly the same work in the same way for the same people at the same place, then the specifications of their jobs will be the same under 1, 2, 3, and 4. All such workers may be easily combined in a single aggregate and supervised together. Their work is homogeneous. But when any of the four items differ, then there must be a selection among the items to determine which shall be given precedence in determining what is and what is not homogeneous and therefore combinable.

A few illustrations may serve to point [out] the problem. Within the City of New York, what shall be done with the doctor who spends all of his time in the public schools examining and attending to children in the Bronx? Shall we (1) say that he is primarily working for the school system, and therefore place him under the department of education? (2) say that he is a medical man, and that we will have all physicians in the department of health? (3) say that he is working with children, and that he should therefore be in a youth administration? or (4) say that he is working in the Bronx and must therefore be attached to the Bronx borough president's office? Whichever answer we give will ignore one or the other of the four elements characterizing his work. The same problem arises with the lawyer serving the street construction gang on damage cases in Brooklyn, the engineer who is working for the department of health in Richmond, and the accountant examining vouchers and records in Queens for the district attorney. . . .

## Organization by Major Purpose

Organization by major purpose, such as water supply, crime control, or education, serves to bring together in a single large department all of those who are at work endeavoring to render a particular service. Under such a policy, the department of education will contain not only teachers and school administrators, but also architects, engineers, chauffeurs, auto mechanics, electricians, carpenters, janitors, gardeners, nurses, doctors, lawyers, and accountants. Everything that has to do with the schools would be included, extending perhaps even to the control of traffic about school properties. Similarly, the department of water supply would include not only engineers and maintenance gangs, but also planners, statisticians, lawyers, architects, accountants, meter readers, bacteriologists, and public health experts.

The advantages of this type of organization are three: first, it makes more certain the accomplishment of any given broad purpose or project by bringing the whole job under a single director with immediate control of all the experts, agencies, and services which are required in the performance of the work. No one can interfere. The director does not have to wait for others nor negotiate for their help and cooperation; nor appeal to the chief executive to untangle a conflict. He can devote all his energies to getting on with the job.

Second, from the standpoint of self-government, organization by purpose seems to conform best to the objectives of government as they are recognized and understood by the public. The public sees the end result, and cannot understand the methodology. It can therefore express its approval or disapproval with less confusion and more effectiveness regarding major purposes than it can regarding the processes.

Third, it apparently serves as the best basis for eliciting the energies and loyalties of the personnel and for giving a focus and central drive to the whole activity, because purpose is understandable by the entire personnel down to the last clerk and inspector.

The statement of these strong points of organization by major purpose points the way to its dangers. These are to be found, first, in the impossibility of cleanly dividing all of the work of any government into a few such major purposes which do not overlap extensively. For example, education overlaps immediately with health and with recreation, as does public works with law enforcement. The strong internal coordination and drive tends to precipitate extensive and serious external conflict and confusion, just as there is more danger of accident with a high-powered motor car. This is apparent particularly in the development of a reasonable city plan, or in arriving at a consistent policy throughout the departments for the maintenance of properties, or in handling legal matters, or arranging similar work and salary conditions. The lawyers, engineers, accountants, doctors of different departments will all have their own ideas as to how similar matters are to be dealt with.

Second, there is danger that an organization erected on the basis of purpose will fail to make use of the most up-to-date technical devices and specialists because the dominance of purpose generally tends to obscure the element of process, and because there may not be enough work of a given technical sort to permit efficient subdivision.

Third, there is also danger in such an organization that subordinate parts of the work will be unduly suppressed or lost sight of because of the singleness of purpose, enthusiasm, and drive of the head of the department. For example, medical work with children when established under the department of education as a division is likely to receive less encouragement than it would if independently established in the health department, because after all the department of education is primarily interested in schools and has its own great needs and problems.

Fourth, a department established on the basis of purpose falls easily into the habit of overcentralization, and thus fails to fit its service effectively to the people. Or if it does decentralize its services, as do the fire department, the police department, the health department, and the department of education of New York City, the representatives of these departments in the field do not always make the best use of each other's assistance and cooperation, and when any difficulty does arise, it is such a long way to the top where coordination can be worked out, that it is easier to get along without it.

Fifth, an organization fully equipped from top to bottom with all of the direct and collateral services required for the accomplishment of its central purpose, without the need of any assistance from other departments, drifts very easily into an attitude and position of complete independence from all other activities and even from democratic control itself.

## Organization by Major Process

Organization by major process, such as engineering, teaching, the law, or medicine, tends to bring together in a single department all of those who are at work making use of a given special skill or technology, or are members of a given profession. Under such a policy the department of law would comprise all of the lawyers and law clerks, including those who are devoting their time to school matters, or water supply suits, or drafting ordinances. The department of engineering and public works would have all the engineers, including those concerned with planning, design, construction, maintenance, and other phases of engineering work, wherever that work was found. This would include the work in the parks, on the streets, in the schools, and in connection with water, sewer, waste, and other services. The department of health would include all of the doctors, nurses, and bacteriologists, and would not only carry on the general public health work, but would do the medical and nursing work for the schools, the water department, the department of social welfare, etc., as has been outlined above.

In every one of these cases it will be observed that the basis of organization is the bringing together in a single office or department of all the workers who are using some particular kind of skill, knowledge, machinery, or profession. This principle of organization has the following advantages:

First, it guarantees the maximum utilization of up-to-date technical skill and by bringing together in a single office a large amount of each kind of work (technologically measured), makes it possible in each case to make use of the most effective divisions of work and specialization.

Second, it makes possible also the economies of the maximum use of labor-saving machinery and mass production. These economies arise not from the total mass of the work to be performed, not from the fact that the work performed serves the same general purpose, but from the fact that the work is performed with the same machine, with the same technique, with the same motions. For example, economy in printing comes from skill in typesetting, printing, and binding and the use of modern equipment. It makes no difference to the printer whether he is printing a pamphlet for the schools, a report for the police department, or a form for the comptroller.

Unit costs, efficiency in the doing of the job, rest upon the process, not the purpose.[5]

Third, organization by process encourages coordination in all of the technical and skilled work of the enterprise, because all of those engaged in any field are brought together under the same supervision, instead of being scattered in several departments as is the case when organization is based upon some other principle.

Fourth, it furnishes an excellent approach to the development of central coordination and control when certain of the services such as budgeting, accounting, purchasing, and planning are set up on a process basis and used as instruments of integration even where other activities are set up on some other basis.

Fifth, organization by process is best adapted to the development of career service, and the stimulation of professional standards and pride. A career ladder can be erected very much more easily in a department which is from top to bottom engineers, or doctors, or statisticians, or clerks, than it can in a department which is partly engineers, partly doctors, partly statisticians, partly clerks. . . .

These are the major advantages of organization on the basis of process. There are, of course, offsetting difficulties. As in the case of any other principle of organization, it is impossible to aggregate all of the work of the government on such a basis alone. It is not difficult to do so for engineering and medicine and teaching, but it becomes impossible when we reach typing and clerical work. It cannot furnish a satisfactory basis for doing the whole job in any large or complicated enterprise.

In the second place, there is always the danger that organization by process will hinder the accomplishment of major purposes, because the process departments may be more interested in *how* things are done than in *what* is accomplished. For example, a housing department which must clear the slums, build new low-cost tenements and manage them, and inspect existing housing and approve new building plans, may find it difficult to make rapid progress if it must draw its legal help from the corporation counsel, its architects from the department of engineering, its enforcement officers from the police department, and its plans from the planning commission, particularly if one or more of these departments regards public housing as a nuisance and passing fad. There are also accountants who think that the only reason for the running of a government is the keeping of books!

Third, experience seems to indicate that a department built around a given profession or skill tends to show a greater degree of arrogance and unwillingness to accept democratic control. This is perhaps a natural outgrowth of the insolence of professionalism to which reference has already been made.

Fourth, organization by process is perhaps less favorable to the development of a separate administrative service, because it tends to bring rather narrow professional specialists to the top of each department, men who are thereby disqualified for transfer to administrative posts in other fields.

And finally, the necessity of effective coordination is greatly increased. Purpose departments must be coordinated so that they will not conflict but will work shoulder to shoulder. But whether they do, or do not, the individual major purposes will be accomplished to a considerable extent, and a failure in any service is limited in its effect to that service. Process departments must be coordinated not only to prevent conflict, but also to guarantee positive cooperation. They work hand in hand. They must also time their work so that it will fit together, a factor of lesser significance in the purpose departments. A failure in one process affects the whole enterprise, and a failure to coordinate one process division may destroy the effectiveness of all of the work that is being done.

While organization by process thus puts great efficiency within our reach, this efficiency cannot be realized unless the compensating structure of coordination is developed.

## Organization by Clientele or Matériel

Organization on the basis of the persons served or dealt with, or on the basis of the things dealt with, tends to bring together in a single department, regardless of the purpose of the service or the techniques used, all of those who are working with a given group or a given set of things. Examples are the veterans' administration which deals with all of the problems of the veteran, be they in health, in hospitals, in insurance, in welfare, or in education; and the immigration bureau which deals with immigrants at all points, including legal, financial, and medical services. Departmentalization on the basis of *matériel* is more common in private business than in public. Department stores, for example, have separate departments for furniture, hardware, drugs, jewelry, shoes, etc., and have separate buyers and sales forces for each. In many communities the school is in reality such a service, as it concentrates most of the community services touching children in school, including medical inspection, corrective treatment, free lunches and recreation, and certain phases of juvenile crime. The Forest Service is another organization based on *matériel*—in this case, trees.

The great advantage of this type of organization is the simplification and coordination of the service of government in its contact with the consumer. He does not encounter first one and then another representative, each of whom does or demands something different or even something contradictory. . . .

A second advantage is found in the increasing skill which attends the handling over and over of the same material.

A third gain arises from the elimination of duplicate travel, particularly in dealing with widely separated or sparsely distributed work.

The disadvantages of an organization which brings together all of the contacts with a given individual or thing are:

First, it tends to sacrifice the efficiency of specialization, because it must after all perform several otherwise specialized functions through the same organization or even at times through the same agent. . . .

A second difficulty is found in the impossibility of applying the principle of division by persons served to all of the work of a government, without encountering extensive conflict and duplication. It is not difficult to pick out special groups like the aged, the youth, the criminal, the veteran, the real estate owner, etc., but when all is said and done there remains a great number of the ordinary citizens that does not fall into *any single* grouping. Each individual will appear in various groups at various times, and in the general group known as "the public" the rest of the time. And it is clearly impossible to organize a special department for the public, with all of the heterogeneous elements which this would entail from the standpoint of dissimilar technologies and conflicting objectives. It must be remembered also that even such departments as seem to be organized on the basis of persons served do not as a matter of fact cover all of the services rendered to or government contacts with a class of individuals. . . .

A third difficulty arises from the danger of dominance by favor-seeking pressure groups. Departments set up by clientele seldom escape political dominance by those groups and are generally found to be special pleaders for those groups, at times in opposition to the general interest of society as a whole. This is in part due to the fact that the organization itself is often brought into being through the action of a pressure group and its demand for a special agency to serve it, but it is also continued through the efforts of the agency once established to marshal and maintain a group in its support. It follows that agencies so set up as to maintain or develop their own pressure backing are peculiarly difficult for democratic control and tend not to fit into a coordinated social policy.

## Organization by Place

Organization on the basis of the place at which the service is performed brings together all of those who work in a limited area regardless of the service they are performing or of the techniques they represent. . . .

. . . [For example,] in some of the largest city police systems the city is divided into precincts, and most of the police activities within a given area are under the complete direction of a precinct officer through whom all communication to and from headquarters must go. . . .

The real work of government is done out among the people in the various sections of the state or city. In the supervision of these forces it is often necessary to establish some form of regional organization, if for no other reason than to save the time of the supervisory officers, who cannot be in two places at once. It is thus generally a question as to how high up in the organization geographical subdivision shall be introduced. Obviously this may be done at the very top, as the first division of the work under the chief executive of an enterprise, or it may be introduced far down the line after the major divisions have been set up by purpose, by process, or by clientele. The former may be termed *primary* geographical subdivision and the latter *secondary*, *tertiary*, or *subordinate* geographical subdivision. A department or major activity, like the Tennessee Valley Authority, which is set up on the basis of geographical boundaries is in fact a primary geographical subdivision of the government. . . .

The advantages of departmentalization on the basis of geographical areas, that is on the basis of superior geographical subdivision are fairly obvious in practice. They consist first of the greater ease of coordination of services rendered and controls exercised within a given area; second, of the greater tendency to adapt the total program to the needs of the areas served, not alone because of the discretion resting within the divisions, but also because the needs and differences of the areas will be more vigorously represented at headquarters in the general consideration of broad policy; and third, of the greater ease with which cooperative relations may be established with subordinate governmental units, which are of necessity first of all geographically defined units. Decentralization of geographical divisions strengthens these tendencies and serves, moreover, to reduce travel costs, short circuit adjustment problems, cut red tape, and speed up all joint activities and administrative decisions. It increases not only the awareness of the officials to local needs and to the interrelation of service and planning problems, but develops a new sensitivity to the process of democratic control through intimate association of the officials with the people served.

With decentralized subdivision a large amount of discretion must be delegated to the men in charge of field offices; in fact, they must be men of ability equal to if not superior to those who would be selected to head centralized departments of similar scope.

The difficulties of primary geographic subdivision are also not far to seek. They consist of the increased difficulty of maintaining a uniform nation-wide, state-wide, or city-wide policy; the danger of too narrow and short-sighted management; and the increased difficulty of making full use of technical services and the highest specialization because of the division of the work into limited blocks. Decentralization tends to enhance these difficulties by reason of physical isolation. It introduces other factors as well, such as higher costs for supervisory personnel, the general hesitancy of central administrative heads to delegate sufficient real power, the lesser prestige of localized officials, and the increased tendency of such a system to come under the control of localized logrolling pressure groups. Political parties under our system of representation are based upon geographical areas. An administrative system also set up by areas is peculiarly subject to spoliation by politicians as long as we have the spoils system.

Whenever the concept of geographic areas is introduced into the structure of organization, either as a primary or as a subordinate plan of division of work, there is always the further practical problem of delineating appropriate boundaries. This is particularly difficult when it is planned to deal with several activities widely differing in their nature and technology. There is always the danger that the tasks to be dealt with do not follow compact geographic boundaries and that the administrative separation introduced by the geographic division will complicate rather than simplify the work.

## Line and Staff

. . . When the work of government is subjected to the dichotomy of "line" and "staff," there are included in staff all of those persons who devote their time exclusively to the knowing, thinking and planning functions, and in the line all of the remainder who are, thus, chiefly concerned with the doing functions. The overhead directing authority of the staff group, usually a board or committee, is the "general staff."

Obviously those in the line are also thinking and planning and making suggestions to superior officers. They cannot operate otherwise. But this does not make them staff officers. Those also in the staff are *doing* something; they do not merely sit and twiddle their thumbs. But they do not organize others, they do not direct or appoint personnel, they do not issue commands, they do not take responsibility for the job. Everything they suggest is referred up, not down, and is carried out, if at all, on the responsibility and under the direction of a line officer.

The important point of confusion in considering line and staff has arisen in speaking of the budget director, the purchasing agent, the controller, the public relations secretary, as "staff" officers. On the basis of the definition it is clear that they are all line officers. They have important duties of direction and control. When administrative responsibility and power are added to any staff function, that function thereby becomes immediately and completely a line function. There is no middle ground.

The chief value of the line and staff classification is to point to the need (1) of developing an independent planning agency as an aid to the chief executive, and (2) of refusing to inject any element of administrative authority and control into such an agency.

The necessity for central purchase, for personnel administration, for budgeting, and for fiscal control rests on other considerations and not on the philosophy of the general staff.

## 4. INTERRELATION OF SYSTEMS OF DEPARTMENTALIZATION

Students of administration have long sought a single principle of effective departmentalization just as alchemists sought the philosophers' stone. But they have sought in vain. There is apparently no one most effective system of departmentalism.

Each of the four basic systems of organization is intimately related with the other three, because in any enterprise all four elements are present in the doing of the work and are embodied in every individual workman. Each member of the enterprise is working for some major purpose, uses some process, deals with some persons, and serves or works at some place.

If an organization is erected about any one of these four characteristics of work, it becomes immediately necessary to recognize the other characteristics in constructing the secondary and tertiary divisions of the work. For example, a government which is first divided on the basis of place will, in each geographical department, find it necessary to divide by purpose, by process, by clientele, or even again by place; and one divided in the first instance by purpose, may well be divided next by process and then by place. While the first or primary division of any enterprise is of very great significance, it must none the less be said that there is no one most effective pattern for determining the priority and order for the introduction of these interdependent principles. It will depend in any case upon the results which are desired at a given time and place.

An organization is a living and dynamic entity. Each activity is born, has its periods of experimental development, of vigorous and stable activity, and, in some cases, of decline. A principle of organization appropriate at one stage may not be appropriate at all during a succeeding stage, particularly in view of the different elements of strength and of weakness which we have seen to exist in the various systems of departmentalization. In any government various parts of its work will always stand at different stages of their life cycle. It will therefore be found that not all of the activities of any government may be appropriately departmentalized neatly on the basis of a single universal plan. Time is an essential element in the formula.

Another variable is technological development. The invention of machines, the advance of applied science, the rise of new specializations and professions, changes in society and in the way men work and move in their private life must be continually reflected in the work of government, and therefore in the structure of government. Medieval governments made use of warriors, priests, artists, builders, and tax gatherers; they had no place for sanitary engineers, chemists, entomologists, pneumatic drill operators and typists. Before you organize a statistical division there must be statistical machinery and statistical science, but as soon as there are such machinery and science, any large organization which fails to recognize the fact in its organization may greatly lessen its utilization of the newly available tools and skills.

A further variable influencing the structure of any enterprise is its size, measured not so much by the amount of work done as by the number of men at work and their geographical dispersion. A drug store is an excellent illustration of the problem encountered. It must have a prescription department with a licensed pharmacist, no matter how small it is, because of the technological requirements involved. But it does not need to have a separate medicine and supply department, refreshment department, book department, toy department, sporting goods department, cigar department, and delivery department, each with a trained manager, buyer and sales force, unless it is a big store. In the small store, the pharmacist may even be the manager, the soda jerker, and the book dispenser. If the business is big enough, it may be desirable to have more than one store in order to reach the customers, thus introducing geographical subdivision. Similarly, in government the nature of the organization must be adapted not only to the technological requirements but also to the size of the undertaking and the dispersion of its work. . . .

## Structure and Coordination

The major purpose of organization is coordination, as has been pointed out above. It should therefore be noted that each of the four principles of departmentalization plays a different role in coordination. In each case the highest degree of coordination takes place within the departments set up, and the greatest lack of coordination and danger of friction occurs between the departments, or at the points where they overlap.

If all of the departments are set up on the basis of purpose, then the task of the chief executive in the field of coordination will be to see that the major purposes are not in conflict and that the various processes which are used are consistent, and that the government as it touches classes of citizens or reaches areas of the community is appropriate, rational, and effective. He will not have to concern himself with coordination within the departments, as each department head will look after this.

If all of the departments are set up on the basis of process, the work methods will be well standardized on professional lines, and the chief executive will have to see that these are coordinated and timed to produce the results and render the services for which the government exists, and that the service rendered actually fits the needs of the persons or areas served.

If place be the basis of departmentalization, that is, if the services be decentralized, then the task of the chief executive is not to see that the activities are coordinated locally and fit the locality, but to see that each of these services makes use of the standard techniques and that the work in each area is part of a general program and policy.

If the work of the government be departmentalized in part on the basis of purpose, in part on the basis of process, in part on the basis of clientele, and in part on the basis of place, it will be seen that the problems of coordination and smooth operation are multiplied and that the task of the executive is increased. Moreover, the nature of his work is altered. In an organization in which all of the major divisions follow one philosophy, the executive himself must furnish the interdepartmental coordination and see that things do not fall between two stools. In an organization built on two or more bases of departmentalization, the executive may use, for example, the process departments as a routine means of coordinating the purpose departments. None the less, the task of the executive is extraordinarily complicated. There is also great danger in such an organization that one department may fail to aid or actually proceed to obstruct another department. When departments cross each other at right angles, the danger of collision is far greater and far more serious than when their contacts are along parallel lines at their respective outer limits. . . .

## The Means of Interdepartmental Coordination

In the discussion thus far it has been assumed that the normal method of interdepartmental coordination is hierarchical in its operation. That is, if trouble develops between a field representive (X) of one department and the field representative (A) of another department, that the solution will be found by carrying the matter up the line from inferior to superior until the complaint of Mr. X and the complaint of Mr. A finally reach their common superior, be he mayor, governor, or President. In actual practice, there are also other means of interdepartmental coordination which must be regarded as part of the organization as such. Among these must be included planning boards and committees, interdepartmental committees, coordinators, and officially arranged regional meetings, etc. These are all organizational devices for bringing about the coordination of the work of government. Coordination of this type is essential. It greatly lessens the military stiffness and red tape of the strictly hierarchical structure. It greatly increases the consultative process in administration. It must be recognized, however, that it is to be used only to deal with abnormal situations and where matters of policy are involved, as in planning. The organization itself should be set up so that it can dispose of the routine work without such devices, because these devices are too dilatory, irresponsible, and time-consuming for normal administration. Wherever an organization needs continual resort to special coordinating devices in the discharge of its regular work, this is proof that the organization is bad. These special agencies of coordination draw their sanction from the hierarchical structure and should receive the particular attention of the executive authority. They should not be set up and forgotten, ignored, or permitted to assume an independent status. . . .

In the devices of coordination, one must recognize also joint service contract and coincident personnel appointments. Independent agencies may be pulled together in operation through such use of the same staff or service. There are many illustrations of the former, especially in engineering services. The county agent who is at the same time a county, a state, and a federal official is an example of the latter.

A great obstacle in the way of all of these plans of coordination is found in the danger of introducing confusion in direction through the violation of the principle of unity of command, and also in the difference in the level of authority of those who are brought together in any interdepartmental or intergovernmental coordinating arrangement. The representatives of the Department of Agriculture, for example, may have a large measure of responsibility and power, and may therefore be in a position to work out an adjustment of program through conference and to agree to a new line of conduct, but the representatives of the Army, coming from an entirely different kind of an organization are sure to be in a position where they cannot make any adjustments without passing the decision back to headquarters.

## 5. COORDINATION BY IDEAS

Any large and complicated enterprise would be incapable of effective operation if reliance for coordination were placed in organization alone. Organization . . . does not take the place of a dominant central idea as the foundation of action and self-coordination in the daily operation of all of the parts of the enterprise. Accordingly, the most difficult task of the chief executive is not command, it is leadership, that is, the development of the desire and will to work together for a purpose in the minds of those who are associated in any activity.

Human beings are compounded of cogitation and emotion and do not function well when treated as though they were merely cogs in motion. Their capacity for great and productive labor, creative cooperative work, and loyal self-sacrifice knows no limits provided the whole man, body-mind-and-spirit, is thrown into the program.

*Implications*

. . . The following specific elements . . . bear directly upon the problem of coordination:

1. Personnel administration becomes of extraordinary significance, not merely from the standpoint of finding qualified appointees for the various positions, but even more from the standpoint of assisting in the selection of individuals and in the maintenance of conditions which will serve to create a foundation of loyalty and enthusiasm. . . .

2. Even where the structure of the organization is arranged to produce coordination by authority, and certainly in those realms in which the structure as such is wanting, the effort should be made to develop the driving ideas by cooperative effort and compromise so that there may be an understanding of the program, a sense of participation in its formulation, and enthusiasm in its realization.

3. Proper reporting on the results of the work of the departments and of the government as a whole to the public and to the controlling legislative body, and public appreciation of good service rendered by public employees is essential, not merely as a part of the process of democratic control, but also as a means to the development of service morale.

4. As a matter of public policy the government should encourage the development of professional associations among the employees of the government, in recognition of the fact that such associations can assist powerfully in the development of standards and ideals. . . .

5. A developing organization must be continually engaged in research bearing upon the major technical and policy problems encountered, and upon the efficiency of the processes of work. In both types of research, but particularly in the latter, members of the staff at every level should be led to participate in the inquiries and in the development of solutions.

6. There is need for a national system of honor awards which may be conspicuously conferred upon men and women who render distinguished and faithful, though not necessarily highly advertised, public service.

7. The structure of any organization must reflect not only the logic of the work to be done, but also the special aptitudes of the particular human beings who are brought together in the organization to carry through a particular project. It is the men and not the organization chart that do the work.

## Dominant Ideals

The power of an idea to serve as the foundation of coordination is so great that one may observe many examples of coordination even in the absence of any single leader or of any framework of authority. The best illustration is perhaps a nation at war. Every element steps into line and swings into high gear "to help win the war." The coordination is enthusiastic and complete, within the limits of knowledge of course. In an old stable community, small enough for each person to know the other, even competing businesses generally work along together in harmony. The town board, the school board, the park commission, the overseer of the poor, though answerable to no single executive, manage to get along with each other and each to fit his part of the work into that of the others to arrive at a sensible result for the whole picture. Men of intelligence and good will find little difficulty in working together for a given purpose even without an organization. They do not need to be held in line or driven to do a specific task in a specific way at a specific time. They carry on because of their inner compulsion, and may in the end accomplish a far better result for that very reason. . . .

It becomes increasingly clear, therefore, that the task of the administrator must be accomplished less and less by coercion and discipline and more and more by persuasion. In other words, management of the future must look more to leadership and less to authority as the primary means of coordination.

. . . The more important and the more difficult part of coordination is to be sought not through systems of authority, but through ideas and persuasion, and to make clear the point that the absurdities of the hierarchical system of authority are made sweet and reasonable through unity of purpose. It may well be that the system of organization, the structure of authority, is primarily important in coordination because it makes it easy to deal with the routine affairs, and thereby lessens the strain placed upon leadership so that it can thus devote itself more fully to the supreme task of developing consent, participation, loyalty, enthusiasm, and creative devotion.

## 6. COORDINATION AND CHANGE

### The Limits of Coordination

Are there limits to coordination? Is mankind capable of undertaking activities which though interrelated are beyond man's power of systematic coordination? . . .

It is clear . . . in which direction the limitations of coordination lie. The difficulties arise from:

1. The uncertainty of the future, not only as to natural phenomena like rain and crops, but even more as to the behavior of individuals and of peoples;

2. The lack of knowledge, experience, wisdom, and character among leaders and their confused and conflicting ideals and objectives;

3. The lack of administrative skill and technique;

4. The vast number of variables involved and the incompleteness of human knowledge, particularly with regard to man and life;

5. The lack of orderly methods of developing, considering, perfecting and adopting new ideas and programs. . . .

## The Accretion of Functions

In view of the fact that organization must conform to the functions performed, attention must be given to the process by which new functions are assumed by governmental units. . . .

In view of the growth processes of governmental functions, those who are concerned with the mechanics of organization will fail to develop a satisfactory theory of organization unless they regard their basic problem as dynamic. In considering the organization of government we deal not alone with living men, but with an organism which has its own life.

## The Evolution of Government

To what extent is this organism subject to the Darwinian laws of survival? It was a basic theory of classical economists that business enterprises survive only in so far as they adapt themselves to the changing economic environment, and that only the fittest survive, fitness being measured in terms of prices and profits. Whatever the truth of that hypothesis, mankind has determined not to try it out. At one end business has upset the free competitive test by monopolies and cartels, and at the other end the public has refused to let itself be pushed around freely by such combinations or to let business enterprises go to the wall in any wholesale fashion, when a whole system cannot meet the economic judgment day.

When we turn to governmental organizations we find even less "survival of the fittest." Governmental organizations seem to be extraordinarily immune to evolutionary changes. Next to the church, they are in all civilizations the most vigorous embodiments of immortality. A governmental unit is by nature a monopoly, and is thus not subject to the purifying influence of competition. It does not have a profit and loss record; its balance sheet is buoyed up by "good will"; its product is priceless and often imponderable;

its deficits are met from taxes, loans and hope. Under these conditions a governmental unit can continue for many years after its utility has passed, or its form of organization or program have become obsolete. . . .

The struggle for survival in government [is] not so much a fight to the death, a test to destruction, but an endless process of adaptation to changed conditions and ideas. In this sense, governmental institutions are in continual evolution. But the process of evolution of human institutions is quite different from the process of evolution of living organisms.

The process of adaptation falls partly in the field of politics and partly in the field of administration. The two are so closely related, however, that the political aspects cannot be ignored completely even here, where we are concerned only with administrative organization. A glance at the present world situation makes it clear that the modern state faces as never before the need of rapid and radical adaptation to changed conditions. Governments which cannot make the necessary evolutionary changes will not survive. It becomes necessary, therefore, in the structure of the organization to make more elaborate provision for those agencies of management which concern themselves with the processes of adaptation. . . .

In periods of change, government must strengthen those agencies which deal with administrative management, that is, with coordination, with planning, with personnel, with fiscal control, and with research. These services constitute the brain and will of any enterprise. It is they that need development when we pass from a regime of habit to one demanding new thinking and new acting.

## NOTES

1. I.e., when *organization is the basis of coordination.* Wherever the central executive authority is composed of several who exercise their functions jointly by majority vote, as on a board, this is from the standpoint of organization still a "single authority"; where the central executive is in reality composed of several men acting freely and independently, then organization cannot be said to be the basis of coordination; it is rather the dominance of an idea and falls under the second principle stated above.

2. Henri Fayol, "Industrial and General Administration." English translation by J. A. Coubrough. International Management Association, Geneva, 1930.

3. Fayol terms the latter "unity of direction."

4. Frederick Winslow Taylor, "Shop Management." Harper and Brothers, New York and London, 1911, p. 99.

5. Of course overall efficiency by the same token rests on the purpose, not the process. For example, a report may be printed at a phenomenally low cost, but if the pamphlet has no purpose, the whole thing is a waste of effort.

# Informal
# Organization
# and Human Relations

♦

CLASSICAL ORGANIZATION THEORY, WITH its emphasis on formal structure and assumptions regarding people's behavior in large-scale organizations, has proven inadequate as a basis for a science of organization and as a practical guide to managing people in organizations. By emphasizing the formal aspects, traditional theorists neglected what Charles H. Page has called "bureaucracy's other face"—informal organization.[1]

The crucial role informal groups play in organizations was identified in the twenties and thirties by a team of researchers from Harvard. The team, headed by Elton Mayo and Fritz Roethlisberger, was engaged in a study of the Hawthorne (Chicago) Works of the Western Electric Company. What began as a study of the effects of illumination on output uncovered a psychological rather than a physiological variable in organizational effectiveness. The initial findings prompted a full-scale study, with plant-wide interviews and experimental work situations, aimed at clarifying the role of informal, small group activity within the formal structure of the organization. Some of the experimental situations—the Relay Assembly Test Room and the Bank Wiring Observation Room—have become classics in social psychology. These experiments showed the development and importance of group solidarity that enabled the employees to control various aspects of their work situation despite the formal commands of the hierarchy.[2]

The Hawthorne studies sparked interest in informal groups in all kinds of organizations. The studies that followed the pioneering efforts of Mayo and Roethlisberger led to the development of a management school that saw "human relations" as the primary method by which management could weld people into an effective organization. Although the human relations movement has often been characterized as glad-handing and back-slapping in order to manipulate subordinates, the intellectual basis of the human relations movement was its concern for the effect of informal group behavior on authority within formal organizations. Research into small group behavior developed several important concepts on which more modern management practices have been based. . . .

The Hawthorne studies reveal that informal groups actually regulate, to a degree, aspects of work in violation of hierarchically prescribed rules. This finding suggests a change in the notion of authority that had been implicit in the traditional organization theories. In the classical theories, authority was assumed to come from the top of the hierarchy and flow downward. Superiors commanded; subordinates obeyed. The research into informal groups showed that the subordinates actually had quite a bit to say about whether they would obey certain orders that came down through the hierarchy. Authority began to be considered more of a relational concept than had formerly been the case.[3]

Chester I. Barnard, the late president of New Jersey Bell Telephone Company, recognized that informal organization was inseparable from formal organization, and he noted the changed nature of authority. To Barnard, a particular communication would be considered authoritative only if the subordinate accepted it as such.[4] Communications would be accepted if they fell within the subordinate's *zone of indifference* or, as Herbert Simon later renamed it, the *zone of acceptance*.[5] (See Figure 1.) The zone of indifference is that area in which subordinates accept communication from the hierarchy as legitimate. Subordinates expect their

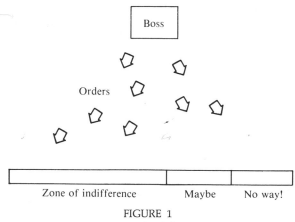

FIGURE 1
*The zone of indifference.*

superiors to make certain demands on them. Socially defined roles govern what kinds of demands will be perceived as legitimate in a given situation. As long as the communication from a superior is viewed as consistent with the role, the subordinates will be indifferent to the communication and will obey. If, however, a superior makes an extraordinary demand—one that is not sanctioned by his role—the subordinates will not be indifferent. They will consider the demand: upon reflection, they may decide that the demand is beyond what *they believe* to be the legitimate power of the superior, and they will refuse to obey. They may, however, consider the demand and upon reflection decide to comply. If they do comply with a demand that was previously perceived to be beyond the role of the superior, they have, *de facto*, enlarged his role and accepted his authority. The crucial point is that the subordinate, as well as the superior, contributes to the definition of roles of both parties in any superior-subordinate interaction. This gives the subordinate an active part in determining authority within the organization—a part that had been substantially overlooked by classical theories.

Barnard suggests that motivation is an important part of organization theory and practical management. He posits a contribution-satisfaction equilibrium model by which people contribute to an organization in return for satisfactions. To get more cooperation from people, management must provide sufficient inducements. These inducements have the effect of broadening the zone of indifference to get more productivity from subordinates.

The reader should note the kinds of inducements with which Barnard deals. Was traditional theory interested in these variables? Can government offer such incentives as readily as private business? What is the effect of organizational size as an incentive factor according to Barnard? Do you agree? Is it possible to develop an organization-wide incentive policy that would elicit a favorable response among a large majority of organization members? If incentives fail to secure cooperation, what forms of persuasion can be effective? What is the function of the group in gaining cooperation?

Peter Blau studied informal group behavior in several public bureaucracies. In the selection reprinted in this volume, he deals with the development of informal norms that arise in direct violation of the formal rules of a law enforcement agency. Furthermore, he suggests that without the informal *modus vivendi* worked out by the participants in the organization, the objectives of the agency would be much harder to attain.

While reading the Blau piece, one might want to consider the degree to which the supervisors—the hierarchy—took part in the informal organization of the agency. What control mechanisms did the hierarchy retain over the agents? Why did the agents violate the no-consultation-with-colleagues rule? What social factors governed the agent's choice of consultants? Did the informal structure tend to support the formal structure or subvert it?

Blau's findings concerning how groups enforce their norms have been corroborated by several behavioral science studies in the last twenty years. Harold Leavitt has presented an extremely clear account of the stages of group pressure. According to Leavitt, the first stage of group pressure on a deviant is *reason*. Group members will try to get the deviant to agree with the group's views by logical arguments. If that does not work, group members will try *seduction*. They will try humor or informal social means to attract the deviant. If seduction fails, the group will *attack*. No more Mr. Nice Guy. The gloves are off, and the deviant is subjected to abuse for destroying group cohesion. If the deviant still does not recant, the group brings out its ultimate weapon, *excommunication*, or, as Blau called it, ostracism.[6]

Depending on what group norms develop, informal group behavior can be a force for innovation and service that will enable the formal organization to accomplish its mission, or group behavior will enforce a conformity that will prevent any changes that might upset established, group-sanctified routines.

## NOTES

1. Attributed to Page by Peter M. Blau, *Bureaucracy in Modern Society* (New York: Random House, Inc., 1956), p. 46.

2. For an excellent summary of the Hawthorne studies, see George C. Homans, "The Western Electric Researches," in Schuyler D. Hoslett, ed., *Human Factors in Management*, rev. ed. (New York: Harper and Brothers, 1951). Available as a Bobbs-Merrill reprint, number S-123.

3. Fritz J. Roethlisberger and William J. Dixon, *Management and the Worker* (Cambridge, Mass.: Harvard University Press, 1939). This book emphasizes the extent to which group attitudes affect an individual's reactions to authority.

4. Chester I. Barnard, *The Functions of the Executive* (Cambridge, Mass.: Harvard University Press, 1937), chapter 12.

5. Herbert A. Simon, *Administrative Behavior: A Study of Decision Making Processes in Administrative Organizations* (New York: The Macmillan Company, Free Press, 1965).

6. Harold J. Leavitt, *Managerial Psychology*, 4th, ed. (Chicago: University of Chicago Press, 1978), pp. 119–25.

# 5

## The Economy
## of
## Incentives

♦

*Chester I. Barnard*

IT HAS ALREADY BEEN demonstrated that an essential element of organizations is the willingness of persons to contribute their individual efforts to the cooperative system. The power of cooperation, which is often spectacularly great when contrasted with that even of large numbers of individuals unorganized, is nevertheless dependent upon the willingness of individuals to cooperate and to contribute their efforts to the cooperative system. The contributions of personal efforts which constitute the energies of organizations are yielded by individuals because of incentives. The egotistical motives of self-preservation and of self-satisfaction are dominating forces; on the whole, organizations can exist only when consistent with the satisfaction of these motives, unless, alternatively, they can change these motives. The individual is always the basic strategic factor in organization. Regardless of his history or his obligations, he must be induced to cooperate, or there can be no cooperation.

It needs no further introduction to suggest that the subject of incentives is fundamental in formal organizations and in conscious efforts to organize. Inadequate incentives mean dissolution, or changes of organization purpose, or failure of cooperation. Hence, in all sorts of organizations the affording of adequate incentives becomes the most definitely emphasized task in their existence. It is probably in this aspect of executive work that failure

*Reprinted by permission of the publishers from Chester I. Barnard,* The Functions of the Executive, *Cambridge, Mass.: Harvard University Press, Copyright, 1938, 1968, by the President and Fellows of Harvard College; 1966 by Grace F. Noera Barnard.*

is most pronounced, though the causes may be due either to inadequate understanding or to the breakdown of the effectiveness of organization.

I

The net satisfactions which induce a man to contribute his efforts to an organization result from the positive advantages as against the disadvantages which are entailed. It follows that a net advantage may be increased or a negative advantage made positive either by increasing the number or the strength of the positive inducements or by reducing the number or the strength of the disadvantages. It often occurs that the positive advantages are few and meager, but the burdens involved are also negligible, so that there is a strong net advantage. Many "social" organizations are able to exist under such a state of affairs. Conversely, when the burdens involved are numerous or heavy, the offsetting positive advantages must be either numerous or powerful.

Hence, from the viewpoint of the organization requiring or seeking contributions from individuals, the problem of effective incentives may be either one of finding positive incentives or of reducing or eliminating negative incentives or burdens. For example, employment may be made attractive either by reducing the work required—say, by shortening hours or supplying tools or power, that is, by making conditions of employment less onerous—or by increasing positive inducement, such as wages.

In practice, although there are many cases where it is clear which side of the "equation" is being adjusted, on the whole specific practices and conditions affect both sides simultaneously or it is impossible to determine which they affect. Most specific factors in so-called working conditions may be viewed either as making employment positively attractive or as making work less onerous. We shall, therefore, make no attempt to treat specific inducements as increasing advantages or as decreasing disadvantages; but this underlying aspect is to be kept in mind.

More important than this is the distinction between the objective and the subjective aspects of incentives. Certain common positive incentives, such as material goods and in some senses money, clearly have an objective existence; and this is true also of negative incentives like working hours, conditions of work. Given a man of a certain state of mind, of certain attitudes, or governed by certain motives, he can be induced to contribute to an organization by a given combination of these objective incentives, positive or negative. It is often the case, however, that the organization is unable to offer objective incentives that will serve as an inducement to that state of mind, or to those attitudes, or to one governed by those motives. The only alternative then available is to change the state of mind, or attitudes, or motives, so that the available objective incentives can become effective.

An organization can secure the efforts necessary to its existence, then, either by the objective inducements it provides or by changing states of mind. It seems to me improbable that any organization can exist as a practical matter which does not employ both methods in combination. In some organizations the emphasis is on the offering of objective incentives—this is true of most industrial organizations. In others the preponderance is on the state of mind—this is true of most patriotic and religious organizations.

We shall call the processes of offering objective incentives "the method of incentives"; and the processes of changing subjective attitudes "the method of persuasion." Using these new terms, let us repeat what we have said: In commercial organizations the professed emphasis is apparently almost wholly on the side of the method of incentives. In religious and political organizations the professed emphasis is apparently almost wholly on the side of persuasion. But in fact, especially if account be taken of the different kinds of contributions required from different individuals, both methods are used in all types of organizations. Moreover, the centrifugal forces of individualism and the competition between organizations for individual contributions result in both methods being ineffective, with few exceptions, for more than short periods or a few years.

## I. The Method of Incentives

We shall first discuss the method of incentives. It will facilitate our consideration of the subject if at the outset we distinguish two classes of incentives; first, those that are specific and can be specifically offered to an individual; and second, those that are general, not personal, that cannot be specifically offered. We shall call the first class specific inducements, the second general incentives.

The specific inducements that may be offered are of several classes, for example: (a) material inducements; (b) personal non-material opportunities; (c) desirable physical conditions; (d) ideal benefactions. General incentives afforded are, for example: (e) associational attractiveness; (f) adaptation of conditions to habitual methods and attitudes; (g) the opportunity of enlarged participation; (h) the condition of communion. Each of these classes of incentives is known under various names, and the list does not purport to be complete, since our purpose now is illustrative. But to accomplish this purpose it is necessary briefly to discuss the incentives named.

(a) Material inducements are money, things, or physical conditions that are offered to the individual as inducements to accepting employment, compensation for service, reward for contribution. Under a money economy and the highly specialized production of material goods, the range and profusion of material inducements are very great. The complexity of schedules of money compensation, the difficulty of securing the monetary means of compensation, and the power of exchange which money gives in organized markets have served to exaggerate the importance of money in particular and material inducements in general as incentives to personal contributions to organized effort. It goes without elaboration that where a large part of the time of an individual is devoted to one organization, the physiological necessities—food, shelter, clothing—require that material inducements should be present in most cases; but these requirements are so limited that they are satisfied with small quantities. The unaided power of material incentives, when the minimum necessities are satisfied, in my opinion is exceedingly limited as to most men, depending almost entirely for its development upon persuasion. Notwithstanding the great emphasis upon material incentives in modern times and especially in current affairs, there is no doubt in my mind that, unaided by other motives, they constitute weak incentives beyond the level of the bare physiological necessities.

To many this view will not be readily acceptable. The emphasis upon material rewards has been a natural result of the success of technological developments—relative to other incentives it is the material things which have been progressively easier to produce, and therefore to offer. Hence there has been a forced cultivation of the love of material things among those above the level of subsistence. Since existing incentives seem always inadequate to the degree of cooperation and of social integration theoretically possible and ideally desirable, the success of the sciences and the arts of material production would have been partly ineffective, and in turn would have been partly impossible, without inculcating the desire of the material. The most significant result of this situation has been the expansion of population, most of which has been necessarily at the bare subsistence level, at which level material inducements are, on the whole, powerful incentives. This has perpetuated the illusion that beyond this subsistence level material incentives are also the most effective.

A concurrent result has been the creation of sentiments in individuals that they *ought* to want material things. The inculcation of "proper" ambitions in youth have greatly stressed material possessions as an evidence of good citizenship, social adequacy, etc. Hence, when underlying and governing motives have not been satisfied, there has been strong influence to rationalize the default as one of material compensation, and not to be conscious of the controlling motives or at least not to admit them.

Yet it seems to me to be a matter of common experience that material rewards are ineffective beyond the subsistence level excepting to a very limited proportion of men; that most men neither work harder for more material things nor can be induced thereby to devote more than a fraction of their possible contribution to organized effort. It is likewise a matter of both present experience and past history that many of the most effective and powerful organizations are built up on incentives in which the materialistic elements, above bare subsistence, are either relatively lacking or absolutely absent. Military organizations have been relatively lacking in material incentives. The greater part of the work of political organizations is without material incentive. Religious organizations are characterized on the whole by material sacrifice. It seems to me to be definitely a general fact that even in purely commercial organizations material incentives are so weak as to be almost negligible except when reinforced by other incentives, and then only because of wholesale general persuasion in the form of salesmanship and advertising.

It will be noted that the reference has been to material incentives rather than to money. What has been said requires some, but not great, qualification with reference to money as an incentive—solely for the reason that money in our economy may be used as the indirect means of satisfying non-materialistic motives—philanthropic, artistic, intellectual, and religious motives for example—and because money income becomes an index of social status, personal development, etc.

(b) Inducements of a personal, non-materialistic character are of great importance to secure cooperative effort above the minimum material rewards essential to subsistence. The opportunities for distinction, prestige, personal power, and the attainment of dominating position are much more important than material rewards in the development of all sorts of organizations, including commercial organizations. In various ways this fact applies to many types of human beings, including those of limited ability and children. Even in strictly commercial organizations, where it is least supposed to be true, money without distinction, prestige, position is so utterly ineffective that it is rare that greater income can be made to serve even temporarily as an inducement if accompanied by suppression of prestige. At least for short periods inferior material rewards are often accepted if assurance of distinction is present; and usually the presumption is that material rewards ought to follow or arise from or even are made necessary by the attainment of distinction and prestige. There is unlimited experience to show that among many men, and especially among women, the real value of differences of money rewards lies in the recognition or distinction assumed to be conferred thereby, or to be procured therewith—one of the reasons why differentials either in money income or in material possessions are a source of jealousy and disruption if not accompanied by other factors of distinction.

(c) Desirable physical conditions of work are often important conscious, and more often important unconscious, inducements to cooperation.

(d) Ideal benefactions as inducements to cooperation are among the most powerful and the most neglected. By ideal benefaction I mean the capacity of organizations to satisfy personal ideals usually relating to non-material, future, or altruistic relations. They include pride of workmanship, sense of adequacy, altruistic service for family or others, loyalty to organization in patriotism, etc., aesthetic and religious feeling. They also include the opportunities for the satisfaction of the motives of hate and revenge, often the controlling factor in adherence to and intensity of effort in some organizations.

All of these inducements—material rewards, personal non-material opportunities, desirable physical conditions, and ideal benefactions—may be and frequently are definitely offered as inducements to contribute to organizations. But there are other conditions which cannot usually be definitely offered, and which are known or recognized by their absence in particular cases. Of these I consider associational attractiveness as exceedingly, and often critically, important.

(e) By associational attractiveness I mean social compatibility. It is in many cases obvious that racial hostility, class antagonism, and national enmities absolutely prevent cooperation, in others decrease its effectiveness, and in still others make it impossible to secure cooperation except by great strengthening of other incentives. But it seems clear that the question of personal compatibility or incompatibility is much more far-reaching in limiting cooperative effort than is recognized, because an intimate knowledge of particular organizations is usually necessary to understand its precise character. When such an intimate knowledge exists, personal compatibility or incompatibility is so thoroughly sensed, and the related problems are so difficult to deal with, that only in special or critical cases is conscious attention given to them. But they can be neglected only at peril of disruption. Men often will not work at all, and will rarely work well, under other incentives if the social situation *from their point of view* is unsatisfactory. Thus often men of inferior education cannot work well with those of superior education, and vice versa. Differences not merely of race, nation, religion, but of customs, morals, social status, education, ambition are frequently controlling. Hence, a powerful incentive to the effort of almost all men is favorable associational conditions from their viewpoint.

Personal aversions based upon racial, national, color, and class differences often seem distinctly pernicious; but on the whole they are, in the immediate sense, I believe, based upon a sound feeling of organization necessities. For when there is incompatibility or even merely lack of compatibility, both formal communication and especially communication through informal organization become difficult and sometimes impossible.

(f) Another incentive of the general type is that of customary working conditions and conformity to habitual practices and attitudes. This is made obvious by the universal practice, in all kinds of organization, of rejecting recruits trained in different methods or possessing "foreign" attitudes. It is taken for granted that men will not or cannot do well by strange methods or under strange conditions. What is not so obvious is that men will frequently not attempt to cooperate if they recognize that such methods or conditions are to be accepted.

(g) Another indirect incentive that we may regard as of general and often of controlling importance is the opportunity for the feeling of enlarged participation in the course of events. It affects all classes of men under some conditions. It is sometimes, though not necessarily, related to love of personal distinction and prestige. Its realization is the feeling of importance of result of effort because of the importance of the cooperative effort as a whole. Thus, *other things being equal,* many men prefer association with large organizations, organizations which they regard as useful, or organizations they regard as effective, as against those they consider small, useless, ineffective.

(h) The most intangible and subtle of incentives is that which I have called the condition of communion. It is related to social compatibility, but is essentially different. It is the feeling of personal comfort in social relations that is sometimes called solidarity, social integration, the gregarious instinct, or social security (in the original, not in its present debased economic, sense). It is the opportunity for comradeship, for mutual support in personal attitudes. The need for communion is a basis of informal organization that is essential to the operation of every formal organization. It is likewise the basis for informal organization within but hostile to formal organization.

It is unnecessary for our purpose to exhaust the list of inducements and incentives to cooperative contributions of individuals to organization. Enough has been said to suggest that the subject of incentives is important and complex when viewed in its objective aspects. One fact of interest now is that different men are moved by different incentives or combinations of incentives, and by different incentives or combinations at different times. Men are unstable in their desires, a fact partly reflecting the instability of their environments. A second fact is that organizations are probably never able to offer *all* the incentives that move men to cooperative effort, and are usually unable to offer adequate incentives. To the reasons for this fact we shall advert later; but a result of it to which we shall turn our attention now is the necessity of persuasion.

## II. The Method of Persuasion

If an organization is unable to afford incentives adequate to the personal contributions it requires it will perish unless it can by persuasion so change the desires of enough men that the incentives it can offer will be adequate.

Persuasion in the broad sense in which I am here using the word includes: (a) the creation of coercive conditions; (b) the rationalization of opportunity; (c) the inculcation of motives.

(a) Coercion is employed both to exclude and to secure the contribution of individuals to an organization. Exclusion is often intended to be exclusion permanently and nothing more. It is an aspect of competition or hostility between organizations or between organizations and individuals with which we shall not further be concerned, except to note that exclusion of undesirables is a necessary method of maintaining organization efficiency. But forced exclusion is also employed as a means of persuasion *by example*, to create fear among those not directly affected so that they will be disposed to render to an organization certain contributions. It presents realistically the alternative either of making these contributions or of foregoing the advantages of association. The grades of exclusion are numerous, beginning with homicide, outlawing, ostracism, corporal punishment, incarceration, withholding of specific benefits, discharge, etc.

Contributions secured by force seem to have been often a necessary process of cooperation. Thus slavery is the creation of conditions by force under which bare subsistence and protection are made sufficient incentives to give certain contributions to the organization; although often it has been the result of conditions not purposely created, that is, slavery has been sometimes a voluntary means to being admitted to benefits of cooperation otherwise withheld. However, usually slavery is evidence of an unstable efficiency, except when it can be combined with other incentives (as in forced military service). But it has undoubtedly often been an effective process of persuasion to those not directly affected. Those who observe homicide, ostracism, outlawing, incarceration, discharge, and other expressions of the power of organizations to persuade by force have unquestionably been affected in their views of the adequacy of offered incentives. Nevertheless, I suppose it is generally accepted that no superior permanent or very complex system of cooperation can be supported to a great extent merely by coercion.

(b) The rationalization of opportunity is a method of persuasion of much greater importance in most modern activities. Even under political and economic regimes in which coercion of individuals is at least temporarily and in some degree the basic process of persuasion, as in Russia, Germany, and Italy, it is observed that the processes of rationalization of other incentives, that is, propaganda, are carried on more extensively than anywhere else.

The rationalization of incentives occurs in two degrees; the general rationalization that is an expression of social organization as a whole and has chiefly occurred in connection with religious and political organizations, and the specific rationalization that consists in attempting to convince individuals or groups that they "ought," "it is to their interest," to perform services or conform to requirements of specific organizations.

The general rationalization of incentives on a noteworthy scale has occurred many times. The rationalization of religious motives as a basis of the Crusades is one of the most striking. The rationalization of communist doctrine in Russia is another. The rationalization of hate as a means of increasing organization (national) "solidarity" is well known. One of the most interesting of these general rationalizations is that of materialistic progress, to which we have already referred. It is an important basis of the characteristic forms of modern western organization. In its most general form it consists in the cult of science as a means to material ends; the glorification of inventions and inventive talent, including patent legislation; and the exaltation of the exploitation of land, forests, mineral resources, and of the means of transportation. In its more obvious current forms it consists in extensive and intensive salesmanship, advertising, and propaganda concerning the satisfactions to be had from the use of material products.

It is the pleasure of many idealists to decry this rationalization of the material. If materialism is to be made an incentive to cooperation as an alternative to other incentives, there is grave reason to question its social value except as it may be the process whereby many millions are enabled to survive and live on a bare subsistence level who otherwise would have perished. But if it is regarded as in the nature of making an *additional* incentive effective, with the result of more effective social cooperation, its justification is not, in my opinion, questionable. It is then the process by which, to use current economic phraseology, purchasing power in material things and services is created. In everyday language, people will not work for what they are not convinced is "worthwhile"; if the conviction that material things are worthwhile detracts from other non-material things as incentives it may be harmful; but if it succeeds in capturing waste[d] effort or wasted time or in minimizing harmful incentives, such as hate, it is clearly advantageous.

Specific rationalization of incentives is the process of personal appeal to "join" an organization, to accept a job or position, to undertake a service, to contribute to a cause. It is the process of proselyting or recruiting that is commonly observed in connection with industrial, military, political, and religious organizations. It consists in emphasizing opportunities for satisfaction that are offered, usually in contrast with those available otherwise; and in attempting to elicit interest in those incentives which are most easily or most outstandingly afforded.

The background of the individual to whom incentives are rationalized consists of his physiological requirements, his geographical and social location, and the general rationalization and especially the social influences to which he has previously been subjected by his society, his government, and his church.

Thus specific rationalization is concerned usually with a small marginal area of choice and with competition. This background differs so widely among individuals that at any given time only a few individuals are deemed to be within range of specific rationalization; and for those that are within that range there are wide differences in the composition of incentives that will be effective.

(c) The form of persuasion that is most important is the inculcation of motives. In its formal aspects this is a process of deliberate education of the young, and propaganda for adults. Thus the persuasion of religious incentives, except at comparatively infrequent intervals, is chiefly accomplished by religious instruction of children. Similarly, the inculcation of ideas of patriotism and much of the other incentives to cooperation are part of the family and general educational process.

Associated with these formal processes are those which are informal and indirect. Precept, example, suggestion, imitation and emulation, habitual attitudes, chiefly condition the motives and the emotional response of individuals to incentives. These are the controlling and fundamental conditions of whole peoples and of groups and classes with respect to the power of incentives. They furnish the greatest limitations to which organizations must adapt their processes both of offering incentives and of persuading individuals.

This brief discussion of the incentives has been a necessary introduction to the considerations that are important to our study of the subject of organization and the executive functions. The processes concerned are each of them difficult in themselves, and are subject to highly developed techniques and skills. Their importance as a whole arises from the inherent difficulty that organizations experience either in supplying incentives or in exercising persuasion. The most appropriate phrase to apply to this inherent difficulty is "economy of incentives"; but it should be understood that "economy" is used in a broad sense and refers not merely to material or monetary economy.

II

In the economy of incentives we are concerned with the net effects of the income and outgo of things resulting from the production of objective incentives and the exercise of persuasion. An organization which makes material things the principal incentive will be unable long to offer this kind of incentive if it is unable to secure at least as much material or money as it pays out. This is the ordinary economic aspect which is well understood. But the same principle applies to other incentives. The possibilities of offering non-material opportunities, desirable conditions, ideal benefactions, desirable associations, stability of practice, enlarged participation, or communion advantages are limited and usually insufficient, so that the utmost economy is ordinarily essential not only in the material sense but in the broader sense as well. The limitations are not alone due to the relationship of the organization to the external physical environment, but also to its relationship to the social environment, and to its internal efficiency.

A complete exposition of the economy of incentives would, among other things, involve some duplication of the theories of general economics, rewritten from the point of view of organization. This is not the place to attempt such an exposition; but as the economy of incentives as a whole in terms of organization is not usually stressed in economic theory and is certainly not well understood, I shall attempt to indicate the outlines of the theory. It will be convenient to do this with reference to organizations of three radically different purposes: (a) an industrial organization; (b) a political organization; and (c) a religious organization.

(a) In an industrial organization the purpose is the production of material goods or services. For the sake of simplicity we may assume that it requires no capital. It secures material production by applying the energies of men to the physical environment. These energies will result in a gross production; but if the inducements offered to secure these energies are themselves material and are sufficient, then it will pay out of its production something on this account. If the amount paid out is no more than the production, the organization can survive; but if the amount paid out is more than the production, it must cease, since it cannot then continue to offer inducements.

Whether this occurs depends upon the combined effect of four factors: the difficulties of the environment, the effectiveness of organization effort, the internal efficiency of organization, and the amount of inducements paid. Obviously many cooperative efforts fail because the environment is too resistant, others because the organization is ineffective, others because internal losses are large, other because the price paid for services is too large. Within the range of ordinary experience, these are mutually dependent variables, or mutually interacting factors. Under very favorable environmental conditions, relative ineffectiveness and relative internal inefficiency with high outgo for inducements are possible. Under unfavorable conditions, effectiveness, efficiency, and low inducements are necessary.

In most cases the limitations of conditions, of effectiveness, and of efficiency permit only limited material inducements; and both effectiveness and efficiency require an output of individual energies that cannot be elicited from most men by material inducements in any event. Hence, in practice other inducements also must be offered. But in such an organization such inducements in some degree, and usually to a considerable degree, require again material inducements. Thus, satisfactory physical conditions of work mean material inducements to factors not directly productive; satisfactory social conditions mean the rejection of some of those best able to contribute to the material production and acceptance of some less able. Almost every type of incentive that can be, or is, necessary will itself in some degree call for material outgo, so that the question is one of choice of methods and degree of emphasis upon different incentives to find the most efficient combination of incentives determined from the material viewpoint. Hence, the various incentives are in competition with each other even from the material point of view.

But the economy of incentives in an industrial organization only begins with the analysis of incentives from the standpoint of material; that is, dollars and cents, costs. The non-material incentives often conflict with each other or are incompatible. Thus opportunity for personal prestige as an incentive for one person necessarily involves a relative depression of others; so that if this incentive is emphasized as to one person, it must be in conjunction with other persons to whom personal prestige is relatively an unimportant inducement.

The difficulties of finding the workable balance of incentives are so great that recourse must be had to persuasion. But persuasion in connection with an industrial effort itself involves material outgo. Thus if coercion is the available method of persuasion, the maintenance of force for this purpose is involved; and if the contribution that can be secured by coercion is limited, as it usually is, except for short periods, the cost of coercion exceeds its effect. The limited efficiencies of slavery systems is an example.

If the method of persuasion is rationalization, either in the form of general propaganda or that of specific argument to individuals (including processes of "selection"), again the overhead cost is usually not negligible. When the general social conditioning is favorable, of course, it is a windfall like favorable physical environment.

(b) A political organization is not ordinarily productive in the materialistic sense. The motives which lie at its roots are ideal benefactions and community satisfactions. Such organizations appear not to survive long unless they can afford these incentives; yet it is obvious that every extensive political organization requires the use of "inferior" incentives. Of these, opportunity for personal prestige and material rewards are most prominent. Hence the necessity, under all forms of political organization, for obtaining great supplies of material inducements for use either in the form of direct payments or of "paying jobs." Accordingly, a striking characteristic of political organizations has been the necessity for securing material contributions from "members" either to capture the opportunities to secure additional material (through taxation) or for direct payment (as in campaigns). But here again the balancing of incentives is necessary. For the limitations of material resources, the impossibility of giving more than is received, the discrimination between recipients as respects either material benefits ,or prestige granted, all tend either to destroy the vital idealism upon which political organization is based or to minimize the *general* material advantages which are perhaps an alternative basis of political organization in many cases.

It is hardly necessary to add that persuasion in its many forms is an important aspect of political recruiting—and that much of the material expenditure goes for this purpose; but this thereby decreases the material available as an incentive to intensive efforts of the "faithful."

(c) In religious organizations the predominant incentives appear to be ideal benefactions and the communion of "kindred spirits," although inferior incentives no doubt often are effective. The fundamental contributions required of members are intensity of faith and loyalty to organization. A most important effort of religious organizations has been persuasion, known as missionary or proselyting effort. But both the maintenance of organization and missionary effort (and coercion when this is used) require material means, so that superficially, and often primarily, members are required by various methods to make material contributions to permit great material expenditures. The material aspects of religious organizations have been often prominent and always inescapable. As a result, the combination and adjustment of incentives in religious organizations appear even more delicate and difficult to administer than in political, military, or industrial organizations. Consider, for example, the conflict between sacrifice by individuals on one hand as a means of intensifying faith and loyalty—which it does in many cases—and sacrifice as a deterrent to adherence and membership, and the resulting dilemma as respects both quality and numbers of communicants. Or the necessity for prestige and display—which are both individual and group incentives—and humility, which is a contrary ideal benefaction.

It will be evident, perhaps, without more elaborate illustration, that in every type of organization, for whatever purpose, several incentives are necessary, and some degree of persuasion likewise, in order to secure and maintain the contributions to organization that are required. It will also be clear that, excepting in rare instances, the difficulties of securing the means of offering incentives, of avoiding conflict of incentives, and of making effective persuasive efforts are inherently great; and that the determination of the precise combination of incentives and of persuasion that will be both effective and feasible is a matter of great delicacy. Indeed, it is so delicate and complex that rarely, if ever, is the scheme of incentives determinable in advance of application. It can only evolve; and the questions relating to it become chiefly those of strategic factors from time to time in the course of the life of the organization. It is also true, of course, that the scheme of incentives is probably the most unstable of the elements of the cooperative system, since invariably external conditions affect the possibilities of material incentives; and human motives are likewise highly variable. Thus incentives represent the final residual of all the conflicting forces involved in organization, a very slight change in underlying forces often making a great change in the power of incentives; and yet it is only by the incentives that the effective balancing of these forces is to be secured, it it can be secured at all.

Two general consequences of this inherent instability are to be noted. One is the innate propensity of all organizations to expand. The maintenance of incentives, particularly those relating to prestige, pride of association, and community satisfaction, calls for growth, enlargement, extension. It is, I think, the basic and, in a sense, the legitimate reason for bureaucratic aggrandizement in corporate, governmental, labor, university, and church organizations everywhere observed. To grow seems to offer opportunity for the realization of all kinds of active incentives—as may be observed by the repeated emphasis in all organizations upon size as an index of the existence of desirable incentives, or the alternative rationalization of other incentives when size is small or growth is discouraged. The overreaching which arises from this cause is the source of destruction of organizations otherwise successful, since growth often so upsets the economy of incentives, through its reactions upon the effectiveness and efficiency of organization, that it is no longer possible to make them adequate.

A second and more important result of the inherent difficulty of securing an adequate scheme of incentives is the highly selective character of the organizational recruiting practice. This has two aspects, the acceptance of desirable and the rejection of undesirable contributions or contributors; and its chief process is the maintenance of differential incentives. Since all incentives are costly to organization, and the costs tend to prevent its survival, and since the balancing of organization outgo and income is initially to be regarded as impossible without the utmost economy, the distribution of incentives must be proportioned to the value and effectiveness of the various contributions sought.

This is only too much accepted as respects material incentives, that is, material things or money payment. No enduring or complex formal organization of any kind seems to have existed without differential material payments, though material compensation may be indirect to a considerable extent. This seems true up to the present even though contrary to the expressed attitude of the organization or not in harmony with its major purpose, as often is the case of churches and socialistic states.

The same doctrine applies in principle and practice even more to nonmaterial incentives. The hierarchy of positions, with gradation of honors and privileges, which is the universal accompaniment of all complex organization, is essential to the adjustment of non-material incentives to induce the services of the most able individuals or the most valuable potential contributors to organization, and it is likewise necessary to the maintenance of pride of organization, community sense, etc., which are important general incentives to all classes of contributors.

# 6

## Consultation among Colleagues and Informal Norms

♦

*Peter M. Blau*

DEPARTMENT Y, THE UNIT UNDER intensive study, had eighteen members. The department supervisor was in charge of sixteen agents and one clerk. The principal duties of agents were carried out in the field. Cases of firms to be investigated were assigned to them individually by the supervisor. Processing a case involved an audit of the books and records of the firm, interviews with the employer (or his representative) and a sample of employees, the determination of the existence of legal violations and of the appropriate action to be taken, and negotiations with the employer. The time spent on a case varied between half a day and several months. On the average, an agent worked seventeen hours on an investigation.

The agent had to evaluate the reliability of the information he obtained—since concealment of violations occurred, of course—and had to decide whether violations had taken place on the basis of a large and complex body of legal regulations. This was a difficult task, which often required extensive research and consultation with the supervisor or with an attorney on the agency's staff. Upon completion of a case, a full report was written. All these activities were carried out in the office. Besides, agents sometimes interviewed employees or negotiated with employers in the office and had to attend biweekly departmental meetings as well as occa-

*Reprinted from* The Dynamics of Bureaucracy: A Study of Interpersonal Relationships in Two Governmental Agencies, *2d ed. by Peter M. Blau by permission of The University of Chicago Press. Copyright by The University of Chicago Press, 1955, 1963. Used with permission. Footnotes deleted.*

sional special conferences. An average of 42 percent of their working time was spent in the office. . . .

. . . Every federal agent . . . possessed a manual containing over a thou sand pages of regulations, to which he constantly referred. Often this manual did not suffice, and agents consulted the volumes of administrative explications and court opinions, which occupied two library shelves. . . . The provisions of the two congressional acts that the federal agency was charged to enforce had become specified and extended through a host of legislative amendments, administrative interpretations, and court opinions setting precedent. Any of these might be pertinent to a given case. The agent's conduct had to be oriented in terms of these regulations, which defined the violations he was required to discover. . . .

. . . Although the federal manual contained operating rules as well as legal regulations, these rules were usually less specific, and most specific ones were not enforced. For example, the manual specified eleven topics to be discussed with the employer during the first interview. None of the observed agents inquired about more than six of these at that time, and the supervisor never checked conformity with this rule. As long as all the necessary information was obtained, it seemed to matter little precisely how and when it was done. . . . Federal supervisors rarely told an agent what he should do at a certain time. . . .

There was less emphasis on strict conformity with operating rules in the federal agency because control over operations was effected by a different method. Rigid and precise legal standards governed the results that agents were required to accomplish in their work. Their findings and the actions they had taken were twice checked for accuracy—by the supervisor and by the review section. Any mistake counted heavily against an agent's record. This evaluation of precision, by itself, might well have engendered over-caution or even a tendency not to report very complex violations, lest mistakes be made in dealing with them. To guard against such tendencies, success in investigations were [sic] also quantitatively evaluated.

. . . In the federal agency, quantitative records were used . . . extensively for evaluating accomplishments. . . . Thirty categories of performance, such as the number and types of violations found, were supplemented by another thirty categories based on the supervisor's standardized evaluation of every completed case. Most of these indices measured results achieved in investigations rather than techniques used. . . . These statistical records influenced ratings in the federal agency. . . . Finally, federal supervisors also tended to stress accomplishments more than conformity with procedures when they judged the qualitative factors that influenced the rating, such as "dependability."

Evaluation on the basis of the end results of operations rather than the particular means used in reaching them constrained agents to choose, on their own initiative, the most effective course of action for the attainment of clearly specified objectives. This fostered uniformity in most respects in which it was bureaucratically relevant and simultaneously permitted agents to employ diverse means in the interest of the successful performance of their duties, for instance, in order to discover a concealed violation. Operating rules, in this situation, could be largely confined to prohibiting certain methods of investigation as illegitimate, such as threatening employers in negotiations by the illicit use of authority. . . .

Specification of results promoted a professional orientation toward the discharge of responsibilities. This evaluation system therefore influenced operations without producing a feeling of being continuously hamstrung by detailed rules. Agents actually exercised a considerable amount of discretion, and the constraints that governed their conduct were experienced as self-imposed rather than arbitrary. There was no "silly" rule prescribing that fifty pages of bookkeeping records be examined in all firms, but the law specified the evidence with which the claim that a violation existed must be supported. This necessitated the examination of fifty or more pages of these records often, but not always. The agent decided rationally how to proceed in terms of the objective he was required to attain.

Operating rules, on the other hand, eliminate discretion in principle and thus restrain conduct also in cases in which there is no rational basis for it. They were experienced as more restrictive than the self-imposed constraints generated by the responsibility for achieving given results. . . . [The] agents objected to detailed operating rules, but there were [relatively few] such rules. . . . The feeling of freedom of action and the professional interest that prevailed among the agents contrasted sharply with the attitudes of most [people in an agency with many operating rules], who considered their jobs routine and confining. This difference in work satisfaction was due, at least partly, to the different control mechanisms employed.

However, the exercise of discretion that made the job more stimulating also engendered anxiety over decision making. The agent was free to make his own decisions, but their legal validity and effectiveness determined his rating. His consequent anxious concern about the correctness of his decisions sometimes actually prevented an agent from making final commitments. The supervisor mentioned that some agents keep difficult cases on their desks instead of completing them, "being afraid to make a decision."

Official provisions were made to assist agents with their difficult cases. Decisions of specified complexity or significance—for example, if the amount of money involved exceeded a certain sum—had to be authorized by the supervisor, who, in turn, had to obtain authorization from his superiors in special cases. Similarly, if an agent encountered a problem he could not solve, he was expected to consult his supervisor, who, if he could not furnish the requested advice himself, gave the agent permission to consult a staff attorney. Agents were not allowed to consult anyone else directly, not even their colleagues.

This rule requiring agents to come to their supervisor with their problems was an integral part of the authority structure of the agency. The supervisor was responsible to his superior for the legal accuracy of all actions taken in his department. In order to be able to discharge this responsibility, he had the authority to control all official decisions of his subordinates. As a last resort, he could correct mistakes when he reviewed their cases and order agents to revise the erroneous actions they had taken. Since this involved much wasted effort and sometimes bad public relations, two other ways of exercising authority were more efficient. First, the supervisor could prevent mistakes by advising agents in difficult cases or by guiding them to expert legal consultants. The requirement that they see him when they had problems, that is, in cases in which mistakes were most likely, facilitated his control over decisions for which he was held responsible. Second, he could discourage the repetition of types of decisions he considered erroneous, because his evaluation of subordinates influenced their career chances. To use this evaluation judiciously and as an effective control device, he had to be able to place responsibility for all decisions made. This would have been impossible if a half-dozen agents had collaborated on a case. The rule prohibiting consultation with colleagues was designed to prevent such collaboration.

Agents, however, were reluctant to reveal to their supervisor their inability to solve a problem for fear that their ratings would be adversely affected. The need for assistance and the requirement that it be obtained only from the supervisor put officials under cross-pressure.

### THE PATTERN OF CONSULTATION

"They are not permitted to consult other agents. If they have a problem, they have to take it up with me," said the department supervisor Yet an agent averaged five contacts per hour with his colleagues. Hardly any of these were officially required, since each agent worked independently on the cases assigned to him. Some of them were purely private conversations, but many were discussions of their work, ranging from simple requests for information that could be answered in a sentence to consultations about complex problems.

This unofficial practice had developed in response to a need for advice from a source other than the supervisor. Anxiety over the correctness of his findings and actions, on which his rating was based, inhibited the agent in the process of making decisions and raised doubts in his mind regarding the validity of the decisions he had made. Consulting the supervisor, the only legitimate source of assistance, could not relieve the anxiety generated by concern over his opinion of an agent's competence. On the contrary, this anxiety induced agents to conceal their difficulties from the supervisor, as one of them explained: "I try to stay away from the supervisor as much as possible. The reason is that the more often you go to the supervisor, the more you show your stupidity." At best, even if an official had made correct tentative decisions, repeatedly asking the supervisor for confirmation would reveal his inability to act independently, which would also affect his rating adversely. Their need for getting advice without exposing their difficulties to the supervisor constrained agents to consult one another, in violation of the official rule.

Requests for information were a time-saving device, which must be distinguished from other consultations. An agent who did not recall a regulation or a reference often turned to ask a colleague instead of conducting a lengthy search. Since any agent might have this knowledge, depending primarily on the kinds of cases on which he had recently worked, proximity largely determined who was asked. An official requested information from his neighbors or from a colleague who passed his desk. This lack of discrimination had the result that every agent was often consulted.

When an agent had trouble solving a problem, on the other hand, he was more selective in his choice of consultant. The sixteen members of Department Y were asked with whom they usually conferred when they encountered difficulties. Seven agents were named by two or more colleagues in answer to this question, namely, all but two of the nine agents whom the supervisor considered highly competent, but none of the seven whose competence was below average.

Competence was clearly related to popularity as a consultant, but consultations were not confined to a few experts. A record was kept of all contacts between agents that lasted for three minutes or more. Most of these discussions were consultations. Two particular officials who spent at least fifteen minutes during thirty hours of observation together in such conferences are defined as a consultation pair. . . .

Most of these officials had one or two regular partners with whom they discussed problems. One partnership involved two agents whose competence, as indicated by the supervisor's rating and the estimation of colleagues, differed greatly, which suggests that one generally advised the other. Typically, however, each member of a pair was in the habit of consulting the other. All four agents without partners were experts, and three of them were also very popular consultants. These three were by no means isolated from the exchange of advice. On the contrary, they participated so widely in it that they did not spend much time with any single co-worker.

A consultation can be considered an exchange of values; both participants gain something, and both have to pay a price. The questioning agent is enabled to perform better than he could otherwise have done, without exposing his difficulties to the supervisor. By asking for advice, he implicitly pays his respect to the superior proficiency of his colleague. This acknowledgment of inferiority is the cost of receiving assistance. The consultant gains prestige, in return for which he is willing to devote some time to the consultation and permit it to disrupt his own work. The following remark of an agent illustrates this: "I like giving advice. It's flattering, I suppose, if you feel that the others come to you for advice."

The expert whose advice was often sought by colleagues obtained social evidence of his superior abilities. This increased his confidence in his own decisions and thus improved his performance as an investigator. Such a popular consultant not only needed advice on fewer occasions than did others, but he could also distribute discussions of his own problems among several colleagues, since most of them were obligated to him for his assistance. Besides, to refrain from asking any particular individual too many questions helped to maintain his reputation as an expert. Consequently, three of the most popular consultants had no regular partner.

All agents liked being consulted, but the value of any one of very many consultations became deflated for experts, and the price they paid in frequent interruptions became inflated. One of them referred to the numerous requests for his advice by saying "I never object, although sometimes it's annoying." . . . Being approached for help was too valuable an experience to be refused, but popular consultants were not inclined to encourage further questions.

The role of the agent who frequently solicited advice was less enviable, even though he benefited most directly from this unofficial practice. Asking a colleague for guidance was less threatening than asking the supervisor, but the repeated admission by an agent of his inability to solve his own problems also undermined his self-confidence and his standing in the group. The cost of advice became prohibitive if the consultant, after the questioner had subordinated himself by asking for help, was in the least discouraging—by postponing a discussion or by revealing his impatience during one. To avoid such rejections, agents usually consulted a colleague with whom they were friendly, even if he was not an expert. One agent explained, when asked whether he ever consults a colleague whom he considers outstandingly competent: "I sometimes would like to, but I'm hesitant. I always have the feeling that I don't have the right to pick his brain. I ask the ones I know well because I don't feel any reluctance about asking them."

The establishment of partnerships of mutual consultation virtually eliminated the danger of rejections as well as the status threat implicit in asking for help, since the roles of questioner and consultant were intermittently reversed. These partnerships also enabled agents to reserve their consultations with an expert whom they did not know very well for their most complicated problems. They could therefore approach him in these cases with less fear of courting a rejection. If the complexity of a problem prevented the agent from solving it, he needed expert guidance. Often, however, anxiety over the correctness of his findings rather than lack of knowledge interfered with his ability to arrive at decisions. In this situation, the counsel of a colleague who was not outstandingly competent could furnish the reassurance that facilitated decision-making.

The prevailing practice of consulting colleagues removed the agent from the isolation in which he otherwise would have been, since his work on his own cases officially required hardly any contact with co-workers. The evidence it supplied that he was not alone in having difficulties and the knowledge it provided that advice could be obtained without revealing his troubles to the supervisor lessened his anxiety about making decisions. The repeated experience of being consulted did so even more effectively. By reducing such anxiety, this unofficial practice made the job less strenuous for agents and improved their ability to make accurate decisions in general and not only in those cases where a consultation took place.

However, consulting others also had disadvantages. It was a source of possible conflict with the supervisor, since it violated an official rule. Although the supervisor tolerated consultations, he did express his disapproval of agents "who are shopping around for the answers to their questions." Moreover, admitting ignorance by asking many questions lowered the group's estimation of an agent and his own self-confidence. The more competent an official was, the greater was his reluctance to admit inability to solve a problem. But even experts needed assistance in making difficult decisions.

### CONSULTATION IN DISGUISE

An agent who worked on an interesting case and encountered strange problems often told his fellow-agents about it. All members of the department liked these discussions and considered them educational. One expressed her disappointment that superiors sometimes discouraged them by saying: "I wish they would not frown upon it. I used to like our gab-fests. You used to learn so much discussing cases somebody came across, which you would never get. I guess they feel that you waste too much time that way." The fact that agents devoted their free time to such discussions—lunch periods were filled with them, despite occasional protests, "No shop talk!"—indicates that they were enjoyed. Officials found it interesting to hear how unusual problems were solved, perhaps after suggesting a possible solution themselves.

Generally, the discussant did not solicit the opinions of his listeners. For instance, an agent explained that one of the experts occasionally discussed a case with him: "He mentions a problem once in a while, because he finds it interesting. I'm sure that he's not going to ask *my* opinion. Usually, you don't want the opinion of somebody else in these discussions. What you're doing is thinking out loud." Even when no advice was expected and none was given, these presentations of complex cases assisted the speaker in solving his problems. They were consultations in disguise.

Making decisions in an investigation involved the coordination of many pieces of information, the selection of the appropriate regulations from a large body of such regulations, and the appraisal of the specific data in terms of these legal principles. Anxiety resulted in "blocking" of ideas and associations, which increased the difficulties inherent in this intellectual process. The agent who attempted to arrive at decisions while sitting alone at his desk defined the situation as preparing the case for submission to the supervisor. His anxiety, engendered by the supervisor's evaluation of his decisions, interfered most with clear thinking in this situation. Instead of trying to make important official decisions, an agent could discuss the interesting aspects of his case with one of his colleagues. This situation, defined as a discussion among friends, did not evoke anxiety. On the contrary, it destroyed the anxiety that pervaded the decision-making process.

The listener was not merely a friend but a fellow-specialist in solving the problems that occurred in investigations. This created the possibility of interruption, if the suggested interpretation required correction. A listener might remind the speaker that he forgot to take some factor into account or that the data lend themselves to alternative conclusions. The assent implicit in the absence of interruptions and in attentive listening destroyed the doubts that continuously arose in the process of making many minor decisions in order to arrive at a conclusion. The admiration for the clever solution of the problem advanced expressed the speaker's confidence in his partial solutions while groping for the final one. By reducing his anxiety, "thinking out loud" enabled an official to associate relevant pieces of information and pertinent regulations and thus arrive at decisions which he might not have thought of while alone.

These discussions of problems were functional substitutes for consultations. They served the same functions for the discussant without having the same disadvantages for him. An explanation of a complex case did not violate the rule against asking other agents for advice, and it did not threaten the speaker's prestige or his self-confidence. In contrast to asking a question, presenting an interesting discussion *enhanced* the respect of his colleagues for an agent. Of course, this was the case only if his conclusions were correct; presenting false conclusions that were corrected by his listeners hurt an agent's standing in the group. Agents who were not confident of their abilities, therefore, did not feel so free as experts to present their own solutions of problems. Besides, experts more often worked on intricate cases with unusual problems that others found interesting. Consequently, they, the very agents most reluctant to admit ignorance by asking for advice, were in the best position to use this substitute for consultations.

The recognition of both participants in a consultation that one provided an intellectual service to the other raised the status of the consultant and subordinated or obligated the questioner to him. These were the inducements for the consultant to give advice and, simultaneously, the cost incurred by the questioner for receiving it. Discussions of interesting problems, on the other hand, were not recognized as providing a service to the speaker, and he did not start them because he experienced a need for *advice*. Manifestly, both he and the listeners, who sometimes commented, participated in these discussions because they were stimulating. The fact that they facilitated his solving of problems was disguised from the speaker as well as from his listeners; this was a latent function of such discussions.

In the absence of awareness that a service was furnished, no need existed for the speaker to reciprocate for the help he did, in fact, obtain. He did not subordinate or obligate himself to listeners. Such inducements were unnecessary for finding an audience, since interest in the problem and its solution supplied sufficient motivation for listening. This constituted the major advantage of consultations in disguise over direct consultations. We find . . . that the extraneous factors that motivate an interaction pattern that is *not intended* to, but does, fulfill a given function make it more efficient than a different pattern *intended* to fulfill this same function. Only a service intentionally rendered creates obligations, which make it costly. . . .

The practice of consulting co-workers, directly or in disguised form, served social, as well as psychological, functions. First, it transformed an aggregate of individuals who happened to have the same supervisor into a cohesive group. The recurrent experience of being dependent on the group, whose members furnished needed help, and of being appreciated by the others in the group, as indicated by their solicitations for assistance, created strong mutual bonds. Requests for information, which were indiscriminately made of any agent near by, permitted all agents, even the least competent ones, to experience being needed by several other members of the department. Social cohesion, in turn, contributed to operations in a variety of ways. . . .

Second, consultation among colleagues made more effective law enforcement possible because it improved the quality of the decisions of agents. Every agent knew that he could obtain help with solving problems whenever he needed it. This knowledge, reinforced by the feeling of being an integrated member of a cohesive group, decreased anxiety about making decisions. Simultaneously, being often approached for advice raised the self-confidence of an investigator. The very existence of this practice enhanced the ability of all agents, experts as well as others, to make decisions independently, even when they were alone in the field.

Third, discussions of problems increased the agent's interest in his work and his knowledge about it. They provided, not only opportunities for learning, from the examples of experts, how intricate problems can be solved, but also incentives for becoming more skilful in this task, since the presentation of an ingenious solution raised an agent's standing in the group. These stimulating discussions, moreover, contributed to the great interest that agents took in their work and their professional pride in being responsible for such complex duties. Most federal officials, in contrast to those in the state agency, considered the interesting and important nature of their tasks the most attractive feature of their job. Such work satisfaction furnishes inducements for exerting greater efforts. Its existence, and that of social cohesion, are perhaps particularly important for the American civil servant, who does not enjoy the emoluments of high status and authority that fortify the *esprit de corps* of his European counterpart, the *Herr Geheimrat*.

Fourth, the pattern of consultations stabilized the relationships among the members of the department and forestalled conflict. It gave agents accurate knowledge of the differences in proficiency among them, as indicated by the close correspondence between his colleagues' ranking of an agent's competence and that of the supervisor, who had evaluated every case. . . . Besides, officials *socially* acknowledged the superior ability of others in the process of asking for advice and in the course of listening admiringly, sometimes in a small group, to presentations of clever solutions of problems. This reduced the chances of friction when agents were differently rewarded for their performance. A high rating, or even a promotion, was less likely to create resentment against the supervisor or the agent involved, since his superior competence had been socially recognized in advance. Indeed, promotion expectations in this department were most realistic. Only two agents expected to become supervisors within ten years, the same ones who were considered to be the two most competent members of Department Y by all co-workers and by the supervisor.

The mechanisms through which these functions were fulfilled also entailed dysfunctions. Thus this pattern of interaction tended to reinforce competence differentials in the process of making them known. The high esteem of agents frequently consulted reinforced their self-confidence as investigators at the expense of lessened self-confidence on the part of others. Furthermore, by creating social cohesion, this pattern also generated resistance to the frequent transfers of personnel from one department to another. Agents disliked being transferred because they felt loyal to their departmental group and because it required adaptation to new consultation relationships. Finally, this practice weakened the authority of the supervisor. It decreased not only the frequency with which agents consulted him but also their respect for his judgment, which they compared unfavorably with that of their most competent colleagues. The comment of one agent is typical: "If you can't get an answer from [either one of two agents], the likelihood of getting an answer from any supervisor is remote." It is quite possible that the anxiety evoked by consulting the supervisor, and its absence in consultations with colleagues, produced a bias in favor of the advice received from peers. In any case, the fact that his judgment did not command their full respect diminished the supervisor's control over subordinates and made it more difficult for him to discharge his responsibilities. . . .

## UNOFFICIAL NORMS

Statistical records of performance enabled the supervisor in Department Y to set production quotas for his subordinates. He expected every agent to complete eight cases a month, to find violations in half of them, and to obtain the employer's agreement to make voluntary adjustments in at least two-thirds of these. The repeated emphasis on these standards and invidious comparisons of one agent's record with those of others were intended to encourage speedy and effective work.

This method of supervision generated some competition between agents. How close they had come to meeting the production standards constituted "the prime topic of discussion," said one agent, exaggerating somewhat; and another confirmed this in principle: "That's what you usually talk about when you're kidding. For example, one month I had *nine* cases. [Simon] was kidding me about it."

This remark indicates the existence of unofficial norms that curbed competitive tendencies. Officials who produced too much were warned by being teased. If one did not heed this warning and persistently exceeded the group's limits, he was ostracized. These norms induced agents, who had strong incentives to perform well, to conceal their accomplishments from colleagues, as one of them noted:

All agents tend to run themselves down, I've found out. . . .

(What do you mean?) They try to make themselves appear less good. . . . I may say that out of eight cases this month, I [obtained agreements for voluntary adjustments] in four, and he'll say, "Really?!" Now, he may have just as many or more than I do, and just say this to make me feel good. That's what I mean when I say, the agents run themselves down.

A highly competent agent admitted that he underemphasized the quality of his performance in his discussions with co-workers:

There's the tendency to tone down the amount of work you've done. I know I do. You don't want to seem like an eager beaver.

(How do you do this?) There's a tendency to play up the poorer aspects of your work, and to keep quiet about the better ones. If I have several cases in a row where I don't find anything, I'll mention that.

Agents were ambivalent about their own productivity standards, but they were in unequivocal agreement concerning other unofficial norms, notably the taboo on reporting offers of bribes. . . .

## STANDARDS OF PRODUCTIVITY
## AMONG WHITE-COLLAR WORKERS

. . . [T]he agents in Department Y hardly competed with one another at all. . . . [T]he co-operative practice of consulting with co-workers engendered a cohesive situation, which was fertile soil for the development of social norms to check the rivalry for outstanding performance that superiors encouraged. Actually, none of the members of Department Y exceeded the group's standards to the extent of invoking the serious disapproval of his colleagues, although this had happened in the past, as one agent reported: "We had some agents here for a short while who set up terrific production standards. They worked very fast, and I don't think they did a good job; but they set up impossible production records."

Compared with the clear-cut restrictions of output that are often found among factory workers, however, the production standards among agents appear vague and ineffective. Condemnation of an individual for excessive performance was so rare because large differences in productivity were tolerated. Furthermore, these group norms were very elastic, as indicated by the reaction of agents when their new supervisor raised the monthly quota from six to eight. Despite considerable grumbling, there was no concerted effort to sabotage the new quota. Most agents met it, and their norms adjusted themselves to it.

The effort of these white-collar workers to standardize productivity was half-hearted, at best, because they were conflicted about it. Remaining true to type as middle-class individuals, they believed that superior ability, ambition, and efficient performance should be rewarded. Enforcing the laws under the agency's jurisdiction, the objectives of which they highly approved, was considered too important a task to be discouraged. In the process of consulting, moreover, agents had learned to respect and appreciate the proficiency of experts who willingly helped them solve difficult problems. Attitudes such as these made it well-nigh impossible to condemn excellent performance; yet social cohesion required that competitive endeavors to excel be suppressed. The solution to this dilemma was a set of unofficial norms that served not so much to restrict productivity as to freeze the established differentials in performance.

The practice of working overtime without compensation, to which some officials resorted who had trouble meeting the production quota, was generally disapproved. One agent said: "There was some discussion of an agent who took cases home to work on. It was looked upon with scorn." Four members of Department Y, all of whom had a low rating, reported in the interview that they took work home on occasion, and one added, "I don't think there is an agent who doesn't." This is unlikely, but it is quite possible that more agents than acknowledged it engaged in this practice. Since such excessive efforts were frowned upon, agents tended to conceal them from their co-workers, and probably also from the observer. It was, significantly, a trainee who had made the mistake of admitting to colleagues that he worked overtime. . . .

The less competent agents condemned this practice as unfair to the rest of the group. One of them stated: "It would make one agent look very good in comparison with the others. I don't think that's fair. Maybe he's interested in his work, or maybe he does it for selfish motives. But it puts all the other agents in a bad light." The more competent officials did not think that a member of the department put the others at a disadvantage by working overtime. Nevertheless, they, too, discouraged this practice, if only by their disrespect for those who engaged in it. This is indicated by their very similar answers, exemplified here by one, when asked, "Does this [the fact that an agent works at home] hurt the others?" "No. Only those who aren't competent tend to do this. Generally, it is only the incompetent agent who responds to this kind of pressure."

Most agents thought ill of colleagues who worked after office hours, although their standing as agents determined the form in which they expressed their disapproval. This censure of working overtime can be considered a functional equivalent of restriction of output among manual workers which was compatible with the professional orientation of these white-collar workers. Their identification with professional standards and their respect for experts did not allow agents to object to superior performance. These attitudes permitted, however, and even fostered disrespect for the person who tried to conceal his inferior ability by devoting more time to the job than was required. By discouraging agents from raising their production beyond the level that they could maintain during regular working hours, this group prevented progressive rivalry of this kind from undermining social cohesion.

The unofficial norm against working overtime minimized competitive conflicts, just as restriction of output in a factory does; but, in contrast to such standardization of productivity, it reinforced the differences in the performance of agents. It deterred those who were less skilled from devoting extra hours to their work in order to match the productivity of their more proficient colleagues. This norm, although it applied equally to all, was inequitable in its effects; it benefited particularly the expert who worked fast, since it protected his superior standing in the department.

THE TABOO ON
REPORTING OFFERS OF BRIBES

Agent Croner had uncovered serious violations in a firm. The manager of this firm brought employee Smith to the agency, whose testimony was intended to show that the alleged violations had not taken place. In a cleverly conducted cross-examination, Mr. Croner forced Mr. Smith to admit that his statements were untrue and that the violations had in fact occurred. Upon leaving, Mr. Smith whispered to Mr. Croner, in a foreign language that he knew the latter understood, asking whether they could talk about this informally. Mr. Croner answered loudly in English, "No, nothing can be done; this is what the law says." Such a "feeler," more or less persistently pursued, is the typical starting point of a bribe. And such a blunt rejection usually ends the incident, despite an unequivocal rule that all offers of bribes must be reported to higher authorities for possible prosecution.

Right after this incident, the observer asked Mr. Croner what agents generally do about clients who offer bribes.

> CRONER: We do what I just did. We never get bribes offered, because we usually stop it before we get an offer. [Turning to his neighbor:] Bert, come over here. [To the observer:] You don't mind if I call him over; I like him. [To the other agent:] What do you do about bribe offers, Bert?
>
> BERT LEHMANN: Squelch it right away; you stop his talking, and that's all.
>
> OBSERVER: That's very interesting. You never turn a man in?
>
> LEHMANN: There's no possibility of turning a man in. It doesn't get to that point. Nobody offers you a bribe. The only thing they some-

*123*

times do is to make some vague suggestions. Then you stop it, and no bribe is offered to you. If you don't, you would have to enter into the proposition, and tell him that you're interested. For instance, once a man asked me whether we could talk it over outside. I knew what that was. So I said, "No; why should we go outside?" If somebody makes an offer like that, you would have to enter into collusion with him before you could report it. You would have to accept his suggestion, and meet him some place, and say that you will take the money. If you do that, you're just as guilty as he is.

Clients recurrently made offers of bribes, and some were quite direct, but all agents were strongly opposed to reporting such offers for prosecution, regardless of their attitudes toward clients. They not only failed to make such reports but considered it *wrong* to do so. The taboo on reporting attempted bribes was the strongest unofficial norm of the group. When the observer questioned it by asking whether prosecuting employers who tried to bribe officials would not show the public how honest civil servants are, agents became aggressive and defended the righteousness of the norm in emotional language, for example, by saying, "We don't like squealers!"

Strong mores are rarely violated. . . . [One] violator of this unofficial taboo, a member of Department Y, questioned his own wisdom in having reported the attempt at bribery. He explained that he had received such offers before but had merely discouraged them. Only the special circumstances in this case, the repeated and insistent way in which the offer had been made in the presence of third persons, had induced him to report it. He added that he would not report an offer of a bribe again under any condition—"It's too unpleasant." Even the deviant agreed with the fundamental validity of the norm.

The major reason for this agent's change of attitude was that the group had responded to his violation of an important norm by ostracizing him. One of his colleagues explained, referring to this person without naming him: "One fellow did turn in a guy once. After that, nobody in the office talked to him for a year." This was not literally true, of course, but the others confirmed that he had been ostracized. He himself said: "Nobody talked to me directly, criticizing me for it, but you can feel it if your fellow-agents disapprove of you." Several years later, this agent continued to occupy an isolated position in the group. . . .

Being offered a bribe constituted a special tactical advantage for an agent. An employer who had violated one law was caught in the act of compounding his guilt by violating another one. He could no longer claim ignorance or inadvertence as an excuse for his violation. Agents exploited this situation to strengthen their position in negotiations. This is implied by the following remark concerning offers of small sums of money: "There's no sense in turning in a man for a small thing like that. You assume the role of the judge, and tell him what's right." Such a superordinate position, created by putting the briber in his place and maintained by his fear that this incorruptible public official might report him for prosecution, made it much easier to induce him to make retroactive adjustments. Refusing but not reporting bribes enabled agents more effectively to carry out their duties, which they considered important and on the basis of which they were evaluated.

Since bribe offers helped agents in their work, there existed a perennial temptation, consciously or unconsciously, to provoke employers to make such overtures. Of course, we do not know, and neither do these agents, to what extent their attitudes invited the many offers of bribes that they, according to their own statements, received. In any case, to preserve the advantageous position into which such an offer had put an agent, he had to reject it outright rather than appear hesitant in anticipation of reporting it for prosecution.

The fact that failing to report bribes facilitated the agent's task can explain only why this was rarely done but not why there was a social norm prohibiting it. The existence of this norm suggests that this act might actually have some advantages for the actor and must therefore be proscribed if it also has disadvantages for the rest of the group. . . .

### THE ENFORCEMENT OF GROUP NORMS

The unofficial norms of work groups in a bureaucratic organization are, of course, not labeled as such. Their existence is revealed only by their characteristics, which may be briefly summarized:

1. *Acceptance by all members of the group*, regardless of differences in attitudes on related subjects. Some agents were very friendly, and others were stern or domineering, toward clients; some refused even the offer of a cigar, and others considered the acceptance of small favors, such as invitations to lunch, legitimate; but they all condemned the reporting of bribes. Even the violator of the taboo agreed with it in principle, and explained his violation as resulting from exceptional circumstances. (For less basic norms, this agreement existed only on the verbal level, and agents tried to hide their violations from colleagues.)

2. *Endeavors to conceal violations*, since they are considered to be shameful, not only from other members of the group, but also from outsiders; indeed, in this case, the reticence extends to violations of colleagues. Several agents refused to talk to the observer about the cases in which bribes had been reported, and most of the others did not mention the names of the two officials who had made the reports. Typically, it was the badly integrated official who named violators of norms. The counterpart of this concealment, stemming from the same assumption of the intrinsic

shamefulness of these acts, is the use of the statement that a person has committed such an act as a deliberate insult. Thus an agent climaxed his derogatory remarks about a colleague by saying that he had even "denounced an employer" who had offered him a bribe.

3. *Questioning provokes hostility* and emotional reactions. Many agents became resentful or aggressive when the observer asked why bribes are not reported, and defended the taboo with irrational phrases, such as "We don't like squealers."

4. *Myths develop* with the theme that it is advantageous to conform. For example: "I'll tell you of one case. . . . He did exactly what you say. He went into a bar with a guy who had promised him money. He was supposed to give it to him in the bar. Then the F.B.I. came in, and they actually came in just like in the movies: the sirens were blasting. They happened to be late, and could only get there on time by using their sirens. And they came in with their guns, asking, 'Who is offering a bribe here?' By that time, the client had said, 'Excuse me, I have to go to the washroom,' and left the place. You know what happened? The F.B.I. didn't say it had made a mistake. It wrote to the [commissioner] telling him that the agent had handled the case badly. So, you can get into all kinds of trouble if you turn a man in."

5. *Ostracism is the penalty* only for violations of the most basic norms. Since the agent who had reported a bribe was cold-shouldered, none of the other members of Department Y made such reports, despite demands from superiors to do so. This one violation had provided the group with an opportunity to demonstrate to potential deviants the dire consequences of disobedience, and thus to assure conformity. . . .

Ostracism is only the most extreme form of a much more frequent phenomenon: a reduction in the degree of friendliness with which one person treats another, an almost automatic reaction to an associate's behavior that arouses one's displeasure. . . .

In addition to these sanctions, which found largely inadvertent expression in daily interaction, there also existed *specific* social sanctions for deviant behavior, such as ridiculing an agent, shaming him, or manifesting aggression in other forms. The departmental meeting or any other gathering of several officials provided an opportunity for punishing a deviant. Pair relationships usually were transformed into group situations before an individual who had violated a norm was penalized. For instance, when an agent asked a colleague to do him a favor, he was refused with the words, "Why ask me? There are lots of good men around. Ask them!" The first agent merely turned away in disgust. However, two others, who had overheard this exchange, called across the room, "Yes, but you're the best one" and "You asked the right man!" Now, the agent who had made the request turned back and joined several others in laughing at the culprit, who remained silent. The penalty for lack of cooperation—sarcasm and laughter—had not been administered so long as only one person confronted the deviant.

Specific sanctions were typically administered in group situations and not in the relative privacy of the pair relationship. . . .

Interactions of this type provide an individual who has violated a taboo with a brief but concentrated experience of what it is like to be ostracized. Two agents showed the observer that his opinions conflicted with theirs and rejected him, by making aggressive remarks, for this reason. Simultaneously, they presented him, through their agreement, with a demonstration of the desirability of being accepted by others. Even the observer, not a genuine part of the group, found this disconcerting. If several colleagues treated a member of the departmental group in this way—for example, by laughing together at aggressive remarks directed against him—he was momentarily put into the worst state of anomie: being alone and feeling disoriented, while witnessing the cohesiveness of others. This threat constituted a strong inducement to surrender unorthodox opinions and to cease deviant practices. . . .

Social sanctions were administered not only when a member of the group violated a norm but in the case of some individuals much more frequently. The fact that deviants are more often the subject of the group's aggression than their conduct warrants is well known; this is, after all, what is generally meant by a "scapegoat." One isolate in Department Y, in particular, could scarcely make a remark in the presence of several colleagues without being ridiculed or reprimanded. When he gave an earnest explanation, the others found reasons to laugh at him; when he made a joke about something, he was seriously told that this was no laughing matter. But his statements were neither so funny nor so tasteless as they were made out to be.

The isolate's continued presence in the group was a constant threat to the authority of its norms. His isolated position often prevented the group from penalizing his deviant acts. Since the others rarely included him in their informal gatherings, there was usually no occasion to administer specific social sanctions immediately after he had violated a norm. Neither could they become much less friendly toward an individual with whom they had only few and superficial contacts. The fact that the isolate's deviant action often went unpunished helps to explain his great tendency to violate group standards and also the frequent aggression of others against him. In the opinion of his colleagues, such an individual deserved, at all times, more punishment than he had actually received. Consequently, they seized every opportunity that presented itself to penalize the isolate. . . .

# *Organizational Humanism*

◆

HUMAN RELATIONS RESEARCH BROADENED classical organization theory to take note of the human factors in management, and through the fifties human relations organizational theory supported the pillars upon which classical theory rested. These pillars are the division of labor, the hierarchical and functional processes, structure, and the span of control.[1] Human relations had been concerned with monotony, alienation, and other problems relating to specialization of work. Authority through the hierarchy and in conflict with functional expertise was a major concern of human relations researchers. Problems of structure and span of control in human relations research were viewed as problems of the individuals who occupied specific roles in organizations. The human relations school accepted the goal of efficiency implicit in traditional organization theory and sought to indicate ways by which management could manipulate human factors to mold the workers to better fit the needs of the organization.

Toward the end of the fifties, however, theorists began to delve behind the more superficial aspects of human activity in organizations, and to deal with the nature of work itself, internalized motivation, and what appeared to be a basic incompatibility between the individual and the organization. The focus was no longer on the organization but on the individual and how his personal growth would affect the organization. This change in emphasis from short-term organizational goals to deep concern for the individual and for the longer-range goals of the organization was the key difference between human relations and organizational humanism.

Chris Argyris, one of the most influential behavioral scientists connected with organizational humanism, sought to delineate the inherent conflict between the individual and the organization. Argyris suggested that healthy personality development takes place along the following seven "developmental dimensions": from passive to active; from dependence to independence; from limited behavior patterns to more complex ones; from casual interests to deep interests; from short time perspectives to long ones; from subordinate roles to peer roles; and from lack of awareness of self to self-awareness. Although Argyris recognized that the world would be a difficult place if everyone progressed toward the more developed end of each continuum, he thought that individuals should have the chance to progress as far as their intelligence and inclinations would permit.

Argyris noted, however, that the traditional type of bureaucratic organization tended to work against the development of mature personalities along the seven developmental dimensions. In large formal organizations individuals have minimal control over their work situation, are expected to be passive and have a short time perspective, and are permitted to develop only a few superficial skills. Furthermore, the organization expects individuals to produce under the conditions that lead to psychological failure.[2]

The organizational humanists, although deeply concerned with the role of the individual, are still concerned with the effectiveness of the overall organization. They claim that an organization that is made up of unhealthy personalities cannot be healthy. An atmosphere conducive to individual growth is necessary. Organizational democracy provides such an atmosphere.

This democratic component of the organizational humanists' thought is brought out most clearly by Warren Bennis and Philip Slater. To Bennis and Slater, democracy is a system of values "which people are *internally* compelled to affirm."[3] Among these values are the following:[4]

1. Full and free *communication*, regardless of rank and power.

2. A reliance on *consensus*, rather than the more customary forms of coercion or compromise, to manage conflict.

3. The idea that *influence* is based on technical competence and knowledge rather than on the vagaries of personal whims or prerogatives of power.

4. An atmosphere that permits and even encourages emotional expression as well as task-oriented acts.

5. A basically human bias, one that accepts the inevitability of conflict between the organization and the individual, but that is willing to cope with and mediate this conflict on rational grounds.

Organizational humanists have great faith in the inner resources of individuals and a positive view of human nature. These assumptions suggest vastly different organizational structures and management behavior than those suggested by the contrary assumptions of traditional theory. The late Douglas McGregor, a college president and successful industrial consultant, sought to spell out an alternative role for management under the assumptions of organizational humanism. Using Abraham Maslow's theory of motivation—the hierarchy of needs—McGregor criticized traditional management practices and suggested new approaches. Often Theory X, the archetype traditional theory, and Theory Y, the organizational humanism approach, have been labeled as "hard" and "soft," respectively, but there is nothing soft about McGregor's insistence that managers operating in a Theory Y environment be held responsible for their results.[5]

The Theory X versus Theory Y formulation sparked research initially aimed at finding *the* best way for motivating people in organizations. Such research quickly evolved into a search for situations in which one or the other of these theories might be useful. Such "contingency theory" has developed the view that change-oriented, unstructured operations like scientific research respond better to the Theory Y approach, whereas routine operations are more effectively managed in a Theory X environment.[6]

When reading the McGregor selection reprinted below, one should deal critically with Maslow's hierarchy of needs theory. Does it seem valid? Can it be proven or disproven? Are only unsatisfied needs motivators? Does Theory Y necessarily stand or fall on the intellectual soundness of the hierarchy of needs? At what levels in a hierarchy might one try a Theory Y approach? How do organizations in the real world attempt to deal with motivation?

Frederick Herzberg discussed this last question.[7] Herzberg identified several motivation factors, all of which are intrinsic to the job. These factors encourage the growth and development needs of people in a work situation: (1) achievement, (2) recognition for achievement, (3) the work itself, (4) responsibility, and (5) growth or advancement. According to Herzberg, if these factors were not present in a work situation, the internal motivators within people would not begin to function. The kind of motivation that Herzberg is concerned with is perfectly in agreement with Douglas McGregor's Theory Y view of organizations.

But Herzberg recognized another group of factors, whose presence does not produce motivation but whose absence produces job dissatisfaction. Generally, these factors were not specifically related to the job. Herzberg called these dissatisfaction avoidance factors "hygiene factors." Among the hygiene factors that Herzberg identified were these: (1) company policy and administration, (2) supervision, (3) interpersonal relationships, (4) working conditions, (5) salary, (6) status, and (7) security. A worker in any field expects a certain degree of salary, status, security. He or she expects pleasant working conditions and good interpersonal relationships. If these things are not forthcoming, the employee will be dissatisfied. If they are forthcoming, the employee will not necessarily be either satisfied or motivated. He or she will simply be not dissatisfied. Herzberg concluded that the opposite of job dissatisfaction was not job satisfaction. It was simply no job dissatisfaction.

Herzberg saw that most organizational efforts to "motivate" employees are really aimed at affecting the hygiene factors. Herzberg derided the efforts to motivate people by cutting the work week. Motivated people do not seek less time on the job; they want more hours of work, according to him. Similarly, spiraling wages and fringe benefits, in Herzberg's eyes, merely motivate the employee to seek another salary increase and join the "fringe benefit of the month club." Human relations and sensitivity training merely deal with improved supervision and interpersonal relationships, which, according to Herzberg, cannot motivate employees but can merely make them not dissatisfied.

Because Herzberg saw motivational factors related to the work itself, he advocated a strategy of job enrichment. Rather than rationalizing work to increase efficiency, which is the way industrial engineers had approached job development, Herzberg wanted to see jobs changed to use the talents of people more effectively. J. Richard Hackman, Greg Oldham, Robert Janson, and Kenneth Purdy build from the Herzberg efforts at job enrichment. They present a set of tools for diagnosing existing jobs to identify cases where job enrichment can be used successfully to motivate employees. Furthermore, they suggest an implementation strategy.

One of the main advances of the Hackman et al. strategy for job enrichment is the frank recognition that job enrichment may not work for everybody. Many managers become turned off to management techniques based on ideas that do not conform to the behavior of people with whom they have been used to dealing. Herzberg's motivators and McGregor's Theory Y, unless qualified, have an air of unreality about them. Many people, especially the stereotypical government bureaucrat, have "low growth needs." Hackman et al. address this problem.

While reading this selection, consider the types of jobs most susceptible to successful job enrichment. Are these jobs well represented in government bureaucracies? Hackman and his associates report on the job enrichment activities of a private insurance company. What aspects of public-sector employment might affect the outcome of job enrichment efforts? Specifically, consider civil service rules and the role of public sector unions. Do you think government could be more effective if job-enrichment plans became more widespread? Would you like to work in an organization managed by Theory Y principles and Herzberg's theory of motivation or in one managed according to more traditional management concepts?

## NOTES

1. William G. Scott, "Organization Theory: An Overview and an Appraisal," *Journal of the Academy of Management* 4, no. 1 (April 1961): 4, 7–27. I have substituted the term "hierarchical" for Scott's term "scalar." The term "organizational humanism" is derived from Scott's discussion of "industrial humanism" in "Organizational Government: Prospects for a Truly Participative System," *Public Administrative Review* 29, no. 1 (January/February 1969): 44–45. Among the people identified with the organizational humanists are Chris Argyris, Robert Blake, Warren Bennis, Rensis Likert, Jane Mouton, and Douglas McGregor.

2. Chris Argyris, *Personality and Organization* (New York: Harper & Row, 1957) fully develops the argument. The discussion of the developmental dimensions has appeared in several journals, among them "Being Human and Being Organized," *Transaction* 1, no. 5 (July 1964): 1, 3–6.

3. Warren G. Bennis and Philip E. Slater, *The Temporary Society* (New York: Harper & Row, 1968), p. 4. (Emphasis added.)

4. Ibid., p. 4 (Emphasis in the original.)

5. Douglas McGregor, *The Human Side of Enterprise* (New York: McGraw-Hill Book Company, 1960).

6. John J. Morse and Jay W. Lorsch, "Beyond Theory Y," *Harvard Business Review* 48, no. 3 (May/June 1970): 61–68.

7. Frederick Herzberg, "One More Time: How Do You Motivate Employees," *Harvard Business Review* 46, no. 1 (January–February 1968): 53–62. The theory came out of Frederick Herzberg, Bernard Mausner, and Barbara B. Snyderman, *The Motivation to Work* (New York: John Wiley & Sons, Inc., 1959).

# 7

## The Human Side
## of Enterprise

◆

### Douglas McGregor

IT HAS BECOME TRITE to say that the most significant developments of the next quarter century will take place not in the physical but in the social sciences, that industry—the economic organ of society—has the fundamental know-how to utilize physical science and technology for the material benefit of mankind, and that we must now learn how to utilize the social sciences to make our human organizations truly effective.

Many people agree in principle with such statements; but so far they represent a pious hope—and little else. Consider with me, if you will, something of what may be involved when we attempt to transform the hope into reality.

I

Let me begin with an analogy. A quarter century ago basic conceptions of the nature of matter and energy had changed profoundly from what they had been since Newton's time. The physical scientists were persuaded that under proper conditions new and hitherto unimagined sources of energy could be made available to mankind.

We know what has happened since then. First came the bomb. Then,

*Reprinted from* Leadership and Motivation, Essays of Douglas McGregor, *edited by Warren G. Bennis and Edgar H. Schein, with the collaboration of Caroline McGregor, by permission of The MIT Press, Cambridge, Massachusetts.* © 1966 by *The Massachusetts Institute of Technology.*

during the past decade, have come many other attempts to exploit these scientific discoveries—some successful, some not.

The point of my analogy, however, is that the application of theory in this field is a slow and costly matter. We expect it always to be thus. No one is impatient with the scientist because he cannot tell industry how to build a simple, cheap, all-purpose source of atomic energy today. That it will take at least another decade and the investment of billions of dollars to achieve results which are economically competitive with present sources of power is understood and accepted.

It is transparently pretentious to suggest any *direct* similarity between the developments in the physical sciences leading to the harnessing of atomic energy and potential developments in the social sciences. Nevertheless, the analogy is not as absurd as it might appear to be at first glance.

To a lesser degree, and in a much more tentative fashion, we are in a position in the social sciences today like that of the physical sciences with respect to atomic energy in the thirties. We know that past conceptions of the nature of man are inadequate and in many ways incorrect. We are becoming quite certain that, under proper conditions, unimagined resources of creative human energy could become available within the organizational setting.

We cannot tell industrial management how to apply this new knowledge in simple, economic ways. We know it will require years of exploration, much costly development research, and a substantial amount of creative imagination on the part of management to discover how to apply this growing knowledge to the organization of human effort in industry.

May I ask that you keep this analogy in mind—overdrawn and pretentious though it may be—as a framework for what I have to say. . . .

## Management's Task: Conventional View

The conventional conception of management's task in harnessing human energy to organizational requirements can be stated broadly in terms of three propositions. In order to avoid the complications introduced by a label, I shall call this set of propositions "Theory X":

1. Management is responsible for organizing the elements of productive enterprise—money, materials, equipment, people—in the interest of economic ends.

2. With respect to people, this is a process of directing their efforts, motivating them, controlling their actions, modifying their behavior to fit the needs of the organization.

3. Without this active intervention by management, people would be passive—even resistant—to organizational needs. They must therefore be persuaded, rewarded, punished, controlled—their ac-

tivities must be directed. This is management's task—in managing subordinate managers or workers. We often sum it up by saying that management consists of getting things done through other people.

Behind this conventional theory there are several additional beliefs—less explicit, but widespread:

4. The average man is by nature indolent—he works as little as possible.

5. He lacks ambition, dislikes responsibility, prefers to be led.

6. He is inherently self-centered, indifferent to organizational needs.

7. He is by nature resistant to change.

8. He is gullible, not very bright, the ready dupe of the charlatan and the demagogue.

The human side of economic enterprise today is fashioned from propositions and beliefs such as these. Conventional organization structures, managerial policies, practices, and programs reflect these assumptions.

In accomplishing its task—with these assumptions as guides—management has conceived of a range of possibilities between two extremes.

### The Hard or the Soft Approach?

At one extreme, management can be "hard" or "strong." The methods for directing behavior involve coercion and threat (usually disguised), close supervision, tight controls over behavior. At the other extreme, management can be "soft" or "weak." The methods for directing behavior involve being permissive, satisfying people's demands, achieving harmony. Then they will be tractable, accept direction.

This range has been fairly completely explored during the past half century, and management has learned some things from the exploration. There are difficulties in the "hard" approach. Force breeds counter-forces: restriction of output, antagonism, militant unionism, subtle but effective sabotage of management objectives. This approach is especially difficult during times of full employment.

There are also difficulties in the "soft" approach. It leads frequently to the abdication of management—to harmony, perhaps, but to indifferent performance. People take advantage of the soft approach. They continually expect more, but they give less and less.

Currently, the popular theme is "firm but fair." This is an attempt to gain the advantages of both the hard and the soft approaches. It is reminiscent of Teddy Roosevelt's "speak softly and carry a big stick."

136

## Is the Conventional View Correct?

The findings which are beginning to emerge from the social sciences challenge this whole set of beliefs about man and human nature and about the task of management. The evidence is far from conclusive, certainly, but it is suggestive. It comes from the laboratory, the clinic, the schoolroom, the home, and even to a limited extent from industry itself.

The social scientist does not deny that human behavior in industrial organization today is approximately what management perceives it to be. He has, in fact, observed it and studied it fairly extensively. But he is pretty sure that this behavior is *not* a consequence of man's inherent nature. It is a consequence rather of the nature of industrial organizations, of management philosophy, policy, and practice. The conventional approach of Theory X is based on mistaken notions of what is cause and what is effect.

"Well," you ask, "what then is the *true* nature of man? What evidence leads the social scientist to deny what is obvious?" And, if I am not mistaken, you are also thinking, "Tell me—simply, and without a lot of scientific verbiage—what you think you know that is so unusual. Give me—without a lot of intellectual claptrap and theoretical nonsense—some practical ideas which will enable me to improve the situation in my organization. And remember, I'm faced with increasing costs and narrowing profit margins. I want proof that such ideas won't result simply in new and costly human relations frills. I want practical results, and I want them now."

If these are your wishes, you are going to be disappointed. Such requests can no more be met by the social scientist today than could comparable ones with respect to atomic energy be met by the physicist fifteen years ago. I can, however, indicate a few of the reasons for asserting that conventional assumptions about the human side of enterprise are inadequate. And I can suggest—tentatively—some of the propositions that will comprise a more adequate theory of the management of people. The magnitude of the task that confronts us will then, I think, be apparent.

II

Perhaps the best way to indicate why the conventional approach of management is inadequate is to consider the subject of motivation. In discussing this subject I will draw heavily on the work of my colleague, Abraham Maslow of Brandeis University. His is the most fruitful approach I know. Naturally, what I have to say will be overgeneralized and will ignore important qualifications. In the time at our disposal, this is inevitable.

### Physiological and Safety Needs

Man is a wanting animal—as soon as one of his needs is satisfied, another appears in its place. This process is unending. It continues from birth to death.

Man's needs are organized in a series of levels—a hierarchy of importance. At the lowest level, but preeminent in importance when they are thwarted, are his physiological needs. Man lives by bread alone, when there is no bread. Unless the circumstances are unusual, his needs for love, for status, for recognition are inoperative when his stomach has been empty for a while. But when he eats regularly and adequately, hunger ceases to be an important need. The sated man has hunger only in the sense that a full bottle has emptiness. The same is true of the other physiological needs of man—for rest, exercise, shelter, protection from the elements.

*A satisfied need is not a motivator of behavior!* This is a fact of profound significance. It is a fact which is regularly ignored in the conventional approach to the management of people. I shall return to it later. For the moment, one example will make my point. Consider your own need for air. Except as you are deprived of it, it has no appreciable motivating effect upon your behavior.

When the physiological needs are reasonably satisfied, needs at the next higher level begin to dominate man's behavior—to motivate him. These are called safety needs. They are needs for protection against danger, threat, deprivation. Some people mistakenly refer to these as needs for security. However, unless man is in a dependent relationship where he fears arbitrary deprivation, he does not demand security. The need is for the "fairest possible break." When he is confident of this, he is more than willing to take risks. But when he feels threatened or dependent, his greatest need is for guarantees, for protection, for security.

The fact needs little emphasis that since every industrial employee is in a dependent relationship, safety needs may assume considerable importance. Arbitrary management actions, behavior which arouses uncertainty with respect to continued employment or which reflects favoritism or discrimination, unpredictable administration of policy—these can be powerful motivators of the safety needs in the employment relationship *at every level* from worker to vice president.

### Social Needs

When man's physiological needs are satisfied and he is no longer fearful about his physical welfare, his social needs become important motivators of his behavior—for belonging, for association, for acceptance by his fellows, for giving and receiving friendship and love.

Management knows today of the existence of these needs, but it often assumes quite wrongly that they represent a threat to the organization. Many studies have demonstrated that the tightly knit, cohesive work group may, under proper conditions, be far more effective than an equal number of separate individuals in achieving organizational goals.

Yet management, fearing group hostility to its own objectives, often goes to considerable lengths to control and direct human efforts in ways that are inimical to the natural "groupiness" of human beings. When man's social needs—and perhaps his safety needs, too—are thus thwarted, he behaves in ways which tend to defeat organizational objectives. He becomes resistant, antagonistic, uncooperative. But this behavior is a consequence, not a cause.

## Ego Needs

Above the social needs—in the sense that they do not become motivators until lower needs are reasonably satisfied—are the needs of greatest significance to management and to man himself. They are the egoistic needs, and they are of two kinds:

1. Those needs that relate to one's self-esteem—needs for self-confidence, for independence, for achievement, for competence, for knowledge.

2. Those needs that relate to one's reputation—needs for status, for recognition, for appreciation, for the deserved respect of one's fellows.

Unlike the lower needs, these are rarely satisfied; man seeks indefinitely for more satisfaction of these needs once they have become important to him. But they do not appear in any significant way until physiological, safety, and social needs are all reasonably satisfied.

The typical industrial organization offers few opportunities for the satisfaction of these egoistic needs to people at lower levels in the hierarchy. The conventional methods of organizing work, particularly in mass production industries, give little heed to these aspects of human motivation. If the practices of scientific management were deliberately calculated to thwart these needs—which, of course, they are not—they could hardly accomplish this purpose better than they do.

## Self-Fulfillment Needs

Finally—a capstone, as it were, on the hierarchy of man's needs—there are what we may call the needs for self-fulfillment. These are the needs for realizing one's own potentialities, for continued self-development, for being creative in the broadest sense of that term.

It is clear that the conditions of modern life give only limited opportunity for these relatively weak needs to obtain expression. The deprivation most people experience with respect to other lower-level needs diverts their energies into the struggle to satisfy *those* needs, and the needs for self-fulfillment remain dormant.

III

Now, briefly, a few general comments about motivation:

We recognize readily enough that a man suffering from a severe dietary deficiency is sick. The deprivation of physiological needs has behavioral consequences. The same is true—although less well recognized—of deprivation of higher-level needs. The man whose needs for safety, association, independence, or status are thwarted is sick just as surely as is he who has rickets. And his sickness will be mistaken if we attribute his resultant passivity, his hostility, his refusal to accept responsibility to his inherent "human nature." These forms of behavior are *symptoms* of illness—of deprivation of his social and egoistic needs.

The man whose lower-level needs are satisfied is not motivated to satisfy those needs any longer. For practical purposes they exist no longer. (Remember my point about your need for air.) Management often asks, "Why aren't people more productive? We pay good wages, provide good working conditions, have excellent fringe benefits and steady employment. Yet people do not seem to be willing to put forth more than minimum effort."

The fact that management has provided for these physiological and safety needs has shifted the motivational emphasis to the social and perhaps to the egoistic needs. Unless there are opportunities *at work* to satisfy these higher-level needs, people will be deprived; and their behavior will reflect this deprivation. Under such conditions, if management continues to focus its attention on physiological needs, its efforts are bound to be ineffective.

People *will* make insistent demands for more money under these conditions. It becomes more important than ever to buy the material goods and services which can provide limited satisfaction of the thwarted needs. Although money has only limited value in satisfying many higher-level needs, it can become the focus of interest if it is the *only* means available.

## The Carrot and Stick Approach

The carrot and stick theory of motivation (like Newtonian physical theory) works reasonably well under certain circumstances. The *means* for satisfying man's physiological and (within limits) his safety needs can be provided or withheld by management. Employment itself is such a means, and so are wages, working conditions, and benefits. By these means the individual can be controlled so long as he is struggling for subsistence. Man lives for bread alone when there is no bread.

But the carrot and stick theory does not work at all once man has reached an adequate subsistence level and is motivated primarily by higher needs. Management cannot provide a man with self-respect, or with the respect of his fellows, or with the satisfaction of needs for self-fulfillment. It can create conditions such that he is encouraged and enabled to seek such satisfactions *for himself*, or it can thwart him by failing to create those conditions.

But this creation of conditions is not "control." It is not a good device for directing behavior. And so management finds itself in an odd position. The high standard of living created by our modern technological know-how provides quite adequately for the satisfaction of physiological and safety needs. The only significant exception is where management practices have not created confidence in a "fair break"—and thus where safety needs are thwarted. But by making possible the satisfaction of low-level needs, management has deprived itself of the ability to use as motivators the devices on which conventional theory has taught it to rely—rewards, promises, incentives, or threats and other coercive devices.

## Neither Hard nor Soft

The philosophy of management by direction and control—*regardless of whether it is hard or soft*—is inadequate to motivate because the human needs on which this approach relies are today unimportant motivators of behavior. Direction and control are essentially useless in motivating people whose important needs are social and egoistic. Both the hard and the soft approach fail today because they are simply irrelevant to the situation.

People, deprived of opportunities to satisfy at work the needs which are now important to them, behave exactly as we might predict—with indolence, passivity, resistance to change, lack of responsibility, willingness to follow the demagogue, unreasonable demands for economic benefits. It would seem that we are caught in a web of our own weaving.

In summary, then, of these comments about motivation:

Management by direction and control—whether implemented with the hard, the soft, or the firm but fair approach—fails under today's conditions to provide effective motivation of human efforts toward organizational objectives. It fails because direction and control are useless methods of motivating people whose physiological and safety needs are reasonably satisfied and whose social, egoistic, and self-fulfillment needs are predominant.

*141*

IV

For these and many other reasons, we require a different theory of the task of managing people based on more adequate assumptions about human nature and human motivation. I am going to be so bold as to suggest the broad dimensions of such a theory. Call it "Theory Y," if you will.

1. Management is responsible for organizing the elements of productive enterprise—money, materials, equipment, people—in the interest of economic ends.

2. People are *not* by nature passive or resistant to organizational needs. They have become so as a result of experience in organizations.

3. The motivation, the potential for development, the capacity for assuming responsibility, the readiness to direct behavior toward organizational goals are all present in people. Management does not put them there. It is a responsibility of management to make it possible for people to recognize and develop these human characteristics for themselves.

4. The essential task of management is to arrange organizational conditions and methods of operation so that people can achieve their own goals *best* by directing *their own* efforts toward organizational objectives.

This is a process primarily of creating opportunities, releasing potential, removing obstacles, encouraging growth, providing guidance. It is what Peter Drucker has called "management by objectives" in contrast to "management by control."

And I hasten to add that it does *not* involve the abdication of management, the absence of leadership, the lowering of standards, or the other characteristics usually associated with the "soft" approach under Theory X. Much on the contrary. It is no more possible to create an organization today which will be a fully effective application of this theory than it was to build an atomic power plant in 1945. There are many formidable obstacles to overcome.

## Some Difficulties

The conditions imposed by conventional organization theory and by the approach of scientific management for the past half century have tied men to limited jobs which do not utilize their capabilities, have discouraged the acceptance of responsibility, have encouraged passivity, have eliminated meaning from work. Man's habits, attitudes, expectations—his whole conception of membership in an industrial organization—have been conditioned by his experience under these circumstances. Change in the direction of Theory Y will be slow, and it will require extensive modification of the attitudes of management and workers alike.

People today are accustomed to being directed, manipulated, controlled in industrial organizations and to finding satisfaction for their social, egoistic, and self-fulfillment needs away from the job. This is true of much of management as well as of workers. Genuine "industrial citizenship"—to borrow again a term from Drucker—is a remote and unrealistic idea, the meaning of which has not even been considered by most members of industrial organizations.

Another way of saying this is that Theory X places exclusive reliance upon external control of human behavior, while Theory Y relies heavily on self-control and self-direction. It is worth noting that this difference is the difference between treating people as children and treating them as mature adults. After generations of the former, we cannot expect to shift to the latter overnight.

V

Before we are overwhelmed by the obstacles, let us remember that the application of theory is always slow. Progress is usually achieved in small steps.

Consider with me a few innovative ideas which are entirely consistent with Theory Y and which are today being applied with some success:

## Decentralization and Delegation

These are ways of freeing people from the too-close control of conventional organization, giving them a degree of freedom to direct their own activities, to assume responsibility, and, importantly, to satisfy their egoistic needs. In this connection, the flat organization of Sears, Roebuck and Company provides an interesting example. It forces "management by objectives" since it enlarges the number of people reporting to a manager until he cannot direct and control them in the conventional manner.

## Job Enlargement

This concept, pioneered by I.B.M. and Detroit Edison, is quite consistent with Theory Y. It encourages the acceptance of responsibility at the bottom of the organization; it provides opportunities for satisfying social and egoistic needs. In fact, the reorganization of work at the factory level offers one of the more challenging opportunities for innovation consistent with Theory Y. The studies by A. T. M. Wilson and his associates of British coal mining and Indian textile manufacture have added appreciably to our understanding of work organization. Moreover, the economic and psychological results achieved by this work have been substantial.

## Participation and Consultative Management

Under proper conditions these results provide encouragement to people to direct their creative energies toward organizational objectives, give them some voice in decisions that affect them, provide significant opportunities for the satisfaction of social and egoistic needs. I need only mention the Scanlon Plan as the outstanding embodiment of these ideas in practice.

The not infrequent failure of such ideas as these to work as well as expected is often attributable to the fact that a management has "bought the idea" but applied it within the framework of Theory X and its assumptions.

Delegation is not an effective way of exercising management by control. Participation becomes a farce when it is applied as a sales gimmick or a device for kidding people into thinking they are important. Only the management that has confidence in human capacities and is itself directed toward organizational objectives rather than toward the preservation of personal power can grasp the implications of this emerging theory. Such management will find and apply successfully other innovative ideas as we move slowly toward the full implementation of a theory like Y.

## Performance Appraisal

Before I stop, let me mention one other practical application of Theory Y which—while still highly tentative—may well have important consequences. This has to do with performance appraisal within the ranks of management. Even a cursory examination of conventional programs of performance appraisal will reveal how completely consistent they are with Theory X. In fact, most such programs tend to treat the individual as though he were a product under inspection on the assembly line.

Take the typical plan: substitute "product" for "subordinate being appraised," substitute "inspector" for "superior making the appraisal," substitute "rework" for "training or development," and, except for the attributes being judged, the human appraisal process will be virtually indistinguishable from the product inspection process.

A few companies—among them General Mills, Ansul Chemical, and General Electric—have been experimenting with approaches which involve the individual in setting "targets" or objectives *for himself* and in a *self*-evaluation of performance semi-annually or annually. Of course, the superior plays an important leadership role in this process—one, in fact, which demands substantially more competence that the conventional approach. The role is, however, considerably more congenial to many managers than the role of "judge" or "inspector" which is forced upon them by conventional performance. Above all, the individual is encouraged to take a greater responsibility for planning and appraising his own contribution to organizational objectives; and the accompanying effects on egoistic and self-fulfillment needs are substantial. This approach to performance appraisal represents one more innovative idea being explored by a few managements who are moving toward the implementation of Theory Y.

## VI

And now I am back where I began. I share the belief that we could realize substantial improvements in the effectiveness of industrial organizations during the next decade or two. Moreover, I believe the social sciences can contribute much to such developments. We are only beginning to grasp the implications of the growing body of knowledge in these fields. But if this conviction is to become a reality instead of a pious hope, we will need to view the process much as we view the process of releasing the energy of the atom for constructive human ends—as a slow, costly, sometimes discouraging approach toward a goal which would seem to many to be quite unrealistic.

The ingenuity and the perseverance of industrial management in the pursuit of economic ends have changed many scientific and technological dreams into commonplace realities. It is now becoming clear that the application of these same talents to the human side of enterprise will not only enhance substantially these materialistic achievements but will bring us one step closer to "the good society." Shall we get on with the job?

# 8

# A New Strategy
# for
# Job Enrichment

♦

*J. Richard Hackman,*
*Greg Oldham, Robert Janson,*
*Kenneth Purdy*

PRACTITIONERS OF JOB ENRICHMENT have been living through a time of excitement, even euphoria. Their craft has moved from the psychology and management journals to the front page and the Sunday supplement. Job enrichment, which began with the pioneering work of Herzberg and his associates, originally was intended as a means to increase the motivation and satisfaction of people at work—and to improve productivity in the bargain.[1-5] Now it is being acclaimed in the popular press as a cure for problems ranging from inflation to drug abuse.

Much current writing about job enrichment is enthusiastic, sometimes even messianic, about what it can accomplish. But the hard questions of exactly what should be done to improve jobs, and how, tend to be glossed over. Lately, because the harder questions have not been dealt with adequately, critical winds have begun to blow. Job enrichment has been described as yet another "management fad," as "nothing new," even as a fraud. And reports of job-enrichment failures are beginning to appear in management and psychology journals.

Acknowledgments: The authors acknowledge with great appreciation the editorial assistance of John Hickey in the preparation of this paper, and the help of Kenneth Brousseau, Daniel Feldman, and Linda Frank in collecting the data that are summarized here. The research activities reported were supported in part by the Organizational Effectiveness Research Program of the Office of Naval Research, and the Manpower Administration of the U.S. Department of Labor, both through contracts to Yale University.

This article attempts to redress the excesses that have characterized some of the recent writings about job enrichment. As the technique increases in popularity as a management tool, top managers inevitably will find themselves making decisions about its use. The intent of this paper is to help both managers and behavioral scientists become better able to make those decisions on a solid basis of fact and data.

Succinctly stated, we present here a new strategy for going about the redesign of work. The strategy is based on three years of collaborative work and cross-fertilization among the authors—two of whom are academic researchers and two of whom are active practitioners in job enrichment. Our approach is new, but it has been tested in many organizations. It draws on the contributions of both management practice and psychological theory, but it is firmly in the middle ground between them. It builds on and complements previous work by Herzberg and others, but provides for the first time a set of tools for *diagnosing* existing jobs—and a map for translating the diagnostic results into specific action steps for change.

What we have, then, is the following:

1. A theory that specifies when people will get personally "turned on" to their work. The theory shows what kinds of jobs are most likely to generate excitement and commitment about work, and what kinds of employees it works best for.

2. A set of action steps for job enrichment based on the theory, which prescribe in concrete terms what to do to make jobs more motivating for the people who do them.

3. Evidence that the theory holds water and that it can be used to bring about measurable—and sometimes dramatic—improvements in employee work behavior, in job satisfaction, and in the financial performance of the organizational unit involved.

## THE THEORY BEHIND THE STRATEGY

### What Makes People Get Turned On to Their Work?

For workers who are really prospering in their jobs, work is likely to be a lot like play. Consider, for example, a golfer at a driving range, practicing to get rid of a hook. His activity is *meaningful* to him; he has chosen to do it because he gets a "kick" from testing his skills by playing the game. He knows that he alone is *responsible* for what happens when he hits the ball. And he has *knowledge of the results* within a few seconds.

Behavioral scientists have found that the three "psychological states" experienced by the golfer in the above example also are critical in determining a person's motivation and satisfaction on the job.

147

1. *Experienced meaningfulness:* The individual must perceive his work as worthwhile or important by some system of values he accepts.

2. *Experienced responsibility:* He must believe that he personally is accountable for the outcomes of his efforts.

3. *Knowledge of results:* He must be able to determine, on some fairly regular basis, whether or not the outcomes of his work are satisfactory.

When these three conditions are present, a person tends to feel very good about himself when he performs well. And those good feelings will prompt him to try to continue to do well—so he can continue to earn the positive feelings in the future. That is what is meant by "internal motivation"—being turned on to one's work because of the positive internal feelings that are generated by doing well, rather than being dependent on external factors (such as incentive pay or compliments from the boss) for the motivation to work effectively.

What if one of the three psychological states is missing? Motivation drops markedly. Suppose, for example, that our golfer has settled in at the driving range to practice for a couple of hours. Suddenly a fog drifts in over the range. He can no longer see if the ball starts to tail off to the left a hundred yards out. The satisfaction he got from hitting straight down the middle—and the motivation to try to correct something whenever he didn't—are both gone. If the fog stays, it's likely that he soon will be packing up his clubs.

The relationship between the three psychological states and on-the-job outcomes is illustrated in Figure 1. When all three are high, then internal work motivation, job satisfaction, and work quality are high, and absenteeism and turnover are low.

## What Job Characteristics Make It Happen?

Recent research has identified five "core" characteristics of jobs that elicit the psychological states described above.[6-8] These five core job dimensions provide the key to objectively measuring jobs and to changing them so that they have high potential for motivating people who do them.

*Toward meaningful work.* Three of the five core dimensions contribute to a job's meaningfulness for the worker:

1. *Skill variety*—the degree to which a job requires the worker to perform activities that challenge his skills and abilities. When even a single skill is involved, there is at least a seed of potential meaningfulness. When several are involved, the job has the potential of appealing to more of the whole person, and also of avoiding the monot-

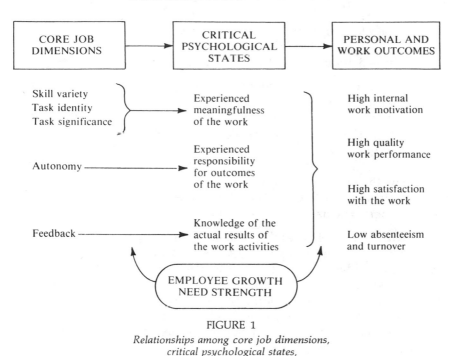

FIGURE 1

*Relationships among core job dimensions,*
*critical psychological states,*
*and on-the-job outcomes.*

ony of performing the same task repeatedly, no matter how much skill it may require.

2. *Task identity*—the degree to which the job requires completion of a "whole" and identifiable piece of work—doing a job from beginning to end with a visible outcome. For example, it is clearly more meaningful to an employee to build complete toasters than to attach electrical cord after electrical cord, especially if he never sees a completed toaster. (Note that the whole job, in this example, probably would involve greater skill variety as well as task identity.)

3. *Task significance*—the degree to which the job has a substantial and perceivable impact on the lives of other people, whether in the immediate organization or the world at large. The worker who tightens nuts on aircraft brake assemblies is more likely to perceive his work as significant than the worker who fills small boxes with paper clips—even though the skill levels involved may be comparable.

Each of these three job dimensions represents an important route to experienced meaningfulness. If the job is high in all three, the worker is quite likely to experience his job as very meaningful. It is not necessary, however, for a job to be very high in all three dimensions. If the job is low

149

in any one of them, there will be a drop in overall experienced meaningfulness. But even when two dimensions are low, the worker may find the job meaningful if the third is high enough.

*Toward personal responsibility.* A fourth core dimension leads a worker to experience increased responsibility in his job. This is *autonomy*, the degree to which the job gives the worker freedom, independence, and discretion in scheduling work and determining how he will carry it out. People in highly autonomous jobs know that they are personally responsible for successes and failures. To the extent that their autonomy is high, then, how the work goes will be felt to depend more on the individual's own efforts and initiatives—rather than on detailed instructions from the boss or from a manual of job procedures.

*Toward knowledge of results.* The fifth and last core dimension is *feedback*. This is the degree to which a worker, in carrying out the work activities required by the job, gets information about the effectiveness of his efforts. Feedback is most powerful when it comes directly from the work itself—for example, when a worker has the responsibility for gauging and otherwise checking a component he has just finished, and learns in the process that he has lowered his reject rate by meeting specifications more consistently.

*The overall "motivating potential" of a job.* Figure 1 shows how the five core dimensions combine to affect the psychological states that are critical in determining whether or not an employee will be internally motivated to work effectively. Indeed, when using an instrument to be described later, it is possible to compute a "motivating potential score" (MPS) for any job. The MPS provides a single summary index of the degree to which the objective characteristics of the job will prompt high internal work motivation. Following the theory outlined above, a job high in motivating potential must be high in at least one (and hopefully more) of the three dimensions that lead to experienced meaningfulness and high in both autonomy and feedback as well. The MPS provides a quantitative index of the degree to which this is in fact the case. (See Appendix for detailed formula.) As will be seen later, the MPS can be very useful in diagnosing jobs and in assessing the effectiveness of job-enrichment activities.

## Does the Theory Work for Everybody?

Unfortunately not. Not everyone is able to become internally motivated in his work, even when the motivating potential of a job is very high indeed.

Research has shown that the *psychological needs* of people are very important in determining who can (and who cannot) become internally motivated at work. Some people have strong needs for personal accomplishment, for learning and developing themselves beyond where they are now, for being stimulated and challenged, and so on. These people are high in "growth-need strength."

Figure 2 shows diagrammatically the proposition that individual growth needs have the power to moderate the relationship between the characteristics of jobs and work outcomes. Many workers with high growth needs will turn on eagerly when they have jobs that are high in the core dimensions. Workers whose growth needs are not so strong may respond less eagerly — or, at first, even balk at being "pushed" or "stretched" too far.

Psychologists who emphasize human potential argue that everyone has within him at least a spark of the need to grow and develop personally. Steadily accumulating evidence shows, however, that unless that spark is pretty strong, chances are it will get snuffed out by one's experiences in typical organizations. So, a person who has worked for twenty years in stultifying jobs may find it difficult or impossible to become internally motivated overnight when given the opportunity.

We should be cautious, however, about creating rigid categories of people based on their measured growth-need strength at any particular time. It is true that we can predict from these measures who is likely to become internally motivated on a job and who will be less willing or able to do so. But what we do not know yet is whether or not the growth-need "spark" can be rekindled for those individuals who have had their growth needs dampened by years of growth-depressing experience in their organizations.

Since it is often the organization that is responsible for currently low levels of growth desires, we believe that the organization also should provide the individual with the chance to reverse that trend whenever possible, even if that means putting a person in a job where he may be "stretched"

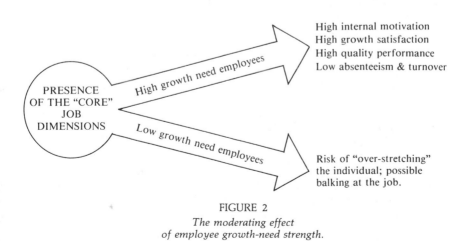

FIGURE 2
*The moderating effect
of employee growth-need strength.*

more than he wants to be. He can always move back later to the old job—and in the meantime the embers of his growth needs just might burst back into flame, to his surprise and pleasure, and for the good of the organization.

FROM THEORY TO PRACTICE:
A TECHNOLOGY FOR JOB ENRICHMENT

When job enrichment fails, it often fails because of inadequate *diagnosis* of the target job and employees' reactions to it. Often, for example, job enrichment is assumed by management to be a solution to "people problems" on the job and is implemented even though there has been no diagnostic activity to indicate that the root of the problem is in fact how the work is designed. At other times, some diagnosis is made—but it provides no concrete guidance about what specific aspects of the job require change. In either case, the success of job enrichment may wind up depending more on the quality of the intuition of the change agent—or his luck—than on a solid base of data about the people and the work.

In the paragraphs to follow, we outline a new technology for use in job enrichment which explicitly addresses the diagnostic as well as the action components of the change process. The technology has two parts: (1) a set of diagnostic tools that are useful in evaluating jobs and people's reactions to them prior to change—and in pinpointing exactly what aspects of specific jobs are most critical to a successful change attempt; and (2) a set of "implementing concepts" that provide concrete guidance for action steps in job enrichment. The implementing concepts are tied directly to the diagnostic tools; the output of the diagnostic activity specifies which action steps are likely to have the most impact in a particular situation.

*The Diagnostic Tools*

Central to the diagnostic procedure we propose is a package of instruments to be used by employees, supervisors, and outside observers in assessing the target job and employees' reactions to it.[9] These instruments gauge the following:

> 1. The objective characteristics of the jobs themselves, including both an overall indication of the "motivating potential" of the job as it exists (that is, the MPS score) and the score of the job on each of the five core dimensions described previously. Because knowing the strengths and weaknesses of the job is critical to any work-redesign effort, assessments of the job are made by supervisors and outside observers as well as the employees themselves—and the final assessment of a job uses data from all three sources.

*152*

2. The current levels of motivation, satisfaction, and work performance of employees on the job. In addition to satisfaction with the work itself, measures are taken of how people feel about other aspects of the work setting, such as pay, supervision, and relationships with co-workers.

3. The level of growth-need strength of the employees. As indicated earlier, employees who have strong growth needs are more likely to be more responsive to job enrichment than employees with weak growth needs. Therefore, it is important to know at the outset just what kinds of satisfactions the people who do the job are (and are not) motivated to obtain from their work. This will make it possible to identify which persons are best to start changes with, and which may need help in adapting to the newly enriched job.

What, then, might be the actual steps one would take in carrying out a job diagnosis using these tools? Although the approach to any particular diagnosis depends upon the specifics of the particular work situation involved, the sequence of questions listed below is fairly typical.

*Step 1. Are motivation and satisfaction central to the problem?* Sometimes organizations undertake job enrichment to improve the work motivation and satisfaction of employees when in fact the real problem with work performance lies elsewhere—for example, in a poorly designed production system, in an error-prone computer, and so on. The first step is to examine the scores of employees on the motivation and satisfaction portions of the diagnostic instrument. (The questionnaire taken by employees is called the Job Diagnostic Survey and will be referred to hereafter as the JDS.) If motivation and satisfaction are problematic, the change agent would continue to Step 2; if not, he would look to other aspects of the work situation to identify the real problem.

*Step 2. Is the job low in motivating potential?* To answer this question, one would examine the motivating potential score of the target job and compare it to the MPS's of other jobs to determine whether or not *the job itself* is a probable cause of the motivational problems documented in Step 1. If the job turns out to be low on the MPS, one would continue to Step 3; if it scores high, attention should be given to other possible reasons for the motivational difficulties (such as the pay system, the nature of supervision, and so on).

*Step 3. What specific aspects of the job are causing the difficulty?* This step involves examining the job on each of the five core dimensions to pinpoint the specific strengths and weaknesses of the job as it is currently structured. It is useful at this stage to construct a "profile" of the target job, to make visually apparent where improvements need to be made. An illustrative profile for two jobs (one "good" job and one job needing improvement) is shown in Figure 3.

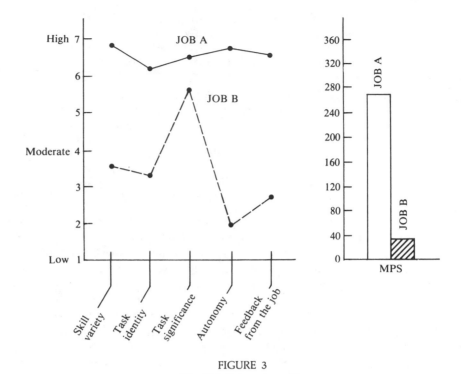

FIGURE 3
*The JDS diagnostic profile*
*for a "good" and a "bad" job.*

Job A is an engineering maintenance job and is high on all of the core dimensions; the MPS of this job is a very high 260. (MPS scores can range from 1 to about 350; an "average" score would be about 125.) Job enrichment would not be recommended for this job; if employees working on the job were unproductive and unhappy, the reasons are likely to have little to do with the nature or design of the work itself.

Job B, on the other hand, has many problems. This job involves the routine and repetitive processing of checks in the "back room" of a bank. The MPS is 30, which is quite low—and indeed, would be even lower if it were not for the moderately high task significance of the job. (Task significance is moderately high because the people are handling large amounts of other people's money, and therefore the quality of their efforts potentially has important consequences for their unseen clients.) The job provides the individuals with very little direct feedback about how effectively they are doing it; the employees have little autonomy in how they go about doing the job; and the job is moderately low in both skill variety and task identity.

For Job B, then, there is plenty of room for improvement—and many avenues to examine in planning job changes. For still other jobs, the avenues for change often turn out to be considerably more specific: for example, feedback and autonomy may be reasonably high, but one or more of the core dimensions that contribute to the experienced meaningfulness of the job (skill variety, task identity, and task significance) may be low. In such a case, attention would turn to ways to increase the standing of the job on these latter three dimensions.

*Step 4. How "ready" are the employees for change?* Once it has been documented that there is a need for improvement in the job—and the particularly troublesome aspects of the job have been identified—then it is time to begin to think about the specific action steps which will be taken to enrich the job. An important factor in such planning is the level of growth needs of the employees, since employees high on growth needs usually respond more readily to job enrichment than do employees with little need for growth. The JDS provides a direct measure of the growth-need strength of the employees. This measure can be very helpful in planning how to introduce the changes to the people (for instance, cautiously versus dramatically), and in deciding who should be among the first group of employees to have their jobs changed.

In actual use of the diagnostic package, additional information is generated which supplements and expands the basic diagnostic questions outlined above. The point of the above discussion is merely to indicate the kinds of questions which we believe to be most important in diagnosing a job prior to changing it. We now turn to how the diagnostic conclusions are translated into specific job changes.

## The Implementing Concepts

Five "implementing concepts" for job enrichment are identified and discussed below.[10] Each one is a specific action step aimed at improving both the quality of the working experience for the individual and his work productivity. They are: (1) forming natural work units; (2) combining tasks; (3) establishing client relationships; (4) vertical loading; (5) opening feedback channels.

The links between the implementing concepts and the core dimensions are shown in Figure 4, which illustrates our theory of job enrichment, ranging from the concrete action steps through the core dimensions and the psychological states to the actual personal and work outcomes.

After completing the diagnosis of a job, a change agent would know which of the core dimensions were most in need of remedial attention. He could then turn to Figure 4 and select those implementing concepts that specifically deal with the most troublesome parts of the existing job. How this would take place in practice will be seen below.

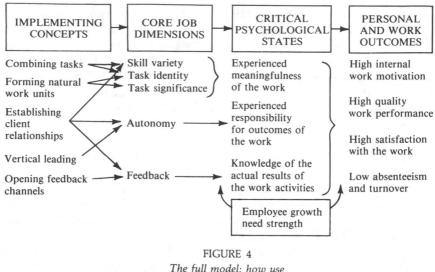

FIGURE 4

*The full model: how use
of the implementing concepts
can lead to positive outcomes.*

*Forming natural work units.* The notion of distributing work in some logical way may seem to be an obvious part of the design of any job. In many cases, however, the logic is one imposed by just about any consideration except jobholder satisfaction and motivation. Such considerations include technological dictates, level of worker training or experience, "efficiency" as defined by industrial engineering, and current workload. In many cases the cluster of tasks a worker faces during a typical day or week is natural to anyone *but* the worker.

For example, suppose that a typing pool (consisting of one supervisor and ten typists) handles all work for one division of a company. Jobs are delivered in rough draft or dictated form to the supervisor, who distributes them as evenly as possible among the typists. In such circumstances the individual letters, reports, and other tasks performed by a given typist in one day or week are randomly assigned. There is no basis for identifying with the work or the person or department for whom it is performed, or for placing any personal value upon it.

The principle underlying natural units of work, by contrast, is "ownership"—a worker's sense of continuing responsibility for an identifiable body of work. Two steps are involved in creating natural work units. The first is to identify the basic work items. In the typing pool, for example, the items might be "pages to be typed." The second step is to group the items in natural categories. For example, each typist might be assigned continuing responsibility for all jobs requested by one or several specific departments.

The assignments should be made, of course, in such a way that workloads are about equal in the long run. (For example, one typist might end up with all the work from one busy department, while another handles jobs from several smaller units.)

At this point we can begin to see specifically how the job-design principles relate to the core dimensions (Figure 4). The ownership fostered by natural units of work can make the difference between a feeling that work is meaningful and rewarding and the feeling that it is irrelevant and boring. As the diagram shows, natural units of work are directly related to two of the core dimensions: task identity and task significance.

A typist whose work is assigned natually rather than randomly—say, by departments—has a much greater chance of performing a whole job to completion. Instead of typing one section of a large report, the individual is likely to type the whole thing, with knowledge of exactly what the product of the work is (task identity). Furthermore, over time the typist will develop a growing sense of how the work affects co-workers in the department serviced (task significance).

*Combining tasks.* The very existence of a pool made up entirely of persons whose sole function is typing reflects a fractionalization of jobs that has been a basic precept of "scientific management." Most obvious in assembly-line work, fractionalization has been applied to nonmanufacturing jobs as well. It is typically justified by efficiency, which is usually defined in terms of either low costs or some time-and-motion type of criteria.

It is hard to find fault with measuring efficiency ultimately in terms of cost-effectiveness. In doing so, however, a manager should be sure to consider *all* the costs involved. It is possible, for example, for highly fractionalized jobs to meet all the time-and-motion criteria of efficiency, but if the resulting job is so unrewarding that performing it day after day leads to high turnover, absenteeism, drugs and alcohol, and strikes, then productivity is really lower (and costs higher) than data on efficiency might indicate.

The principle of combining tasks, then, suggests that whenever possible existing and fractionalized tasks should be put together to form new and larger modules of work. At the Medfield, Massachusetts plant of Corning Glass Works the assembly of a laboratory hot plate has been redesigned along the lines suggested here. Each hot plate now is assembled from start to finish by one operator, instead of going through several separate operations that are performed by different people.

Some tasks, if combined into a meaningfully large module of work, would be more than an individual could do by himself. In such cases, it is often useful to consider assigning the new, larger task to a small *team* of workers, who are given great autonomy for its completion. At the Racine, Wisconsin plant of Emerson Electric, the assembly process for trash disposal appliances was restructured this way. Instead of a sequence of moving the appliance from station to station, the assembly now is done from start to finish by one team. Such teams include both men and women to permit switching off the heavier and more delicate aspects of the work. The team responsible is identified on the appliance. In case of customer complaints, the team often drafts the reply.

As a job-design principle, task combination, like natural units of work, expands the task identity of the job. For example, the hot-plate assembler can see and identify with a finished product ready for shipment, rather than a nearly invisible junction of solder. Moreover, the more tasks that are combined into a single worker's job, the greater the variety of skills he must call on in performing the job. So task combination also leads directly to greater skill variety—the third core dimension that contributes to the overall experienced meaningfulness of the work.

*Establishing client relationships.* One consequence of fractionalization is that the typical worker has little or no contact with (or even awareness of) the ultimate user of his product or service. By encouraging and enabling employees to establish direct relationships with the clients of their work, improvements often can be realized simultaneously on three of the core dimensions. Feedback increases, because of additional opportunities for the individual to receive praise or criticism of his work outputs directly. Skill variety often increases, because of the necessity to develop and exercise one's interpersonal skills in maintaining the client relationship. And autonomy can increase because the individual often is given personal responsibility for deciding how to manage his relationships with the clients of his work.

Creating client relationships is a three-step process. First, the client must be identified. Second, the most direct contact possible between the worker and the client must be established. Third, criteria must be set up by which the client can judge the quality of the product or service he recieves. And whenever possible, the client should have a means of relaying his judgments directly back to the worker.

The contact between worker and client should be as great as possible and as frequent as necessary. Face-to-face contact is highly desirable, at least occasionally. Where that is impossible or impractical, telephone and mail can suffice. In any case, it is important that the performance criteria by which the worker will be rated by the client must be mutually understood and agreed upon.

*Vertical loading.* Typically the split between the "doing" of a job and the "planning" and "controlling" of the work has evolved along with horizontal fractionalization. Its rationale, once again, has been "efficiency through specialization." And once again, the excess of specialization that has emerged has resulted in unexpected but significant costs in motivation, morale, and work quality. In vertical loading, the intent is to partially close the gap between the doing and the controlling parts of the job—and thereby reap some important motivational advantages.

Of all the job-design principles, vertical loading may be the single most crucial one. In some cases, where it has been impossible to implement any other changes, vertical loading alone has had significant motivational effects.

When a job is vertically loaded, responsibilities and controls that formerly were reserved for higher levels of management are added to the job. There are many ways to accomplish this:

1. Return to the jobholder greater discretion in setting schedules, deciding on work methods, checking on quality, and advising or helping to train less experienced workers.

2. Grant additional authority. The objective should be to advance workers from a position of no authority or highly restricted authority to positions of reviewed and, eventually, near-total authority for his own work.

3. Time management. The jobholder should have the greatest possible freedom to decide when to start and stop work, when to break, and how to assign priorities.

4. Troubleshooting and crisis decisions. Workers should be encouraged to seek problem solutions on their own, rather than calling immediately for the supervisor.

5. Financial controls. Some degree of knowledge and control over budgets and other financial aspects of a job can often be highly motivating. However, access to this information frequently tends to be restricted. Workers can benefit from knowing something about the costs of their jobs, the potential effect upon profit, and various financial and budgetary alternatives.

When a job is vertically loaded it will inevitably increase in *autonomy*. And as shown in Figure 4, this increase in objective personal control over the work will also lead to an increased feeling of personal responsibility for the work, and ultimately to higher internal work motivation.

*Opening feedback channels.* In virtually all jobs there are ways to open channels of feedback to individuals or teams to help them learn whether their performance is improving, deteriorating, or remaining at a constant level. While there are numerous channels through which information about performance can be provided, it generally is better for a worker to learn about his performance *directly as he does his job*—rather than from management on an occasional basis.

Job-provided feedback usually is more immediate and private than supervisor-supplied feedback, and it increases the worker's feelings of personal control over his work in the bargain. Moreover, it avoids many of the potentially disruptive interpersonal problems that can develop when the only way a worker has to find out how he is doing is through direct messages or subtle cues from the boss.

Exactly what should be done to open channels for job-provided feedback will vary from job to job and organization to organization. Yet in many cases the changes involve simply removing existing blocks that isolate the worker from naturally occurring data about performance—rather than generating entirely new feedback mechanisms. For example:

1. Establishing direct client relationships often removes blocks between the worker and natural external sources of data about his work.

2. Quality-control efforts in many organizations often eliminate a natural source of feedback. The quality check on a product or service is done by persons other than those responsible for the work. Feedback to the workers—if there is any—is belated and diluted. It often fosters a tendency to think of quality as "someone else's concern." By placing quality control close to the worker (perhaps even in his own hands), the quantity and quality of data about performance available to him can dramatically increase.

3. Tradition and established procedure in many organizations dictate that records about performance be kept by a supervisor and transmitted up (not down) in the organizational hierarchy. Sometimes supervisors even check the work and correct any errors themselves. The worker who made the error never knows it occurred—and is denied the very information that could enhance both his internal work motivation and the technical adequacy of his performance. In many cases it is possible to provide standard summaries of performance records directly to the worker (as well as to his superior), thereby giving him personally and regularly the data he needs to improve his performance.

4. Computers and other automated operations sometimes can be used to provide the individual with data now blocked from him. Many clerical operations, for example, are now performed on computer consoles. These consoles often can be programmed to provide the clerk with immediate feedback in the form of a CRT display or a printout indicating that an error has been made. Some systems even have been programmed to provide the operator with a positive feedback message when a period of error-free performance has been sustained.

Many organizations simply have not recognized the importance of feedback as a motivator. Data on quality and other aspects of performance are viewed as being of interest only to management. Worse still, the *standards* for acceptable performance often are kept from workers as well. As a result, workers who would be interested in following the daily or weekly ups and downs of their performance, and in trying accordingly to improve, are deprived of the very guidelines they need to do so. They are like the golfer we mentioned earlier, whose efforts to correct his hook are stopped dead by fog over the driving range.

### THE STRATEGY IN ACTION:
### HOW WELL DOES IT WORK?

So far we have examined a basic theory of how people get turned on to their work; a set of core dimensions of jobs that create the conditions for such internal work motivation to develop on the job; and a set of five implementing concepts that are the action steps recommended to boost a job on the core dimensions and thereby increase employee motivation, satisfaction, and productivity.

The remaining question is straightforward and important: *Does it work?* In reality, that question is twofold. First, does the theory itself hold water, or are we barking up the wrong conceptual tree? And second, does the change strategy really lead to measurable differences when it is applied in an actual organizational setting?

This section summarizes the findings we have generated to date on these questions.

### *Is the Job-Enrichment Theory Correct?*

In general, the answer seems to be yes. The JDS instrument has been taken by more than 1,000 employees working on about 100 diverse jobs in more than a dozen organizations over the last two years. These data have been analyzed to test the basic motivational theory—and especially the impact of the core job dimensions on worker motivation, satisfaction, and behavior on the job. An illustrative overview of some of the findings is given below.[11]

1. People who work on jobs high on the core dimensions are more motivated and satisfied than are people who work on jobs that score low on the dimensions. Employees with jobs high on the core dimensions (MPS scores greater than 240) were compared to those who held unmotivating jobs (MPS scores less than 40). As shown in Figure 5, employees with high MPS jobs were higher on (a) the three psychological states, (b) internal work motivation, (c) general satisfaction, and (d) "growth" satisfaction.

2. Figure 6 shows that the same is true for measures of actual

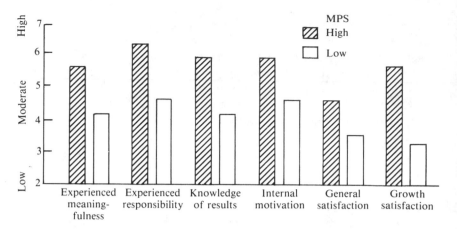

FIGURE 5

*Employee reactions to jobs high and low*
*in motivating potential*
*for two banks and a steel firm.*

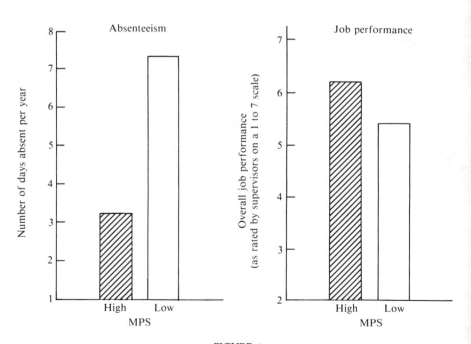

FIGURE 6

*Absenteeism and job performance*
*for employees with jobs*
*high and low in motivating potential.*

behavior at work—absenteeism and performance effectiveness—although less strongly so for the performance measure.

3. Responses to jobs high in motivating potential are more positive for people who have strong growth needs than for people with weak needs for growth. In Figure 7 the linear relationship between the motivating potential of a job and employees' level of internal work motivation is shown, separately for people with high versus low growth needs as measured by the JDS. While both groups of employees show increases in internal motivation as MPS increases, the *rate* of increase is significantly greater for the group of employees who have strong needs of growth.

## How Does the Change Strategy Work in Practice?

The results summarized above suggest that both the theory and the diagnostic instrument work when used with real people in real organizations. In this section, we summarize a job-enrichment project conducted at the Travelers Insurance Companies, which illustrates how the change procedures themselves work in practice.

The Travelers project was designed with two purposes in mind. One was to achieve improvements in morale, productivity, and other indicators of employee well-being. The other was to test the general effectiveness of the strategy for job enrichment we have summarized in this article.

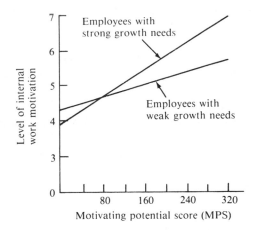

FIGURE 7

*Relationship between the motivating potential of a job and the internal work motivation of employees. (Shown separately for employees with strong versus weak growth-need strength.)*

163

The work group chosen was a keypunching operation. The group's function was to transfer information from printed or written documents onto punched cards for computer input. The work group consisted of ninety-eight keypunch operators and verifiers (both in the same job classification), plus seven assignment clerks. All reported to a supervisor who, in turn, reported to the assistant manager and manager of the data-input division.

The size of individual punching orders varied considerably, from a few cards to as many as 2,500. Some work came to the work group with a specified delivery date, while other orders were to be given routine service on a predetermined schedule.

Assignment clerks received the jobs from the user departments. After reviewing the work for obvious errors, omissions, and legibility problems, the assignment clerk parceled out the work in batches expected to take about one hour. If the clerk found the work not suitable for punching, it went to the supervisor, who either returned the work to the user department or cleared up problems by phone. When work went to operators for punching, it was with the instruction, "Punch only what you see. Don't correct errors, no matter how obvious they look."

Because of the high cost of computer time, keypunched work was 100 percent verified—a task that consumed nearly as many man-hours as the punching itself. Then the cards went to the supervisor, who screened the jobs for due dates before sending them to the computer. Errors detected in verification were assigned to various operators at random to be corrected.

The computer output from the cards was sent to the originating department, accompanied by a printout of errors. Eventually the printout went back to the supervisor for final correction.

A great many phenomena indicated that the problems being experienced in the work group might be the result of poor motivation. As the only person performing supervisory functions of any kind, the supervisor spent most of his time responding to crisis situations, which recurred continually. He also had to deal almost daily with employees' salary grievances or other complaints. Employees frequently showed apathy or outright hostility toward their jobs.

Rates of work output, by accepted work-measurement standards, were inadequate. Error rates were high. Due dates and schedules frequently were missed. Absenteeism was higher than average, especially before and after weekends and holidays.

The single, rather unusual exception was turnover. It was lower than the companywide average for similar jobs. The company has attributed this fact to a poor job market in the base period just before the project began, and to an older, relatively more settled work force—made up, incidentally, entirely of women.

## The Diagnosis

Using some of the tools and techniques we have outlined, a consulting team from the Management Services Department and from Roy W. Walters & Associates concluded that the keypunch-operator's job exhibited the following serious weaknesses in terms of the core dimensions.

1. Skill variety: there was none. Only a single skill was involved—the ability to punch adequately the data on the batch of documents.

2. Task identity: virtually nonexistent. Batches were assembled to provide an even workload, but not whole identifiable jobs.

3. Task significance: not apparent. The keypunching operation was a necessary step in providing service to the company's customers. The individual operator was isolated by an assignment clerk and a supervisor from any knowledge of what the operation meant to the using department, let alone its meaning to the ultimate customer.

4. Autonomy: none. The operators had no freedom to arrange their daily tasks to meet schedules, to resolve problems with the using department, or even to correct, in punching, information that was obviously wrong.

5. Feedback: none. Once a batch was out of the operator's hands, she had no assured chance of seeing evidence of its quality or inadequacy.

## Design of the Experimental Trial

Since the diagnosis indicated that the motivating potential of the job was extremely low, it was decided to attempt to improve the motivation and productivity of the work group through job enrichment. Moreover, it was possible to design an experimental test of the effects of the changes to be introduced: the results of changes made in the target work group were to be compared with trends in a control work group of similar size and demographic make-up. Since the control group was located more than a mile away, there appeared to be little risk of communication between members of the two groups.

A base period was defined before the start of the experimental trial period, and appropriate data were gathered on the productivity, absenteeism, and work attitudes of members of both groups. Data also were available on turnover; but since turnover was already below average in the target group, prospective changes in this measure were deemed insignificant.

An educational session was conducted with supervisors, at which they were given the theory and implementing concepts and actually helped to design the job changes themselves. Out of this session came an active plan consisting of about twenty-five change items that would significantly affect the design of the target jobs.

## The Implementing Concepts and the Changes

Because the job as it existed was rather uniformly low on the core job dimensions, all five of the implementing concepts were used in enriching it.

1. Natural units of work. The random batch assignment of work was replaced by assigning to each operator continuing responsibility for certain accounts—either particular departments or particular recurring jobs. Any work for those accounts now always goes to the same operator.

2. Task combination. Some planning and controlling functions were combined with the central task of keypunching. In this case, however, these additions can be more suitably discussed under the remaining three implementing concepts.

3. Client relationships. Each operator was given several channels of direct contact with clients. The operators, not their assignment clerks, now inspect their documents for correctness and legibility. When problems arise, the operator, not the supervisor, takes them up with the client.

4. Feedback. In addition to feedback from client contact, the operators were provided with a number of additional sources of data about their performance. The computer department now returns incorrect cards to the operators who punched them, and operators correct their own errors. Each operator also keeps her own file of copies of her errors. These can be reviewed to determine trends in error frequency and types of errors. Each operator receives weekly a computer printout of her errors and productivity, which is sent to her directly, rather than given to her by the supervisor.

5. Vertical loading. Besides consulting directly with clients about work questions, operators now have the authority to correct obvious coding errors on their own. Operators may set their own schedules and plan their daily work, as long as they meet schedules. Some competent operators have been given the option of not verifying their work and making their own program changes.

## Results of the Trial

The results were dramatic. The number of operators declined from ninety-eight to sixty. This occurred partly through attrition and partly through transfer to other departments. Some of the operators were promoted to higher-paying jobs in departments whose cards they had been handling—something that had never occurred before. Some details of the results are given below.

1. Quantity of work. The control group, with no job changes made, showed an increase in productivity of 8.1 percent during the trial period. The experimental group showed an increase of 39.6 percent.

2. Error rates. To assess work quality, error rates were recorded for about forty operators in the experimental group. All were experienced, and all had been in their jobs before the job-enrichment program began. For two months before the study, these operators had a collective error rate of 1.53 percent. For two months toward the end of the study, the collective error rate was 0.99 percent. By the end of the study the number of operators with poor performance had dropped from 11.1 percent to 5.5 percent.

3. Absenteeism. The experimental group registered a 24.1 percent decline in absences. The control group, by contrast, showed a 29 percent *increase*.

4. Attitudes toward the job. An attitude survey given at the start of the project showed that the two groups scored about average, and nearly identically, in nine different areas of work satisfaction. At the end of the project the survey was repeated. The control group showed an insignificant 0.5 percent improvement, while the experimental group's overall satisfaction score rose 16.5 percent.

5. Selective elimination of controls. Demonstrated improvements in operator proficiency permitted them to work with fewer controls. Travelers estimates that the reduction of controls had the same effect as adding seven operators—a saving even beyond the effects of improved productivity and lowered absenteeism.

6. Role of the supervisor. One of the most significant findings in the Travelers experiment was the effect of the changes on the supervisor's job, and thus on the rest of the organization. The operators took on many responsibilities that had been reserved at least to the unit leaders and sometimes to the supervisor. The unit leaders, in turn, assumed some of the day-to-day supervisory functions that had plagued the supervisor. Instead of spending his days supervising the behavior of subordinates and dealing with crises, he was able to devote time to developing feedback systems, setting up work modules, and spearheading the enrichment effort—in other words, managing. It should be noted, however, that helping supervisors change their own work activities when their subordinates' jobs have been enriched is itself a challenging task. And if appropriate attention and help are not given to supervisors in such cases, they rapidly can become disaffected—and a job-enrichment "backlash" can result.[11]

*Summary*

By applying work-measurement standards to the changes wrought by job enrichment—attitude and quality, absenteeism, and selective administration of controls—Travelers was able to estimate the total dollar impact of the project. Actual savings in salaries and machine rental charges during the first year totaled $64,305. Potential savings by further application of the changes were put at $91,937 annually. Thus, by almost any measure used—from the work attitudes of individual employees to dollar savings for the company as a whole—The Travelers test of the job-enrichment strategy proved a success.

## CONCLUSIONS

In this article we have presented a new strategy for the redesign of work in general and for job enrichment in particular. The approach has four main characteristics:

1. It is grounded in a basic psychological theory of what motivates people in their work.

2. It emphasizes that planning for job changes should be done on the basis of *data* about the jobs and the people who do them—and a set of diagnostic instruments is provided to collect such data.

3. It provides a set of specific implementing concepts to guide actual job changes, as well as a set of theory-based rules for selecting *which* action steps are likely to be most beneficial in a given situation.

4. The strategy is buttressed by a set of findings showing that the theory holds water, that the diagnostic procedures are practical and informative, and that the implementing concepts can lead to changes that are beneficial both to organizations and to the people who work in them.

We believe that job enrichment is moving beyond the stage where it can be considered "yet another management fad." Instead, it represents a potentially powerful strategy for change that can help organizations achieve their goals for higher quality work—and at the same time further the equally legitimate needs of contemporary employees for a more meaningful work experience. Yet there are pressing questions about job enrichment and its use that remain to be answered.

Prominent among these is the question of employee participation in planning and implementing work redesign. The diagnostic tools and implementing concepts we have presented are neither designed nor intended for use only by management. Rather, our belief is that the effectiveness of job enrichment is likely to be enhanced when the tasks of diagnosing and changing jobs are undertaken *collaboratively* by management and by the employees whose work will be affected.

Moreover, the effects of work redesign on the broader organization remain generally uncharted. Evidence now is accumulating that when jobs are changed, turbulence can appear in the surrounding organization—for example, in supervisory-subordinate relationships, in pay and benefit plans, and so on. Such turbulence can be viewed by management either as a problem with job enrichment, or as an opportunity for further and broader organizational development by teams of managers and employees. To the degree that management takes the latter view, we believe, the oft-espoused goal of achieving basic organizational change through the redesign of work may come increasingly within reach.

The diagnostic tools and implementing concepts we have presented are useful in deciding on and designing basic changes in the jobs themselves. They do not address the broader issues of who plans the changes, how they are carried out, and how they are followed up. The way these broader questions are dealt with, we believe, may determine whether job enrichment will grow up—or whether it will die an early and unfortunate death, like so many other fledgling behavioral-science approaches to organizational change.

## APPENDIX

For the algebraically inclined, the Motivating Potential Score is computed as follows

$$MPS = \left( \frac{\text{Skill Variety} + \text{Task Identity} + \text{Task Significance}}{3} \right) \times \text{Autonomy} \times \text{Feedback}$$

It should be noted that in some cases the MPS score can be *too* high for positive job satisfaction and effective performance—in effect overstimulating the person who holds the job. This paper focuses on jobs which are toward the low end of the scale—and which potentially can be improved through job enrichment.

## NOTES

1. F. Herzberg, B. Mausner, and B. Snyderman, *The Motivation to Work* (New York: John Wiley & Sons, 1959).

2. F. Herzberg, *Work and the Nature of Man* (Cleveland: World, 1966).

3. F. Herzberg, "One More Time: How Do You Motivate Employees?" *Harvard Business Review* (1968), pp. 53–62.

4. W. J. Paul, Jr., K. B. Robertson, and F. Herzberg, "Job Enrichment Pays Off," *Harvard Business Review* (1969), pp. 61–78.

5. R. N. Ford, *Motivation Through the Work Itself* (New York: American Management Association, 1969).

6. A. N. Turner and P. R. Lawrence, *Industrial Jobs and the Worker* (Cambridge, Mass.: Harvard Graduate School of Business Administration, 1965).

7. J. R. Hackman and E. E. Lawler, "Employee Reactions to Job Characteristics," *Journal of Applied Psychology Monograph* (1971), pp. 259–286.

8. J. R. Hackman and G. R. Oldham, *Motivation Through the Design of Work: Test of a Theory*, Technical Report No. 6, Department of Administrative Sciences, Yale University, 1974.

9. J. R. Hackman and G. R. Oldham, "Development of the Job Diagnostic Survey," *Journal of Applied Psychology* (1975), pp. 159–170.

10. R. W. Walters and Associates, *Job Enrichment for Results* (Reading, Mass.: Addison-Wesley, 1975).

11. E. E. Lawler III, J. R. Hackman, and S. Kaufman, "Effects of Job Redesign: A Field Experiment," *Journal of Applied Social Psychology* (1973), pp. 49–62.

# Decision-Making
# Theory

♦

ORGANIZATIONS EXIST TO ACCOMPLISH things, and to accomplish things, the people within an organization must make choices among various alternatives. The factors that they consider and the means they use to assess these factors comprise the heart of decision-making theory as it applies to organizations—especially public organizations.

As William J. Gore has pointed out, a "decision refers to the consideration of the consequences of some act before undertaking it."[1] Consideration is a rational process that unites perceptions of reality and possible consequences with the values that the decision maker places on those consequences. The perceptions of reality that an organization has are dependent upon the information available to it and its manipulation of that information.

Ideally an organization wants to get a picture of reality that approaches reality itself and not one distorted far out of proportion. John Kenneth Galbraith has suggested that organizations have a natural tendency to develop and act on false pictures of reality: "What is done and what is believed are, first and naturally, what serve the goals of the bureaucracy itself."[2] An organization that is to cope with changes in the environment must be able to act flexibly on accurate information. If an organization is a prisoner to its own "bureaucratic truths," it will not be able to deal with change in a positive way.

There are several ways through which an organization attempts to keep its information processes open to reality. Organizational humanism is one way. A Theory Y atmosphere is one in which many views of reality can be suggested, debated, and assessed on their merits and freed from some of the inhibitions of the hierarchy that encourage the propagation of "bureaucratic truths." Supposedly, the views that more closely reflect the true situation will survive. Management science is another way. Management science is the general term covering the application of modern technology to all planes of organizational activity, but especially to information gathering and manipulation. Among the tools associated with this area of management science are computers, systems analysis, and operations research. Still another way that organizations seek to obtain an accurate picture of reality is through contact with other organizations that deal in the same or related functional areas. The aim of all these methods is to get a better view of the real world so that better decisions can be made.

It is this question of how organizations represent the real world that has engendered several decision-making theories. Charles E. Lindblom, the distinguished political economist at Yale, discusses two theories. One he calls the rational-comprehensive theory. Basically, this is the scientific method of problem solving. Lindblom claims that this method, despite modern technology, cannot adequately deal with complex questions because of man's limitations—"the boundaries of rationality," as Herbert Simon has called it.[3] Furthermore, the scientific method of problem-solving assumes agreement on goals—agreement on what the problem is—and this assumption generally does not apply to complex public policy issues.

As an alternative to rational-comprehensive analysis, Lindblom suggests the method of successive limited comparisons. This incremental approach is a practical decision-making method for public policy questions because of its use of the process of *partisan mutual adjustment*.[4] Partisan mutual adjustment is an overtly political means for getting information and making decisions; various interests make demands on the organization and bargain with it and with other interests who are making contradictory demands. It can also be viewed as an attempt by the organization to maintain a liaison with reality through outside organizations. Partisan mutual adjustment, working through increments of change, is pluralism in action. As such it is subject to the most telling criticisms of pluralism—which groups are involved in the bargaining and what are the power positions of these groups in society.[5]

Herbert Simon, a strong advocate of management science, has suggested that decision makers do not engage in comprehensive analysis because they are satisfied with less information and analysis than the rational-comprehensive model posits. Decision makers do not seek to maximize the goodness of any decision. They "satisfice." They are satisfied by a certain level of goodness in their decisions.[6] Taking this into account, has Lindblom presented analysis as a straw man? Is there a place for analysis in the bargaining process? What kinds of change and responses to change can we expect from the incremental strategy? If people can agree on goals and computers can handle the data, are there any arguments for the incremental approach of partisan mutual adjustment?

Even though Lindblom included several reservations in his piece, the thrust of "Muddling Through" denigrates analysis and sanctifies incrementalism. As such, it gives aid and comfort to anti change, anti innovation forces. Furthermore, it unrealistically ignores the middle ground where economic criteria and analytic methods can be integrated with political criteria.[7]

Amitai Etzioni has given the theoretical justification for this middle way between pure economic rationality and pure political rationality. Using a satellite-based weather observation system as an analogy to observing social phenomena, Etzioni suggested how a "mixed-scanning" technique might work:

> The rationalistic approach would seek an exhaustive survey of weather conditions by using cameras capable of detailed observations and by scheduling reviews of the entire sky as often as possible. This would yield an avalanche of details, costly to analyze and likely to overwhelm our action capacities. . . . Incrementalism would focus on those areas in which similar patterns developed in the recent past and, perhaps, on a few nearby regions; it would thus ignore all formations which might deserve attention if they arose in unexpected areas.
>
> A mixed-scanning strategy would include elements of both approaches by employing two cameras: a broad-angle camera that would cover all parts of the sky but not in great detail, and a second one which would zero in on those areas revealed by the first camera to require a more in-depth examination. While mixed-scanning might miss areas in which only a detailed camera could reveal trouble, it is less likely than incrementalism to miss obvious trouble spots in unfamiliar areas.[8]

The common sense of a mixed-scanning approach has, indeed, been characteristic of many aspects of policy making since the mid-1960s. The polar positions of decision theory have not changed, but there is an operational accommodation between the two. Very few people would claim that rational-comprehensive decision making is possible on such major political issues as racism, poverty, the economy, or even national security. Similarly, few people would completely discount the role that systematic planning and analysis can have in clarifying certain aspects of these pressing problems.

E. S. Quade of the Rand Corporation sees a strong future for analytic work on policy problems, yet he is aware of the limitations on the craft.[9] The piece reprinted here was originally written to introduce decision makers to the kind of analysis that was to be the heart of the Planning-Programming-Budgeting System (PPBS). PPBS, it was hoped in the mid-1960s, was supposed to enable the government to make better decisions by identifying national goals, uncovering alternative ways to achieve them and correctly costing out these alternatives. Although PPBS was quietly phased out in the early 1970s, analysis of public policy problems has survived.

Quade suggests specific ways in which one can engage in analysis of public problems. Is he overly optimistic? Does he understate the limitations of the method? Can you think of any examples where policy analysis has actually changed a major policy decision? How can analysis be integrated with politics in decision making? What problems might there be?

## NOTES

1. William J. Gore, *Administrative Decision-Making: A Heuristic Model* (New York: John Wiley & Sons, Inc., 1964), p. 19.

2. John Kenneth Galbraith, *How to Control the Military* (New York: New American Library Inc., Signet Books, 1969), p. 16. "Bureaucratic truth" is also Galbraith's term.

3. James G. March and Herbert A. Simon, *Organizations* (New York: John Wiley & Sons, Inc., 1958), p. 171 and chapter 6.

4. Charles E. Lindblom, *The Intelligence of Democracy* (New York: The Macmillan Company, The Free Press, 1965).

5. For an excellent collection of essays indicting pluralism, see William E. Connolly, ed., *The Bias of Pluralism* (New York: Atherton, 1969).

6. March and Simon, *Organizations*, pp. 140–141, 169.

7. Lindblom's later work explicitly recognized this problem. See his "Still Muddling, Not Yet Through," *Public Administration Review* 39, no. 6 (November/December 1979): 517–26. Much of this issue of the *PAR* is a twentieth-anniversary tribute to the article reprinted in this book.

8. Amitai Etzioni, "Mixed-Scanning: A 'Third' Approach to Decision Making," *Public Administration Review*, 27, no. 5 (December 1967): 388.

9. For a more complete argument, see E. S. Quade, *Analysis for Public Decisions* (New York: American Elsevier Publishing Company, 1975).

# 9

# The Science
# of
# "Muddling Through"

♦

*Charles E. Lindblom*

SUPPOSE AN ADMINISTRATOR IS given responsibility for formulating policy with respect to inflation. He might start by trying to list all related values in order of importance, e.g., full employment, reasonable business profit, protection of small savings, prevention of a stock market crash. Then all possible policy outcomes could be rated as more or less efficient in attaining a maximum of these values. This would of course require a prodigious inquiry into values held by members of society and an equally prodigious set of calculations on how much of each value is equal to how much of each other value. He could then proceed to outline all possible policy alternatives. In a third step, he would undertake systematic comparison of his multitude of alternatives to determine which attains the greatest amount of values.

In comparing policies, he would take advantage of any theory available that generalized about classes of policies. In considering inflation, for example, he would compare all policies in the light of the theory of prices. Since no alternatives are beyond his investigation, he would consider strict central control and the abolition of all prices and markets on the one hand and elimination of all public controls with reliance completely on the free market on the other, both in the light of whatever theoretical generalizations he could find on such hypothetical economies.

Finally, he would try to make the choice that would in fact maximize his values.

An alternative line of attack would be to set as his principal objective, either explicitly or without conscious thought, the relatively simple goal of keeping prices level. This objective might be compromised or complicated by only a few other goals, such as full employment. He would in fact disregard most other social values as beyond his present interest, and he would for the moment not even attempt to rank the few values that he regarded as immediately relevant. Were he pressed, he would quickly admit that he was ignoring many related values and many possible important consequences of his policies.

As a second step, he would outline those relatively few policy alternatives that occurred to him. He would then compare them. In comparing his limited number of alternatives, most of them familiar from past controversies, he would not ordinarily find a body of theory precise enough to carry him through a comparison of their respective consequences. Instead he would rely heavily on the record of past experience with small policy steps to predict the consequences of similar steps extended into the future.

Moreover, he would find that the policy alternatives combined objectives or values in different ways. For example, one policy might offer price-level stability at the cost of some risk of unemployment; another might offer less price stability but also less risk of unemployment. Hence, the next step in his approach—the final selection—would combine into one the choice among values and the choice among instruments for reaching values. It would not, as in the first method of policy making, approximate a more mechanical process of choosing the means that best satisfied goals that were previously clarified and ranked. Because practitioners of the second approach expect to achieve their goals only partially, they would expect to repeat endlessly the sequence just described, as conditions and aspirations changed and as accuracy of prediction improved.

## BY ROOT OR BY BRANCH

For complex problems, the first of these two approaches is of course impossible. Although such an approach can be described, it cannot be practiced except for relatively simple problems and even then only in a somewhat modified form. It assumes intellectual capacities and sources of information that men simply do not possess, and it is even more absurd as an approach to policy when the time and money that can be allocated to a policy problem is limited, as is always the case. Of particular importance to public administrators is the fact that public agencies are in effect usually instructed not to practice the first method. That is to say, their prescribed functions and constraints—the politically or legally possible—restrict their attention to relatively few values and relatively few alternative policies among the countless alternatives that might be imagined. It is the second method that is practiced.

Curiously, however, the literatures of decision-making, policy formulation, planning, and public administration formalize the first approach rather than the second, leaving public administrators who handle complex decisions in the position of practicing what few preach. For emphasis I run some risk of overstatement. True enough, the literature is well aware of limits on man's capacities and of the inevitability that policies will be approached in some such style as the second. But attempts to formalize rational policy formulation—to lay out explicitly the necessary steps in the process—usually describe the first approach and not the second.[1]

The common tendency to describe policy formulation even for complex problems as though it followed the first approach has been strengthened by the attention given to, and successes enjoyed by, operations research, statistical decision theory, and systems analysis. The hallmarks of these procedures, typical of the first approach, are clarity of objective, explicitness of evaluation, a high degree of comprehensiveness of overview, and, wherever possible, quantification of values for mathematical analysis. But these advanced procedures remain largely the appropriate techniques of relatively small-scale problem-solving where the total number of variables to be considered is small and value problems restricted. Charles Hitch, head of the Economics Division of RAND Corporation, one of the leading centers for application of these techniques, has written:

> I would make the empirical generalization from my experience at RAND and elsewhere that operations research is the art of sub-optimizing, i.e., of solving some lower-level problems, and that difficulties increase and our special competence diminishes by an order of magnitude with every level of decision making we attempt to ascend. The sort of simple explicit model which operations researchers are so proficient in using can certainly reflect most of the significant factors influencing traffic control on the George Washington Bridge, but the proportion of the relevant reality which we can represent by any such model or models in studying, say, a major foreign-policy decision, appears to be almost trivial.[2]

Accordingly, I propose in this paper to clarify and formalize the second method, much neglected in the literature. This might be described as the method of *successive limited comparisons.* I will contrast it with the first approach, which might be called the rational-comprehensive method.[3] More impressionistically and briefly—and therefore generally used in this article—they could be characterized as the branch method and root method, the former continually building out from the current situation, step-by-step and by small degrees; the latter starting from fundamentals anew each time, building on the past only as experience is embodied in a theory, and always prepared to start completely from the ground up.

Let us put the characteristics of the two methods side by side in simplest terms.

| Rational-Comprehensive (Root) | Successive Limited Comparisons (Branch) |
|---|---|
| 1a. Clarification of values or objectives distinct from and usually prerequisite to empirical analysis of alternative policies. | 1b. Selection of value goals and empirical analysis of the needed action are not distinct from one another but are closely intertwined. |
| 2a. Policy-formulation is therefore approached through means-end analysis: First the ends are isolated, then the means to achieve them are sought. | 2b. Since means and ends are not distinct, means-end analysis is often inappropriate or limited. |
| 3a. The test of a "good" policy is that is can be shown to be the most appropriate means to desired ends. | 3b. The test of a "good" policy is typically that various analysts find themselves directly agreeing on a policy (without their agreeing that it is the most appropriate means to an agreed objective). |
| 4a. Analysis is comprehensive; every important relevant factor is taken into account. | 4b. Analysis is drastically limited: i) Important possible outcomes are neglected. ii) Important alternative potential policies are neglected. iii) Important affected values are neglected. |
| 5a. Theory is often heavily relied upon. | 5b. A succession of comparisons greatly reduces or eliminates reliance on theory. |

Assuming that the root method is familiar and understandable, we proceed directly to clarification of its alternative by contrast. In explaining the second, we shall be describing how most administrators do in fact approach complex questions, for the root method, the "best" way as a blueprint or model, is in fact not workable for complex policy questions, and administrators are forced to use the method of successive limited comparisons.

INTERTWINING EVALUATION
AND EMPIRICAL ANALYSIS (1b)

The quickest way to understand how values are handled in the method of successive limited comparisons is to see how the root method often breaks down in *its* handling of values or objectives. The idea that values should be clarified, and in advance of the examination of alternative policies, is appealing. But what happens when we attempt it for complex social problems? The first difficulty is that on many critical values or objectives, citizens disagree, congressmen disagree, and public administrators disagree. Even where a fairly specific objective is prescribed for the administrator, there remains considerable room for disagreement on sub-objectives. Consider, for example, the conflict with respect to locating public housing, described in Meyerson and Banfield's study of the Chicago Housing Authority[4]—disagreement which occurred despite the clear objective of providing a certain number of public housing units in the city. Similarly conflicting are objectives in highway location, traffic control, minimum wage administration, development of tourist facilities in national parks, or insect control.

Administrators cannot escape these conflicts by ascertaining the majority's preference, for preferences have not been registered on most issues; indeed, there often *are* no preferences in the absence of public discussion sufficient to bring an issue to the attention of the electorate. Furthermore, there is a question of whether intensity of feeling should be considered as well as the number of persons preferring each alternative. By the impossibility of doing otherwise, administrators often are reduced to deciding policy without clarifying objectives first.

Even when an administrator resolves to follow his own values as a criterion for decisions, he often will not know how to rank them when they conflict with one another, as they usually do. Suppose, for example, that an administrator must relocate tenants living in tenements scheduled for destruction. One objective is to empty the buildings fairly promptly, another is to find suitable accommodation for persons displaced, another is

179

to avoid friction with residents in other areas in which a large influx would be unwelcome, another is to deal with all concerned through persuasion if possible, and so on.

How does one state even to himself the relative importance of these partially conflicting values? A simple ranking of them is not enough; one needs ideally to know how much of one value is worth sacrificing for some of another value. The answer is that typically the administrator chooses—and must choose—directly among policies in which these values are combined in different ways. He cannot first clarify his values and then choose among policies.

A more subtle third point underlies both the first two. Social objectives do not always have the same relative values. One objective may be highly prized in one circumstance, another in another circumstance. If, for example, an administrator values highly both the dispatch with which his agency can carry through its projects *and* good public relations, it matters little which of the two possibly conflicting values he favors in some abstract or general sense. Policy questions arise in forms which put to administrators such a question as: Given the degree to which we are or are not already achieving the values of dispatch and the values of good public relations, is it worth sacrificing a little speed for a happier clientele, or is it better to risk offending the clientele so that we can get on with our work? The answer to such a question varies with circumstances.

The value problem is, as the example shows, always a problem of adjustments at a margin. But there is no practicable way to state marginal objectives or values except in terms of particular policies. That one value is preferred to another in one decision situation does not mean that it will be preferred in another decision situation in which it can be had only at great sacrifice of another value. Attempts to rank or order values in general and abstract terms so that they do not shift from decision to decision end up by ignoring the relevant marginal preferences. The significance of this third point thus goes very far. Even if all administrators had at hand an agreed set of values, objectives, and constraints, their marginal values in actual choice situations would be impossible to formulate.

Unable consequently to formulate the relevant values first and then choose among policies to achieve them, administrators must choose directly among alternative policies that offer different marginal combinations of values. Somewhat paradoxically, the only practicable way to disclose one's relevant marginal values even to oneself is to describe the policy one chooses to achieve them. Except roughly and vaguely, I know of no way to describe—or even to understand—what my relative evaluations are for, say, freedom and security, speed and accuracy in governmental decisions, or low taxes and better schools than to describe my preferences among specific policy choices that might be made between the alternatives in each of the pairs.

In summary, two aspects of the process by which values are actually handled can be distinguished. The first is clear: evaluation and empirical analysis are intertwined; that is, one chooses among values and among policies at one and the same time. Put a little more elaborately, one simultaneously chooses a policy to attain certain objectives and chooses the objectives themselves. The second aspect is related but distinct: the administrator focuses his attention on marginal or incremental values. Whether he is aware of it or not, he does not find general formulations of objectives very helpful and in fact makes specific marginal or incremental comparisons. Two policies, X and Y, confront him. Both promise the same degree of attainment of objectives $a$, $b$, $c$, $d$, and $e$. But X promises him somewhat more of $f$ than does Y, while Y promises him somewhat more of $g$ than does X. In choosing between them, he is in fact offered the alternative of a marginal or incremental amount of $f$ at the expense of a marginal or incremental amount of $g$. The only values that are relevant to his choice are those increments by which the two policies differ; and, when he finally chooses between the two marginal values, he does so by making a choice between policies.[5]

As to whether the attempt to clarify objectives in advance of policy selection is more or less rational than the close intertwining of marginal evaluation and empirical analysis, the principal difference established is that for complex problems, the first is impossible and irrelevant, and the second is both possible and relevant. The second is possible because the administrator need not try to analyze any values except the values by which alternative policies differ and need not be concerned with them except as they differ marginally. His need for information on values or objectives is drastically reduced as compared with the root method; and his capacity for grasping, comprehending, and relating values to one another is not strained beyond the breaking point.

### RELATIONS BETWEEN MEANS AND ENDS (2b)

Decision making is ordinarily formalized as a means-ends relationship: means are conceived to be evaluated and chosen in the light of ends finally selected independently of and prior to the choice of means. This is the means-ends relationship of the root method. But it follows from all that has just been said that such a means-ends relationship is possible only to the extent that values are agreed upon, are reconcilable, and are stable at the margin. Typically, therefore, such a means-ends relationship is absent from the branch method, where means and ends are simultaneously chosen.

*181*

Yet any departure from the means-ends relationship of the root method will strike some readers as inconceivable. For it will appear to them that only in such a relationship is it possible to determine whether one policy choice is better or worse than another. How can an administrator know whether he has made a wise or foolish decision if he is without prior values or objectives by which to judge his decisions? The answer to this question calls up the third distinctive difference between root and branch methods: how to decide the best policy.

## THE TEST OF "GOOD" POLICY (3b)

In the root method, a decision is "correct," "good," or "rational" if it can be shown to attain some specified objective, where the objective can be specified without simply describing the decision itself. Where objectives are defined only through the marginal or incremental approach to values described above, it is still sometimes possible to test whether a policy does in fact attain the desired objectives; but a precise statement of the objectives takes the form of a description of the policy chosen or some alternative to it. To show that a policy is mistaken one cannot offer an abstract argument that important objectives are not achieved; one must instead argue that another policy is more to be preferred.

So far, the departure from customary ways of looking at problem-solving is not troublesome, for many administrators will be quick to agree that the most effective discussion of the correctness of policy does take the form of comparison with other policies that might have been chosen. But what of the situation in which administrators cannot agree on values or objectives, either abstractly or in marginal terms? What then is the test of "good" policy? For the root method, there is no test. Agreement on objectives failing, there is no standard of "correctness." For the method of successive limited comparisons, the test is agreement on policy itself, which remains possible even when agreement on values is not.

It has been suggested that continuing agreement in Congress on the desirability of extending old age insurance stems from liberal desires to strengthen the welfare programs of the federal government and from conservative desires to reduce union demands for private pension plans. If so, this is an excellent demonstration of the ease with which individuals of different ideologies often can agree on concrete policy. Labor mediators report a similar phenomenon: the contestants cannot agree on criteria for settling their disputes but can agree on specific proposals. Similarly, when one administrator's objective turns out to be another's means, they often can agree on policy.

Agreement on policy thus becomes the only practicable test of the policy's correctness. And for one administrator to seek to win the other over to agreement on ends as well would accomplish nothing and create quite unnecessary controversy.

If agreement directly on policy as a test for "best" policy seems a poor substitute for testing the policy against its objectives, it ought to be remembered that objectives themselves have no ultimate validity other than they are agreed upon. Hence agreement is the test of "best" policy in both methods. But where the root method requires agreement on what elements in the decision constitute objectives and on which of these objectives should be sought, the branch method falls back on agreement wherever it can be found.

In an important sense, therefore, it is not irrational for an administrator to defend a policy as good without being able to specify what it is good for.

## NON-COMPREHENSIVE ANALYSIS (4b)

Ideally, rational-comprehensive analysis leaves out nothing important. But it is impossible to take everything important into consideration unless "important" is so narrowly defined that analysis is in fact quite limited. Limits on human intellectual capacities and on available information set definite limits to man's capacity to be comprehensive. In actual fact, therefore, no one can practice the rational-comprehensive method for really complex problems, and every administrator faced with a sufficiently complex problem must find ways drastically to simplify.

An administrator assisting in the formulation of agricultural economic policy cannot in the first place be competent on all possible policies. He cannot even comprehend one policy entirely. In planning a soil bank program, he cannot successfully anticipate the impact of higher or lower farm income on, say, urbanization—the possible consequent loosening of family ties, possible consequent eventual need for revisions in social security and further implications for tax problems arising out of new federal responsibilities for social security and municipal responsibilities for urban services. Nor, to follow another line of repercussions, can he work through the soil bank program's effects on prices for agricultural products in foreign markets and consequent implications for foreign relations, including those arising out of economic rivalry between the United States and the U.S.S.R.

In the method of successive limited comparisons, simplification is systematically achieved in two principal ways. First, it is achieved through limitation of policy comparisons to those policies that differ in relatively small degree from policies presently in effect. Such a limitation immediately reduces the number of alternatives to be investigated and also drastically simplifies the character of the investigation of each. For it is not necessary to undertake fundamental inquiry into an alternative and its consequences; it is necessary only to study those respects in which the proposed alternative and its consequences differ from the status quo. The empirical comparison of marginal differences among alternative policies that differ only marginally is, of course, a counterpart to the incremental or marginal comparison of values discussed above.[6]

### Relevance as Well as Realism

It is a matter of common observation that in Western democracies public administrators and policy analysts in general do largely limit their analyses to incremental or marginal differences in policies that are chosen to differ only incrementally. They do not do so, however, solely because they desperately need some way to simplify their problems; they also do so in order to be relevant. Democracies change their policies almost entirely through incremental adjustments. Policy does not move in leaps and bounds.

The incremental character of political change in the United States has often been remarked. The two major political parties agree on fundamentals; they offer alternative policies to the voters only on relatively small points of difference. Both parties favor full employment, but they define it somewhat differently; both favor the development of water power resources, but in slightly different ways; and both favor unemployment compensation, but not the same level of benefits. Similarly, shifts of policy within a party take place largely through a series of relatively small changes, as can be seen in their only gradual acceptance of the idea of governmental responsibility for support of the unemployed, a change in party positions beginning in the early 1930s and culminating in a sense in the Employment Act of 1946.

Party behavior is in turn rooted in public attitudes, and political theorists cannot conceive of democracy's surviving in the United States in the absence of fundamental agreement on potentially disruptive issues, with consequent limitation of policy debates to relatively small differences in policy.

Since the policies ignored by the administrator are politically impossible and so irrelevant, the simplification of analysis achieved by concentrating on policies that differ only incrementally is not a capricious kind of simplification. In addition, it can be argued that, given the limits on knowledge within which policy-makers are confined, simplifying by limiting the focus to small variations from present policy makes the most of available knowledge. Because policies being considered are like present and past policies, the administrator can obtain information and claim some insight. Non-incremental policy proposals are therefore typically not only politically irrelevant but also unpredictable in their consequences.

The second method of simplification of analysis is the practice of ignoring important possible consequences of possible policies, as well as the values attached to the neglected consequences. If this appears to disclose a shocking shortcoming of successive limited comparisons, it can be replied that, even if the exclusions are random, policies may nevertheless be more intelligently formulated than through futile attempts to achieve a comprehensiveness beyond human capacity. Actually, however, the exclusions, seeming arbitrary or random from one point of view, need be neither.

## Achieving a Degree of Comprehensiveness

Suppose that each value neglected by one policy-making agency were a major concern of at least one other agency. In that case, a helpful division of labor would be achieved, and no agency need find its task beyond its capacities. The shortcomings of such a system would be that one agency might destroy a value either before another agency could be activated to safeguard it or in spite of another agency's efforts. But the possibility that important values may be lost is present in any form of organization, even where agencies attempt to comprehend in planning more than is humanly possible.

The virtue of such a hypothetical division of labor is that every important interest or value has its watchdog. And these watchdogs can protect the interests in their jurisdiction in two quite different ways: first, by redressing damages done by other agencies; and, second, by anticipating and heading off injury before it occurs.

In a society like that of the United States, in which individuals are free to combine to pursue almost any possible common interest they might have and in which government agencies are sensitive to the pressures of these groups, the system described is approximated. Almost every interest has its watchdog. Without claiming that every interest has a sufficiently powerful watchdog, it can be argued that our system often can assure a more comprehensive regard for the values of the whole society than any attempt at intellectual comprehensiveness.

In the United States, for example, no part of government attempts a comprehensive overview of policy on income distribution. A policy nevertheless evolves, and one responding to a wide variety of interests. A process of mutual adjustment among farm groups, labor unions, municipalities and school boards, tax authorities, and government agencies with responsibilities in the fields of housing, health, highways, national parks, fire, and police accomplishes a distribution of income in which particular income problems neglected at one point in the decision processes become central at another point.

Mutual adjustment is more pervasive than the explicit forms it takes in negotiation between groups; it persists through the mutual impacts of groups upon each other even where they are not in communication. For all the imperfections and latent dangers in this ubiquitous process of mutual adjustment, it will often accomplish an adaptation of policies to a wider range of interests than could be done by one group centrally.

Note, too, how the incremental pattern of policy-making fits with the multiple pressure pattern. For when decisions are only incremental—closely related to known policies—it is easier for one group to anticipate the kind of moves another might make and easier too for it to make correction for injury already accomplished.[7]

Even partisanship and narrowness, to use pejorative terms, will sometimes be assets to rational decision making, for they can doubly insure that what one agency neglects, another will not; they specialize personnel to distinct points of view. The claim is valid that effective rational coordination of the federal administration, if possible to achieve at all, would require an agreed set of values[8]—if "rational" is defined as the practice of the root method of decision making. But a high degree of administrative coordination occurs as each agency adjusts its policies to the concerns of the other agencies in the process of fragmented decision making I have just described.

For all the apparent shortcomings of the incremental approach to policy alternatives with its arbitrary exclusion coupled with fragmentation, when compared to the root method, the branch method often looks far superior. In the root method, the inevitable exclusion of factors is accidental, unsystematic, and not defensible by any argument so far developed, while in the branch method the exclusions are deliberate, systematic, and defensible. Ideally, of course, the root method does not exclude; in practice it must.

Nor does the branch method necessarily neglect long-run considerations and objectives. It is clear that important values must be omitted in considering policy, and sometimes the only way long-run objectives can be given adequate attention is through the neglect of short-run considerations. But the values omitted can be either long-run or short-run.

### SUCCESSION OF COMPARISONS (5b)

The final distinctive element in the branch method is that the comparisons, together with the policy choice, proceed in a chronological series. Policy is not made once and for all; it is made and re-made endlessly. Policy making is a process of successive approximation to some desired objectives in which what is desired itself continues to change under reconsideration.

Making policy is at best a very rough process. Neither social scientists, nor politicians, nor public administrators yet know enough about the social world to avoid repeated error in predicting the consequences of policy moves. A wise policy-maker consequently expects that his policies will achieve only part of what he hopes and at the same time will produce unanticipated consequences he would have preferred to avoid. If he proceeds through a *succession* of incremental changes, he avoids serious lasting mistakes in several ways.

In the first place, past sequences of policy steps have given him knowledge about the probable consequences of further similar steps. Second, he need not attempt big jumps toward his goals that would require predictions beyond his or anyone else's knowledge, because he never expects his policy to be a final resolution of a problem. His decision is only one step, one that if successful can quickly be followed by another. Third, he is in effect able to test his previous predictions as he moves on to each further step. Lastly, he often can remedy a past error fairly quickly—more quickly than if policy proceeded through more distinct steps widely spaced in time.

Compare this comparative analysis of incremental changes with the aspiration to employ theory in the root method. Man cannot think without classifying, without subsuming one experience under a more general category of experiences. The attempt to push categorization as far as possible and to find general propositions which can be applied to specific situations is what I refer to with the word "theory." Where root analysis often leans heavily on theory in this sense, the branch method does not.

The assumption of root analysts is that theory is the most systematic and economical way to bring relevant knowledge to bear on a specific problem. Granting the assumption, an unhappy fact is that we do not have adequate theory to apply to problems in any policy area, although theory is more adequate in some areas—monetary policy, for example—than in others. Comparative analysis, as in the branch method, is sometimes a systematic alternative to theory.

Suppose an administrator must choose among a small group of policies that differ only incrementally from each other and from present policy. He might aspire to "understand" each of the alternatives—for example, to know all the consequences of each aspect of each policy. If so, he would indeed require theory. In fact, however, he would usually decide that, *for policy-making purposes*, he need know, as explained above, only the consequences of each of those aspects of the policies in which they differed from one another. For this much more modest aspiration, he requires no theory (although it might be helpful, if available), for he can proceed to isolate probable differences by examining the differences in consequences associated with past differences in policies, a feasible program because he can take his observations from a long sequence of incremental changes.

For example, without a more comprehensive social theory about juvenile delinquency than scholars have yet produced, one cannot possibly understand the ways in which a variety of public policies—say on education, housing, recreation, employment, race relations, and policing—might encourage or discourage delinquency. And one needs such an understanding if he undertakes the comprehensive overview of the problem prescribed in the models of the root method. If, however, one merely wants to mobilize knowledge sufficient to assist in a choice among a small group of similar policies—alternative policies on juvenile court procedures, for example—he can do so by comparative analysis of the results of similar past policy moves.

## THEORISTS AND PRACTITIONERS

This difference explains—in some cases at least—why the administrator often feels that the outside expert or academic problem-solver is sometimes not helpful and why they in turn often urge more theory on him. And it explains why an administrator often feels more confident when "flying by the seat of his pants" than when following the advice of theorists. Theorists often ask the administrator to go the long way round to the solution of his problems, in effect ask him to follow the best canons of the scientific method, when the administrator knows that the best available theory will work less well than more modest incremental comparisons. Theorists do not realize that the administrator is often in fact practicing a systematic method. It would be foolish to push this explanation too far, for sometimes practical decision-makers are pursuing neither a theoretical approach nor successive comparisons, nor any other systematic method.

It may be worth emphasizing that theory is sometimes of extremely limited helpfulness in policy-making for at least two rather different reasons. It is greedy for facts; it can be constructed only through a great collection of observations. And it is typically insufficiently precise for application to a policy process that moves through small changes. In contrast, the comparative method both economizes on the need for facts and directs the analyst's attention to just those facts that are relevant to the fine choices faced by the decision-maker.

With respect to precision of theory, economic theory serves as an example. It predicts that an economy without money or prices would in certain specified ways misallocate resources, but this finding pertains to an alternative far removed from the kind of policies on which administrators need help. On the other hand, it is not precise enough to predict the consequences of policies restricting business mergers, and this is the kind of issue on which the administrators need help. Only in relatively restricted areas does economic theory achieve sufficient precision to go far in resolving policy questions; its helpfulness in policy-making is always so limited that it requires supplementation through comparative analysis.

## SUCCESSIVE COMPARISON AS A SYSTEM

Successive limited comparisons is, then, indeed a method or system; it is not a failure of method for which administrators ought to apologize. None the less, its imperfections, which have not been explored in this paper, are many. For example, the method is without a built-in safeguard for all relevant values, and it also may lead the decision-maker to overlook excellent policies for no other reason than that they are not suggested by the chain of successive policy steps leading up to the present. Hence, it ought to be said that under this method, as well as under some of the most sophisticated variants of the root method—operations research, for example—policies will continue to be as foolish as they are wise.

Why then bother to describe the method in all the above detail? Because it is in fact a common method of policy formulation, and is, for complex problems, the principal reliance of administrators as well as of other policy analysts.[9] And because it will be superior to any other decision-making method available for complex problems in many circumstances, certainly superior to a futile attempt at superhuman comprehensiveness. The reaction of the public administrator to the exposition of method doubtless will be less a discovery of a new method than a better acquaintance with an old. But by becoming more conscious of their practice of this method, administrators might practice it with more skill and know when to extend or constrict its use. (That they sometimes practice it effectively and sometimes not may explain the extremes of opinion on "muddling through," which is both praised as a highly sophisticated form of problem-solving and denounced as no method at all. For I suspect that in so far as there is a system in what is known as "muddling through," this method is it.)

One of the noteworthy incidental consequences of clarification of the method is the light it throws on the suspicion an administrator sometimes entertains that a consultant or adviser is not speaking relevantly and responsibly when in fact by all ordinary objective evidence he is. The trouble lies in the fact that most of us approach policy problems within a framework given by our view of a chain of successive policy choices made up to the present. One's thinking about appropriate policies with respect, say, to urban traffic control is greatly influenced by one's knowledge of the incremental steps taken up to the present. An administrator enjoys an intimate knowledge of his past sequences that "outsiders" do not share, and his thinking and that of the "outsider" will consequently be different in ways that may puzzle both. Both may appear to be talking intelligently, yet each may find the other unsatisfactory. The relevance of the policy chain of succession is even more clear when an American tries to discuss, say, antitrust policy with a Swiss, for the chains of policy in the two countries are strikingly different and the two individuals consequently have organized their knowledge in quite different ways.

If this phenomenon is a barrier to communication, an understanding of it promises an enrichment of intellectual interaction in policy formulation. Once the source of difference is understood, it will sometimes be stimulating for an administrator to seek out a policy analyst whose recent experience is with a policy chain different from his own.

This raises again a question only briefly discussed above on the merits of like-mindedness among government administrators. While much of organization theory argues the virtues of common values and agreed organizational objectives, for complex problems in which the root method is inapplicable, agencies will want among their own personnel two types of diversification: administrators whose thinking is organized by reference to policy chains other than those familiar to most members of the organization and, even more commonly, administrators whose professional or personal values or interests create diversity of view (perhaps coming from different specialties, social classes, geographical areas) so that, even within a single agency, decision-making can be fragmented and parts of the agency can serve as watchdogs for other parts.

## NOTES

1. James G. March and Herbert A. Simon similarly characterize the literature. They also take some important steps, as have Simon's recent articles, to describe a less heroic model of policy making. See *Organizations* (John Wiley and Sons, 1958), p. 137.

2. "Operations Research and National Planning—A Dissent," 5 *Operations Research* 718 (October, 1957). Hitch's dissent is from particular points made in the article to which his paper is a reply; his claim that operations research is for low-level problems is widely accepted.

For examples of the kind of problems to which operations research is applied, see C. W. Churchman, R. L. Ackoff and E. L. Arnoff, *Introduction to Operations Research* (John Wiley and Sons, 1957); and J. F. McCloskey and J. M. Coppinger (eds.), *Operations Research for Management*, Vol. II (The Johns Hopkins Press, 1956).

3. I am assuming that administrators often make policy and advise in the making of policy and am treating decision making and policy making as synonymous for purposes of this paper.

4. Martin Meyerson and Edward C. Banfield, *Politics, Planning, and the Public Interest* (The Free Press, 1955).

5. The line of argument is, of course, an extension of the theory of market choice, especially the theory of consumer choice, to public policy choices.

6. A more precise definition of incremental policies and a discussion of whether a change that appears "small" to one observer might be seen differently by another is to be found in my "Policy Analysis," 48 *American Economic Review* 298 (June 1958).

7. The link between the practice of the method of successive limited comparisons and mutual adjustment of interests in a highly fragmented decision-making process adds a new facet to pluralist theories of government and administration.

8. Herbert Simon, Donald W. Smithburg, and Victor A. Thompson, *Public Administration* (Alfred A. Knopf, 1950), p. 434.

9. Elsewhere I have explored this same method of policy formulation as practiced by academic analysts of policy ("Policy Analysis," 48 *American Economic Review* 298 [June 1958]). Although it has been here presented as a method for public administrators, it is no less necessary to analysts more removed from immediate policy questions, despite their tendencies to describe their own analytical efforts as though they were the rational-comprehensive method with an especially heavy use of theory. Similarly, this same method is inevitably resorted to in personal problem solving, where means and ends are sometimes impossible to separate, where aspirations or objectives undergo constant development, and where drastic simplification of the complexity of the real world is urgent if problems are to be solved in the time that can be given to them. To an economist accustomed to dealing with the marginal or incremental concept in market processes, the central idea in the method is that both evaluation and empirical analysis are incremental. Accordingly, I have referred to the method elsewhere as "the incremental method."

# 10

# Systems Analysis Techniques for Public Policy Problems

◆

*E. S. Quade*

### INTRODUCTION

BROADLY SPEAKING, ANY ORDERLY analytic study designed to help a decision-maker identify a preferred course of action from among possible alternatives might be termed a systems analysis. As commonly used in the defense community, the phrase "systems analysis" refers to formal inquiries intended to advise a decision-maker on the policy choices involved in such matters as weapon development, force posture design, or the determination of strategic objectives. A typical analysis might tackle the question of what might be the possible characteristics of a new strategic bomber and whether one should be developed; whether tactical air wings, carrier task forces, or neither could be substituted for United States ground divisions in Europe; or whether we should modify the test-ban treaty now that the Chinese Communists have nuclear weapons and, if so, how. Systems analysis represents an approach to, or way of looking at complex problems of choice under uncertainty that should have utility in the Planning-Programming-Budgeting (PPB) process. Our purpose is to discuss the question of extending military systems analysis to the civilian activities of the

*Originally entitled "Systems Analysis Techniques for Planning-Programming-Budgeting," Report P-3322 (Santa Monica, California: The Rand Corporation, March, 1966); reprinted by permission of the author and publisher. Any views expressed in this paper are those of the author. They should not be interpreted as reflecting the views of the Rand Corporation or the official opinion or policy of any of its governmental or private research sponsors. Papers are reproduced by the Rand Corporation as a courtesy to the members of its staff.*

government, to point out some of the limitations of analysis in this role, and to call attention to techniques that seem likely to be particularly useful. I will interpret the term "technique" broadly enough to range from proven mathematical algorithms to certain broad principles that often seem to be associated with successful analysis.

Some fifteen years ago a similar extension raised quite some doubt. When weapons system analysts (particularly those at The Rand Corporation) began to include the formulation of national security policy and strategy as part of their field of interest, experienced "military analysts" in the Pentagon and elsewhere were not encouraging. They held that the tools, techniques, and concepts of operations analysis, as practiced in World War II, or of weapons system optimization and selection—in which analysts had been reasonably successful—would not carry over, that strategy and policy planning were arts and would remain so.

Fortunately, these skeptics were only partially right. It is true that additional concepts and methodologies significantly different from those of earlier analysis had to be developed. But there has been substantial progress, and the years since 1961 have seen a marked increase in the extent to which analyses of policy and strategy have influenced decision-makers on the broadest issues of national defense.

Today's contemplated extension to PPB is long overdue and possibly even more radical. Systems analysis has barely entered the domain of the social sciences. Here, in urban planning, in education, in welfare, and in other nonmilitary activities, as Olaf Helmer remarks in his perceptive essay:

> We are faced with an abundance of challenges: how to keep the peace, how to alleviate the hardships of social change, how to provide food and comfort for the inaffluent, how to improve the social institutions and the values of the affluent, how to cope with revolutionary innovations, and so on.[1]

Since systems analysis represents an approach to, or way of looking at, any problem of choice under uncertainty, it should be able to help with these problems.

Actually, systematic analysis of *routine* operations is widespread throughout the civil government as well as in commerce, industry, and the military. Here analysis takes its most mathematical form and, in a certain sense, its most fruitful role. For example, it may help to determine how Post Office pickup trucks should be routed to collect mail from deposit boxes, or whether computers should be rented or purchased to handle warehouse inventories, or what type of all-weather landing system should be installed in new commercial aircraft. Such problems are typically an attempt to increase the efficiency of a man-machine system in a situation where it is clear what "more efficient" means. The analysis can often be reduced to the application of a well-understood mathematical discipline such as linear programming or queuing theory to a generic "model," which, by a specification of its parameters, can be made to fit a wide variety of operations. An "optimum" solution is then obtained by means of a systematic computational routine. The queuing model, for example, is relevant to many aspects of the operations of the Post Office, airports, service facilities, maintenance shops, and so on. In many instances such models may actually tell the client what his decision or plan ought to be. Analysis of this type is usually called operations research or management science rather than systems analysis, however.

There are, however, other decisions or problems, civilian as well as military, where computational techniques can help only with subproblems. Typical decisions of this latter type might be the determination of how much of the federal budget should be allocated to economic development and what fraction of that should be spent on South America; or whether the needs of interstate transportation are better served by improved high-speed rail transport or by higher performance highway turnpikes; or if there is some legislative action that might end the growth of juvenile delinquency. Such problems will normally involve more than the efficient allocation of resources among alternative uses; they are not "solvable" in the same sense as efficiency problems in which one can maximize some "payoff" function that clearly expresses what one is trying to accomplish. Here, rather, the objectives or goals of the action to be taken must be determined first. Decision problems associated with program budgeting are mainly of this type—where the difficulty lies in deciding what ought to be done as well as in how to do it, where it is not clear what "more efficient" means, and where many of the factors in the problem elude quantification. The final program recommendation will thus remain in part a matter of faith and judgment. Studies to help with these problems are systems analyses rather than operations research.[2]

Every systems analysis involves, at one stage, a comparison of alternative courses of action in terms of their costs and their effectiveness in attaining a specified objective. Usually this comparison takes the form of an attempt to designate the alternative that will minimize the costs, subject to some fixed performance requirement (something like reduce unemployment to less than 2 percent in two years, or add a certain number of miles to the interstate highway system); or conversely, it is an attempt to maximize some physical measure of performance subject to a budget constraint. Such evaluations are called cost-effectiveness analyses.[3] Since they often receive the lion's share of attention, the entire study also is frequently called a cost-effectiveness analysis. But this label puts too much emphasis on just one aspect of the decision process. In analyses designed to furnish broad policy advice, other facets of the problem are of greater significance than the comparison of alternatives: the specification of sensible objectives, the determination of a satisfactory way to measure performance, the influence of considerations that cannot be quantified, or the design of better alternatives.

## THE ESSENCE OF THE METHOD

What is there about the analytic approach that makes it better or more useful than other ways to furnish advice—than, say, an expert or a committee? In areas such as urban redevelopment or welfare planning, where there is no accepted theoretical foundation, advice obtained from experts working individually or as a committee must depend largely on judgment and intuition. *So must the advice from systems analysis.* But the virtue of such analysis is that it permits the judgment and intuition of the experts in relevant fields to be combined systematically and efficiently. The essence of the method is to construct and operate within a "model," a simplified abstraction of the real situation appropriate to the question. Such a model, which may take such varied forms as a computer simulation, an operational game, or even a purely verbal "scenario," introduces a precise structure and terminology that serve primarily as an effective means of communication, enabling the participants in the study to exercise their judgment and intuition in a concrete context and in proper relation to others. Moreover, through feedback from the model (the results of computation, the countermoves in the game, or the critique of the scenario), the experts have a chance to revise early judgments and thus arrive at a clearer understanding of the problem and its context, and perhaps of their subject matter.[4]

## The Process of Analysis

The fundamental importance of the model is seen in its relation to the other elements of analysis.[5] There are five all told, and each is present in every analysis of choice and should always be explicitly identified.

1. *The objective (or objectives).* Systems analysis is undertaken primarily to help choose a policy or course of action. The first and most important task of the analyst is to discover what the decision-maker's objectives are (or should be) and then how to measure the extent to which these objectives are, in fact, attained by various choices. This done, strategies, policies, or possible actions can be examined, compared, and recommended on the basis of how well and how cheaply they can accomplish these objectives.

2. *The alternatives.* The alternatives are the means by which it is hoped the objectives can be attained. They may be policies or strategies or specific actions or instrumentalities, and they need not be obvious substitutes for each other or perform the same specific function. Thus, education, anti-poverty measures, police protection, and slum clearance may all be alternatives in combating juvenile delinquency.

3. *The costs.* The choice of a particular alternative for accomplishing the objectives implies that certain specific resources can no longer be used for other purposes. These are the costs. For a future time period, most costs can be measured in money, but their true measure is in terms of the opportunities they preclude. Thus, if the goal is to lower traffic fatalities, the irritation and delay caused to motorists by schemes that lower automobile speed in a particular location must be considered as costs, for such irritation and delay may cause more speeding elsewhere.

4. *A model (or models).* A model is a simplified, stylized representation of the real world that abstracts the cause-and-effect relationships essential to the question studied. The means of representation may range from a set of mathematical equations or a computer program to a purely verbal description of the situation, in which intuition alone is used to predict the consequences of various choices. In systems analysis, or any analysis of choice, the role of the model (or models, for it may be inappropriate or absurd to attempt to incorporate all the aspects of a problem in a single formulation) is to estimate for each alternative the costs that would be incurred and the extent to which the objectives would be attained.

5. *A criterion.* A criterion is a rule or standard by which to rank the alternatives in order of desirability. It provides a means for weighing cost against effectiveness.

The process of analysis takes place in three overlapping stages. In the first, the formulation stage, the issues are clarified, the extent of the inquiry limited, and the elements identified. In the second, the search stage, information is gathered and alternatives generated. The third stage is evaluation.

To start the process of evaluation or comparison (Figure 1), the various *alternatives* (which may have to be discovered or invented as part of the analysis) are examined by means of the *models*. The models tell us what consequences or outcomes can be expected to follow from each alternative; that is, what the *costs* are and the extent to which each *objective* is attained. A *criterion* can then be used to weigh the costs against performance, and thus the alternatives can be arranged in the order of preference.

Unfortunately, things are seldom tidy: too often the objectives are multiple, conflicting, and obscure; alternatives are not adequate to attain the objectives; the measures of effectiveness do not really measure the extent to which the objectives are attained; the predictions from the model are full of uncertainties; and other criteria that look almost as plausible as the one

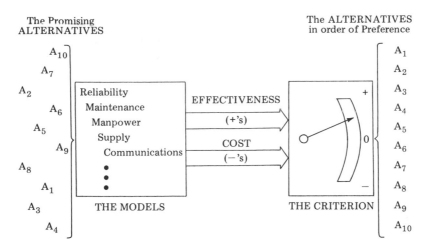

FIGURE 1

*The structure of analysis.*

chosen may lead to a different order of preference. When this happens, we must take another approach. A single attempt or pass at a problem is seldom enough. (See Figure 2.) The key of successful analysis is a continuous cycle of formulating the problem, selecting objectives, designing alternatives, collecting data, building models, weighing cost against performance, testing for sensitivity, questioning assumptions and data, reexamining the objectives, opening new alternatives, building better models, and so on, until satisfaction is obtained or time or money forces a cut-off.

In brief, a systems analysis attempts to look at the entire problem and look at it in its proper context. Characteristically, it will involve a systematic investigation of the decision-maker's objectives and of the relevant criteria; a comparison—quantitative insofar as possible—of the cost, effectiveness, risk, and timing associated with each alternative policy or strategy for achieving the objectives; and an attempt to design better alternatives and select other goals if those examined are found wanting.

Note that there is nothing really new about the procedures I have just sketched. They have been used, more or less successfully, by managers throughout government and industry since ancient times. The need for considering cost relative to performance must have occurred to the earliest planner. Systems analysis is thus not a catchword to suggest we are doing something new; at most, we are doing something better. What may be novel, though, is that this sort of analysis is an attempt to look at the entire problem systematically with emphasis on explicitness, on quantification, and on the recognition of uncertainty. Also novel are the schemes or models used to explore the consequences of various choices and to

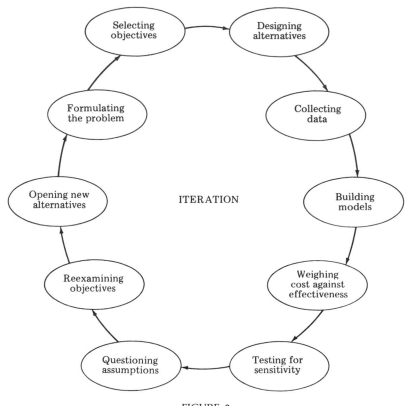

FIGURE 2

*The key to analysis.*

eliminate inferior action in situations where the relationships cannot be represented adequately by a mathematical model.

Note that there is nothing in these procedures that guarantees the advice from the analysis to be good. They do not preclude the possibility that we are addressing the wrong problem or have allowed our personal biases to bar a better solution from consideration. When a study is a poor one it is rarely because the computer was not powerful enough or because the methods of optimization were not sufficiently sophisticated, but because it had the wrong objective or poor criteria. There are some characteristics of a study, however, that seem to be associated with good analysis. Let me identify some of these.

*Principles of Good Analysis*

1. It is all important to tackle the "right" problem. A large part of the investigators' efforts must be invested in thinking about the problem, exploring its proper breadth, and trying to discover the appropriate objectives

and to search out good criteria for choice. If we have not chosen the best set of alternatives to compare we will not discover the best solution. But if we have chosen the wrong objective then we might find a solution to the wrong problem. Getting an accurate answer to the wrong question is likely to be far less helpful than an incomplete answer to the right question.

2. The analysis must be systems oriented. Rather than isolating a part of the problem by neglecting its interactions with other parts, an effort should be made to extend the boundaries of the inquiry as far as required for the problem at hand, to find what interdependencies are important, and to study the entire complex system. This should be done even if it requires the use of purely intuitive judgment.

An interdisciplinary team of persons having a variety of knowledge and skills is helpful here. This is not so merely because a complex problem is likely to involve many diverse factors that cannot be handled by a single discipline. More importantly, a problem looks different to an economist, an engineer, a political scientist, or a professional bureaucrat, and their different approaches may contribute to finding a solution.

3. The presence of uncertainty should be recognized, and an attempt made to take it into account. Most important decisions are fraught with uncertainty. In planning urban redevelopment we are uncertain about city growth patterns, about the extent to which freeways or rapid transit systems will be used, about costs, about tax revenues, about the demand for services. For many of these things, there is no way to say with confidence that a given estimate is correct. The analyst attempts to identify these uncertainties and evaluate their impact. Often he can say the value of a parameter will be more than A but less than B. Sometimes it is possible to indicate how the uncertainty can be reduced by further testing and how long that will take. Most important, the analysis should determine the effect of uncertainty on the answers. This is done by a sensitivity analysis that shows the answers change in response to changes in assumptions and estimates.[6]

The study report should include the presentation of a contingency table showing the effectiveness and cost associated with each significant alternative for various future environments and for each set of assumptions about the uncertainties.

4. The analysis attempts to discover new alternatives as well as to improve the obvious ones. The invention of new alternatives can be much more valuable than an exhaustive comparison of given alternatives, none of which may be very satisfactory.

5. While in problems of public policy or national security the scientific method of controlled repeated experiment cannot be used, the analysis should strive to attain the standards traditional to science. These are (1) intersubjectivity: results obtained by processes that can be duplicated by others to attain the same results; (2) explicitness: use of calculations,

assumptions, data, and judgments that are subject to checking, criticism, and disagreement; and (3) objectivity: conclusions do not depend on personalities, reputations, or vested interests; where possible these conclusions should be in quantitative and experimental terms.

## THE MODELS

As mentioned earlier, systems analysis is flexible in the models it uses. Indeed, it has to be. Mathematics and computing machines, while extremely useful, are limited in the aid they can give in broad policy questions. If the important aspects of the problem can be completely formulated mathematically or represented numerically, techniques such as dynamic programming, game theory, queuing theory, or computer simulation may be the means of providing the best solution. But in most policy analyses, computations and computers are often more valuable for the aid they provide to intuition and understanding, rather than for the results they supply.

While a computer can solve only the problems that the analyst knows conceptually how to solve himself, it can help with many others. The objection that one cannot use results which depend on many uncertain parameters represents a lack of understanding of how systems analysis can help a decision-maker. For a study to be useful it must indicate the *relative* merit of the various alternatives and identify the critical parameters. The great advantage of a computerized model is that it gives the analyst the capability to do numerous excursions, parametric investigations, and sensitivity analyses and thus to investigate the ranking of alternatives under a host of assumptions. This may be of more practical value to the decision-maker than the ability to say with high confidence that a given alternative will have such and such a rank in a very narrowly defined situation.

The type of model appropriate to a problem depends on the problem and what we know or think we know about it.

For example, suppose we are concerned with long-range economic forecasting or decisions about the development of a national economy. The type of model to use will depend on the particular economy and on the kind of questions that must be answered. If the questions were about the United States, the model might be mathematical and possibly programmed for a computer because of its size and complexity. (By a mathematical model I mean one in which the relationships between the variables and parameters are represented by mathematical equations.) In the case of the United States, because of the vast amount of data available in the form of economic and demographic time series regarding just about every conceivable aspect of economic life, numerous mathematical and computer models have been formulated and used with more or less success.

If we are not able to abstract the situation to a series of equations or a mathematical model, some other way to represent the consequences that follow from particular choices must be found. Simulation may work. Here, instead of describing the situation directly, each element making up the real situation may be simulated by a physical object or, most often, by a digital computer using sets of random numbers, and its behavior analyzed by operating with the representation. For example, we might use computer simulation to study the economy of some Latin American country. The distinction between a computer simulation and the use of a computer to analyze a mathematical model is often a fuzzy one, but the fundamental difference is that in simulation the overall behavior of the model is studied through a case-by-case approach.

For studying the economy of a newly emerging nation such as is found in Africa, where the situation is even more poorly structured and where we have little firm knowledge of existing facts and relationships, a possible approach would be through the direct involvement of experts who have knowledge of the problem.

Ordinarily, we would like to have the judgment of more than one expert, even though their advice usually differs. There are several ways to try for a consensus; the traditional way has been to assemble the experts in one place, to let them discuss the problem freely, and to require that they arrive at a joint answer. They could also be put to work individually, letting others seek methods for the best combined use of their findings. Or they could be asked to work in a group exercise—ranging from a simple structured discussion to a sophisticated simulation or an "operational game"—to obtain judgments from the group as a whole.

This latter approach is a laboratory simulation involving role-playing by human subjects who simulate real-world decision-makers. To study the economy of an underdeveloped country the various sectors of the economy might be simulated by specialized experts.[7] They would be expected, in acting out their roles, not so much to play a competitive game against one another, but to use their intuition as experts to simulate as best they could the attitudes and consequent decisions of their real-life counterparts. For instance, a player simulating a goods-producing sector of the economy might, within constraints, shut down or expand manufacturing facilities, modernize, change raw material and labor inputs, vary prices, and so on. There would also need to be government players who could introduce new fiscal or monetary policies and regulations (taxes, subsidies, tariffs, price ceilings, etc.) as well as social and political innovations with only indirect economic implications (social security, education, appeals to patriotism, universal military service, etc.). In laying down the rules governing the players' options and constraints and the actions taken within these rules, expert judgment is essential. It is also clear that for this problem political and sociological experts will be needed, as well as economists.

There is, of course, no guarantee that the projections obtained from such a model would be reliable. But the participating experts might gain a great deal of insight. Here the game structure—again a model—furnishes the participants with an artificial, simulated environment within which they can jointly and simultaneously experiment, acquiring through feedback the insights necessary to make successful predictions within the gaming context and thus indirectly about the real world.

Another useful technique is one that military systems analysts call "scenario writing." This is an effort to show how, starting with the present, a future state might evolve out of the present one. The idea is to show how this might happen plausibly by exhibiting a reasonable chain of events. A scenario is thus a primitive model. A collection of scenarios provides an insight on how future trends can depend on factors under our control and suggests policy options to us.

Another type of group action, somewhat less structured than the operational game, attempts to improve the panel or committee approach by subjecting the views of individual experts to each other's criticism without actual confrontation and its possible psychological shortcomings. In this approach, called the Delphi method, direct debate is replaced by the interchange of information and opinion through a carefully designed sequence of questionnaires. At each successive interrogation, the participants are given new refined information, and opinion feedback is derived by computing a consensus from the earlier part of the program. The process continues until either a consensus is reached, or the conflicting views are documented fully.[8]

It should be emphasized that in many important problems it is not possible to build really quantitative models. The primary function of a model is "explanatory," to organize our thinking. As I have already stated, the essence of systems analysis is not mathematical techniques or procedures, and its recommendations need not follow from computation. What counts is the effort to compare alternatives systematically, in quantitative terms when possible, using a logical sequence of steps that can be retraced and verified by others.

## The Virtues

In spite of many limitations, the decision-makers who have made use of systems analysis find it extremely useful. In fact, for some questions of national defense, analysis is essential. Without calculation there is no way to discover how many missiles may be needed to destroy a target system, or how arms control may affect security. It may be essential in other areas also; one cannot experiment radically with the national economy or even change the traffic patterns in a large city without running the risk of chaos.

Analysis offers an alternative to "muddling though" or to settling national problems by yielding to the strongest pressure group. It forces the devotees of a program to make explicit their lines of argument, to calculate the resources their programs will require as well as the advantages they might produce.

It is easy, unfortunately, to exaggerate the degree of assistance that systems analysis can offer the policy-maker. At most, it can help him understand the relevant alternatives and the key interactions by providing an estimate of the costs, risks, payoffs, and the time span associated with each course of action. It may lead him to consider new and better alternatives. It may sharpen the decision-maker's intuition and will certainly broaden his basis for judgment, thus helping him make a better decision. But value judgments, imprecise knowledge, intuitive estimates, and uncertainties about nature and the actions of others mean that a study can do little more than assess some of the implications of choosing one alternative over another. In practically no case, therefore, should the decision-maker expect the analysis to demonstrate that, beyond all reasonable doubt, a particular course of action is best.

## The Limitations

Every systems analysis has defects. Some of these are limitations inherent in all analyses of choice. Others are a consequence of the difficulties and complexities of the question. Still others are blunders or errors in thinking, which hopefully will disappear as we learn to do better and more complete analyses.

The alternatives to analysis also have their defects. One alternative is pure intuition. This is in no sense analytic, since no effort is made to structure the problem or to establish cause-and-effect relationships and operate on them to arrive at a solution. The intuitive process is to learn everything possible about the problem, to "live with it," and to let the subconscious provide the solution.

Between pure intuition, on one hand, and systems analysis, on the other, other sources of advice can, in a sense, be considered to employ analysis, although ordinarily of a less systematic, explicit, and quantitative kind. One can turn to an expert. His opinion may, in fact, be very helpful if it results from a reasonable and impartial examination of the facts, with due allowance for uncertainty, and if his assumptions and chain of logic are made *explicit*. Only then can others use his information to form their own considered opinions. But an expert, particularly an unbiased expert, may be hard to find.

Another way to handle a problem is to turn it over to a committee. Committees, however, are much less likely than experts to make their reasoning explicit, since their findings are usually obtained by bargaining. This is not to imply that a look by a "blue ribbon" committee into such problems as poverty or the allocation of funds for foreign aid might not be useful, but a committee's greatest usefulness is likely to be in the critique of analysis done by others.

However, no matter whether the advice is supplied by an expert, a committee, or a formal study group, the analysis of a problem of choice involves the same five elements and basic structure we discussed earlier.

It is important to remember that all policy analysis falls short of being scientific research. No matter how we strive to maintain standards of scientific inquiry or how closely we attempt to follow scientific methods, we cannot turn systems analysis into science. Such analysis is designed primarily to recommend—or at least to suggest—a course of action, rather than merely to understand and predict. Like engineering, the aim is to use the results of science to do things well and cheaply. Yet, when applied to national problems, the difference from ordinary engineering is apparent in the enormous responsibility involved in the unusual difficulty of appraising—or even discovering—a value system applicable to the problems, and in the absence of ways to test the validity of the analysis.

Except for this inability to verify, systems analysis may still look like a purely rational approach to decision making, a coldly objective, scientific method free from preconceived ideas, partisan bias, judgment, and intuition.

It really is not. Judgment and intuition are used in designing the models; in deciding what alternatives to consider, what factors are relevant, what the interrelations between these factors are, and what criteria to choose; and in interpreting the results of the analysis. This fact—that judgment and intuition permeate all analysis—should be remembered when we examine the apparently precise results that seem to come with such high-precision analysis.

Many flaws are the results of pitfalls faced by the analyst. It is all too easy for him to begin to believe his own assumptions and to attach undue significance to his calculations, especially if they involve bitter arguments and extended computations. The most dangerous pitfall or source of defects is an unconscious adherence to a "party line." This is frequently caused by a cherished belief or an *attention bias*. All organizations foster one to some extent; Rand, the military services, and the civilian agencies of the government are no exception. The party line is "the most important single reason for the tremendous miscalculations that are made in foreseeing and preparing for technical advances or changes in the strategic situation."[9] Examples are plentiful: the political adviser whose aim is so fixed on maintaining peace that he completely disregards what might happen should deterrence fail; the weaponeer who is so fascinated by the startling new weapons that he has invented that he assumes the politician will allow them to be used; the union leader whose attention is so fixed on current employment that he rejects an automatic device that can spread his craft into scores of new areas. In fact, this failure to realize the vital interdependence of political purpose, diplomacy, military posture, economics, and technical feasibility is the typical flaw in most practitioners' approach to national security analysis.

There are also pitfalls for the bureaucrat who commissions a study or gives inputs to it. For instance, he may specify assumptions and limit the problem arbitrarily. When a problem is first observed in one part of an organization, there is a tendency to seek a solution completely contained in that part. An administrator is thus likely to pose his problems in such a way as to bar from consideration alternatives or criteria that do not fit into his idea of the way things should be done; for example, he may not think of using ships for some tasks now being done by aircraft. Also, to act wisely on the basis of someone else's analysis one should, at the very least, understand the important and fundamental principles involved. One danger associated with analysis is that it may be employed by an administrator who is unaware of or unwilling to accept its limitations.

Pitfalls are one thing, but the inherent limitations of analysis itself are another. These limitations confine analysis to an advisory role. Three are commented on here: analysis is necessarily incomplete; measures of effectiveness are inevitably approximate; and ways to predict the future are lacking.

### Analysis Is Necessarily Incomplete

Time and money costs obviously place sharp limits on how far any inquiry can be carried. The very fact that time moves on means that a correct choice at a given time may soon be outdated by events and that goals set down at the start may not be final. The need for reporting almost always forces a cutoff. Time considerations are particularly important in military analysis, for the decision-maker can wait only so long for an answer. Other costs are important here, too. For instance, we would like to find out what the Chinese Communists would do if we put an end to all military aid to Southeast Asia. One way to get this information would be to stop such aid. But while this would clearly be cheap in immediate dollar costs, the likelihood of other later costs precludes this type of investigation.

Still more important, however, is the general fact that, even with no limitations of time and money, analysis can never treat all the considerations that may be relevant. Some are too intangible—for example, how some unilateral United States action will affect NATO solidarity, or whether Congress will accept economies that disrupt cherished institutions such as the National Guard or radically change the pattern of domestic military spending. Considerations of this type should play as important a role in the recommendation of alternative policies as any idealized cost-effectiveness calculations. But ways to measure these considerations even approximately do not exist today, and they must be handled intuitively. Other immeasurable considerations involve moral judgments—for example, whether national security is better served by an increase in the budget for defense or for welfare, or under what circumstances the preservation of an immediate advantage is worth the compromise of fundamental principles. The analyst can apply his and others' judgment and intuition to these considerations, thus making them part of the study; but *bringing them to the attention of the decision-maker*, the man with the responsibility, is extremely important.

### Measures of Effectiveness Are Approximate

In military comparisons, measures of effectiveness are at best reasonably satisfactory approximations for indicating the attainment of such vaguely defined objectives as deterrence or victory. Sometimes the best that can be done is to find measures that point in the right direction. Consider deterrence, for instance. It exists only in the mind—and in the enemy's mind at that. We cannot, therefore, measure the effectiveness of alternatives we hope will lead to deterrence by some scale of deterrence, but must use instead such approximations as to the potential mortalities that we might inflict or the roof cover we might destroy. Consequently, even if a comparison of two systems indicated that one could inflict 50 percent more casualties on the enemy than the other, we could not conclude that this means the system supplies 50 percent more deterrence. In fact, since in some circumstances it may be important *not* to look too dangerous, we encounter arguments that the system threatening the greatest number of casualties may provide the *least* deterrence!

Similarly, consider the objective of United States government expenditures for health. A usual measure of effectiveness is the dollar value of increased labor force participation. But, this is clearly inadequate; medical services are more often in demand because of a desire to reduce the everyday aches and pains of life. Moreover, we cannot be very confident about the accuracy of our estimates. For example, one recent and authoritative source estimates the yearly cost of cancer to the United States at $11 billion, while another equally authoritative source estimates $2.6 billion.[10]

### No Satisfactory Way to Predict the Future Exists

While it is possible to forecast events in the sense of mapping out possible futures, there is no satisfactory way to predict a single future for which we can work out the best system or determine an optimum policy. Consequently, we must consider a range of possible futures or contingencies. In any one of these we may be able to designate such action for the entire range of possibilities. We can design a force structure for a particular war in a particular place, but we have no way to work out a structure that is good for the entire spectrum of future wars in all the places they may occur.

Consequently, defense planning is rich in the kind of analysis that tells what damage could be done to the United States given a particular enemy force structure; but it is poor in the kinds of analysis that evaluate how we will actually stand in relation to the Soviets in years to come.

In spite of these limitations, it is not sensible to formulate policy or action without careful consideration of whatever relevant numbers can be discovered. In current Department of Defense practice, quantitative estimates of various kinds are used extensively. Many people, however, are vaguely uneasy about the particular way these estimates are made and their increasingly important role not only in military planning but elsewhere throughout the government.

Some skepticism may be justified, for the analytical work may not always be done competently or used with its limitations in mind. There may indeed be some dangers in relying on systems analysis, or on any similar approach to broad decisions. For one thing, since many factors fundamental to problems of federal policy are not readily amenable to quantitative treatment, they may possibly be neglected, or deliberately set aside for later consideration and then forgotten, or improperly weighed in the analysis itself, or in the decision based on such analysis. For another, a study may, on the surface, appear so scientific and quantitative that it may be assigned a validity not justified by the many subjective judgments involved. In other words, we may be so mesmerized by the beauty and precision of the numbers that we overlook the simplifications made to achieve this precision, neglect analysis of the qualitative factors, and overemphasize the importance of idealized calculations in the decision process. But without analysis we face even greater dangers in neglect of considerations and in the assignment of improper weights!

## THE FUTURE

And finally, what of the future? Resistance by the military to the use of systems analysis in broad problems of strategy has gradually broken down. Both government and military planning and strategy have always involved more art than science; what is happening is that the art form is changing from an ad hoc, seat-of-the-pants approach based on intuition to one based on analysis *supported by* intuition and experience. This change may come more slowly in the nonmilitary aspects of government. For one thing, the civilian employees of the government are not so closely controlled "from the top" as those in the military; also, the goals in these areas are just as vague and even more likely to be conflicting.[11] The requirements of the integrated Planning—Programming—Budgeting System will do much to speed the acceptance of analysis for other tasks, however.

With the acceptance of analysis, the computer is becoming increasingly significant—as an automaton, a process-controller, an information processor, and a decision aid. Its usefulness in serving these ends can be expected to grow. But at the same time, it is important to note that even the best computer is no more than a tool to expedite analysis. Even in the narrowest decisions, considerations not subject to any sort of quantitative analysis can always be present. Big decisions, therefore, cannot be the *automatic* consequence of a computer program or of any application of mathematical models.

For broad studies, intuitive, subjective, even ad hoc study schemes must continue to be used—but supplemented to an increasing extent by systems analysis. The ingredients of this analysis must include not only an increasing use of computer-based models for those problems where they are appropriate, but for treatment of the non-quantifiable aspects, a greater use of techniques for better employment of judgment, intuition, and experience. These techniques—operational gaming, "scenario" writing, and the systematic interrogation of experts—are on the way to becoming an integral part of systems analysis.

## CONCLUDING REMARKS

And now to review. A systems analysis is an analytic study designed to help a decision-maker identify a preferred choice among possible alternatives. It is characterized by a systematic and rational approach, with assumptions made explicit, objectives and criteria clearly defined, and alternative courses of action compared in the light of their possible consequences. An effort is made to use quantitative methods, but computers are not essential. What is essential is a model that enables expert intuition and judgment to be applied efficiently. The method provides its answer by processes that are accessible to critical examination, capable of duplication by others, and, more or less, readily modified as new information becomes available. And, in contrast to other aids to decision making, which share the same limitations, it extracts everything possible from scientific methods, and therefore its virtues are the virtues of those methods. At its narrowest, systems analysis has offered a way to choose the numerical quantities related to a weapon system so that they are logically consistent with each other, with an assumed objective, and with the calculator's expectation of the future. At its broadest, through providing the analytic backup for the plans, programs, and budgets of the various executive departments and establishments of the federal government, it can help guide national policy. But, even within the Department of Defense, its capabilities have yet to be fully exploited.

## NOTES

1. O. Helmer, *Social Technology*, P-3063 (The Rand Corporation, February, 1965); presented at the Futuribles Conference in Paris, April 1965.

2. For a further discussion of this distinction, see J. R. Schlesinger, "Quantitative Analysis and National Security," *World Politics* 15, no. 2 (January 1963): 295–315.

3. Or, alternatively, cost-utility and cost-benefit analysis.

4. C. J. Hitch in E. S. Quade (ed.), *Analysis for Military Decisions* (Chicago: Rand McNally, 1964), p. 23, states: "Systems analyses should be looked upon not as the antithesis of judgment but as a framework which permits the judgment of experts in numerous subfields to be utilized—to yield results which transcend any individual judgment. This is its aim and opportunity."

5. Olaf Helmer, op. cit., p. 7, puts it this way: "The advantage of employing a model lies in forcing the analyst to make explicit what elements of a situation he is taking into consideration and in imposing upon him the discipline of clarifying the concepts he is using. The model thus serves the important purpose of establishing unambiguous intersubjective communication about the subject matter at hand. Whatever intrinsic uncertainties may becloud the area of investigation, they are thus less likely to be further compounded by uncertainties due to disparate subjective interpretations."

6. See, for example, Donald M. Fort, *Systems Analysis as an Aid in Air Transportation Planning*, P-3293 (Santa Monica, Calif.: The Rand Corporation, January 1966), pp. 12–14.

7. O. Helmer and E. S. Quade, "An Approach to the Study of a Developing Economy by Operational Gaming," in *Recherche Operationnelle et Problemes du Tiers-Monde*, Colloquium organized by the French Society of Operational Research, with the participation of the Institute of Management Sciences, Operations Research Society of America (Paris: Dunod, 1964), pp. 43–54.

8. O. Helmer and Norman C. Dalkey, "An Experimental Application of the Delphi Method to the Use of Experts," *Management Sciences* 9, no. 3 (April 1963): 458–67; and O. Helmer and Nicholas Rescher, "On the Epistemology of the Inexact Sciences," *Management Sciences* 6, no. 1 (October 1959): 25–52.

9. Ibid.

10. H. Kahn and I. Mann, *Ten Common Pitfalls*, RM-1937 (Santa Monica, Calif.: The Rand Corporation, July 17, 1957).

11. James R. Schlesinger, op. cit., has a slightly different view: "Thus the mere uncovering of ways to increase efficiency is not sufficient. Even where a decision is clear to the disinterested observer, it is difficult to persuade committed men that their programs or activities should be reduced or abandoned. The price of enthusiasm is that those who have commitment will be 'sold' on their specialty and are incapable of viewing it in cold analytic terms. This may be especially true of the

military establishment, where the concepts of duty, honor, and country *when particularized* lead to a certain inflexibility in adjusting to technological change and the new claims of efficiency. But it is also true in the civilian world: for conservationists, foresters, water resource specialists, businessmen, union leaders, or agrarians, some aspects of their value-systems run directly counter to the claims of efficiency. The economic view strikes them all as immoral as well as misleading. (After all, is it not a value judgment on the part of economists that efficiency calculations are important?)

"Even in the case of fairly low-level decisions, if they are political, systematic quantitative analysis does not necessarily solve problems. It will not convince ardent supporters that their program is submarginal. Nevertheless, quantitative analysis remains most useful. For certain operational decisions, it either provides the decision-maker with the justification he may desire for cutting off a project or forces him to come up with a nonnumerical rationalization. It eliminates the purely subjective approach on the part of devotees of a program and forces them to change their lines of argument. They must talk about reality rather than morality. Operational research creates a bridge to budgetary problems over which planners, who previously could assume resources were free, are forced, willingly or unwillingly, to walk."

## REFERENCES

Dorfman, Robert (ed.), *Measuring Benefits of Government Investments* (Washington, D.C.: The Brookings Institution, 1965).

Ellis, J. W., Jr., and T. E. Greene, "The Contextual Study: A Structured Approach to the Study of Limited War," *Operations Research* 8, no. 5 (September-October 1960): 639-51.

Fisher, G. H., *The World of Program Budgeting,* P-3361 (Santa Monica, Calif.: The Rand Corporation, May 1966).

Hitch, C. J., and R. N. McKean, *The Economics of Defense in the Nuclear Age* (Cambridge, Mass.: Harvard University Press, 1960).

McKean, R. N., *Efficiency in Government Through Systems Analysis* (New York: Wiley, 1958).

Marshall, A. W., *Cost/Benefit Analysis in Health,* P-3274 (Santa Monica, Calif.: The Rand Corporation, December, 1965).

Mood, Alex M., "Diversification of Operations Research," *Operations Research* 13, no. 2 (March-April 1965): 169-78.

Novick, D. (ed.), *Program Budgeting: Program Analysis and the Federal Budget* (Washington, D.C.: Government Printing Office, 1965; Cambridge, Mass.: Harvard University Press, 1965).

Peck, M. J., and F. M. Scherer, *The Weapons Acquisition Process: An Economic Analysis* (Cambridge, Mass.: Harvard University Press, 1962).

# Managing
# Public
# Bureaucracy

◆

PUBLIC SECTOR MANAGERS FACE constraints not found in the private sector. Political executives tend to have short time horizons because they want results that can benefit them by the next election. Organizational response times, however, are long. To a degree, public sector managers find they lack information to manage effectively because impact measures are hard to develop in many kinds of government work. Generally, public accounting systems tend to be control-oriented rather than geared to provide information needed for management and planning. Even if management had the information it wanted, civil service rules would insulate many workers from the management pressures that can be used in the private sector to see that tasks are accomplished.[1]

Yet a case can be made that management in both the public and private sectors face many similar problems and might be able to use similar solutions. As Joseph L. Bower, an observer who emphasizes the differences between private and public management, has pointed out: "With enough time and persistence a public administrator can move structure and people to produce the ends he [or she] wishes. The organization then becomes as efficient a producer of a well-defined product as any private organization."[2] For examples, he pointed to J. Edgar Hoover of the F.B.I. and Robert Moses of the Triborough Bridge Authority and the New York State Park Commission,[3] and several others. The secret of success of these notorious or acclaimed—depending on your perspective—public managers was to gain enough power so they could control their agencies' structure, personnel, and access to funds without the intervention of elected political executives. Of course, this violates the basic premise of accountability in public bureaucracy. This notion of accountability to a larger public does affect the style of public managers, but one does not have to become a minor league dictator to improve upon typical public sector management.

One cannot talk about public administration without dealing with power. Earlier we dealt with Norton Long's observation that power had to be cultivated by public managers because the hierarchy did not supply enough power to allow these managers to get their assigned jobs done.[4] Public managerial power relationships center on constituents and legislative committees, as Eugene Lewis has pointed out because the agencies, the constituents, and the legislative committees are mutually dependent on one another.[5]

In recent years observers of private organizations have also discovered power,[6] and they see its need for the same reasons as did Long and Lewis. Managers in both the public and private sectors are dependent on others for their performance. John P. Kotter, who is concerned with power in private organizations, notes that dependency is inherent in managerial jobs:

> Because the work in organizations is divided into specialized divisions, departments and jobs, managers are made directly or indirectly dependent on many others for information, staff services, and cooperation in general. Because of their organizations' limited resources, managers are also dependent on their external environments for support. Without some minimal cooperation from suppliers, competitors, unions, regulatory agencies, and customers, managers cannot help their organizations survive and achieve their objectives.[7]

Perhaps management is more a generic process than public administrators have been willing to admit. Perhaps notions of power in the public sector differ only in degrees from power in the private sector.

Usually public administrators' concern for power focuses on power relations outside the agency, but these power relations may have implications for effective management within the agency. Using a private sector organization, Rosabeth Moss Kanter discusses the sources of managerial power and how some jobs inhibit the development of the power needed to carry out the tasks assigned to that job. Are her "three lines of power" relevant to the public sector? Do public sector jobs encourage the development of lines of power or inhibit that development? How would you define a powerful manager in the public sector? Are women and minority group individuals set up for failure in government? Does this notion of power and the job shed light on the failures of public management?

Peter F. Drucker, a highly influential consultant to private industries and the father of management by objectives (MBO) has paid an increasing amount of attention to public institutions in the last decade.[8] He sees many similarities between the public service institutions and private businesses and suggests ways in which the former can borrow techniques from the private sector to become more effective. The crux of his suggestions for public sector improvement rest with defining organizational objectives and using measures to indicate the degree to which those objectives are being met.[9]

While reading the Drucker selection, consider whether his public and private analogies are valid. Can you think of political factors that might upset his notions of an efficient public service organization? How does Drucker think public managers can get better results? What conditions are necessary for this to be achieved? How can public managers work to develop these conditions? How might these reforms relate to Kanter's notions of power?

## NOTES

1. Joseph L. Bower, "Effective Public Management," *Harvard Business Review* 55, no. 2 (March/April 1977): 137–40.

2. *Ibid.*, p. 138.

3. One of the best books on public administration describes the career of Robert Moses. See Robert A. Caro, *The Power Broker: Robert Moses and the Fall of New York* (New York: Alfred A. Knopf, Inc., 1974).

4. Norton Long, "Power and Administration," *Public Administration Review* 9 (Autumn 1949): 257–64.

5. Eugene Lewis, *American Politics in a Bureaucratic Age: Citizens, Constituents, Clients and Victims* (Cambridge, Mass.: Winthrop Publishers, Inc., 1977) and the selection reprinted *supra*.

6. David C. McClelland, *Power: The Inner Experience* (New York: Irvington Publishers, 1975); John P. Kotter, "Power, Dependence and Effective Management," *Harvard Business Review*, 55, no. 4 (July/August 1977): 125–36. For a guide to using power and manipulating people, see Michael Kordo, *Power! How to Get It. How to Use It* (New York: Random House, 1975).

7. Kotter, *op. cit.*, pp. 126–27.

8. See his "What Results Should You Expect? A User's Guide to MBO," *Public Administration Review* 36, no. 1 (January/February 1976): 12–19 and his "Managing the Public Service Institution," *The Public Interest*, no. 33 (Fall 1973): 43–59.

9. The Urban Institute has done some fine work in developing measures for a variety of public activities. See Harry P. Hatry, Louis H. Blair, Donald M. Fisk, John M. Greiner, John R. Hall, Jr., and Philip S. Schaenman, *How Effective Are Your Community Services* (Washington; D.C.: Urban Institute, 1977).

# 11

## Power Failure
## in Management
## Circuits

♦

*Rosabeth Moss Kanter*

POWER IS AMERICA'S LAST dirty word. It is easier to talk about money—and much easier to talk about sex—than it is talk about power. People who have it deny it; people who want it do not want to appear to hunger for it; and people who engage in its machinations do so secretly.

Yet, because it turns out to be a critical element in effective managerial behavior, power should come out from undercover. Having searched for years for those styles or skills that would identify capable organization leaders, many analysts, like myself, are rejecting individual traits or situational appropriateness as key and finding the sources of a leader's real power.

Access to resources and information and the ability to act quickly make it possible to accomplish more and to pass on more resources and information to subordinates. For this reason, people tend to prefer bosses with "clout." When employees perceive their manager as influential upward and outward, their status is enhanced by association and they generally have high morale and feel less critical or resistant to their boss.[1] More powerful leaders are also more likely to delegate (they are too busy to do it all themselves), to reward talent, and to build a team that places subordinates in significant positions.

Powerlessness, in contrast, tends to breed bossiness rather than true leadership. In large organizations, at least, it is powerlessness that often creates ineffective, desultory management and petty, dictatorial, rules-minded managerial styles. Accountability without power—responsibility for results without the resources to get them—creates frustration and failure. People who see themselves as weak and powerless and find their subordinates resisting or discounting them tend to use more punishing forms of influence. If organizational power can "ennoble," then, recent research shows, organizational powerlessness can (with apologies to Lord Acton) "corrupt."[2]

So perhaps power, in the organization at least, does not deserve such a bad reputation. Rather than connoting only dominance, control, and oppression, *power* can mean efficacy and capacity—something managers and executives need to move the organization toward its goals. Power in organizations is analogous in simple terms to physical power: it is the ability to mobilize resources (human and material) to get things done. The true sign of power, then, is accomplishment—not fear, terror, or tyranny. Where the power is "on," the system can be productive; where the power is "off," the system bogs down.

But saying that people need power to be effective in organizations does not tell us where it comes from or why some people, in some jobs, systematically seem to have more of it than others. In this article I want to show that to discover the sources of productive power, we have to look not at the *person*—as conventional classifications of effective managers and employees do—but at the *position* the person occupies in the organization.

## WHERE DOES POWER COME FROM?

The effectiveness that power brings evolves from two kinds of capacities: first, access to the resources, information, and support necessary to carry out a task; and second, ability to get cooperation in doing what is necessary. (Exhibit 1 identifies some symbols of an individual manager's power.)

Both capacities derive not so much from a leader's style and skill as from his or her location in the formal and informal systems of the organization—in both job definition and connection to other important people in the company. Even the ability to get cooperation from subordinates is strongly defined by the manager's clout outward. People are more responsive to bosses who look as if they can get more for them from the organization.

We can regard the uniquely organizational sources of power as consisting of three "lines":

1. *Lines of supply.* Influence outward, over the environment, means that managers have the capacity to bring in the things that their own

EXHIBIT 1. *Some common symbols of a manager's organizational power (influence upward and outward)*

To what extent a manager can—
Intercede favorably on behalf of someone in trouble with the organization
Get a desirable placement for a talented subordinate
Get approval for expenditures beyond the budget
Get above-average salary increases for subordinates
Get items on the agenda at policy meetings
Get fast access to top decision makers
Get regular, frequent access to top decision makers
Get early information about decisions and policy shifts

organizational domain needs—materials, money, resources to distribute as rewards, and perhaps even prestige.

2. *Lines of information.* To be effective, managers need to be "in the know" in both the formal and the informal sense.

3. *Lines of support.* In a formal framework, a manager's job parameters need to allow for nonordinary action, for a show of discretion or exercise of judgment. Thus, managers need to know that they can assume innovative, risk-taking activities without having to go through the stifling multilayered approval process. And, informally, managers need the backing of other important figures in the organization whose tacit approval becomes another resource they bring to their own work unit as well as a sign of the manager's being "in."

Note that productive power has to do with *connections* with other parts of a system. Such systemic aspects of power derive from two sources—job activities and political alliances:

1. Power is most easily accumulated when one has a job that is designed and located to allow *discretion* (nonroutinized action permitting flexible, adaptive, and creative contributions), *recognition* (visibility and notice), and *relevance* (being central to pressing organizational problems).

2. Power also comes when one has relatively close contact with *sponsors* (higher-level people who confer approval, prestige, or backing), *peer networks* (circles of acquaintanceship that provide reputation and information, the grapevine often being faster than formal communication channels), and *subordinates* (who can be developed to relieve managers of some of their burdens and to represent the manager's point of view).

When managers are in powerful situations, it is easier for them to accomplish more. Because the tools are there, they are likely to be highly motivated and, in turn, to be able to motivate subordinates. Their activities are more likely to be on target and to net them successes. They can flexibly interpret or shape policy to meet the needs of particular areas, emergent situations, or sudden environmental shifts. They gain the respect and cooperation that attributed power brings. Subordinates' talents are resources rather than threats. And because powerful managers have so many lines of connection and thus are oriented outward, they tend to let go of control downward, developing more independently functioning lieutenants.

The powerless live in a different world. Lacking the supplies, information, or support to make things happen easily, they may turn instead to the ultimate weapon of those who lack productive power—oppressive power: holding others back and punishing with whatever threats they can muster.

Exhibit II summarizes some of the major ways in which variables in the organization and in job design contribute to either power or powerlessness.

EXHIBIT 2. *Ways organizational factors contribute to power or powerlessness*

| Factors | Generates power *when factor is* | Generates powerlessness *when factor is* |
|---|---|---|
| Rules inherent in the job | Few | Many |
| Predecessors in the job | Few | Many |
| Established routines | Few | Many |
| Task variety | High | Low |
| Rewards for reliability/ predictability | Few | Many |
| Rewards for unusual performance/innovation | Many | Few |
| Flexibility around use of people | High | Low |
| Approvals needed for nonroutine decisions | Few | Many |
| Physical location | Central | Distant |
| Publicity about job activities | High | Low |
| Relation of tasks to current problem areas | Central | Peripheral |
| Focus of tasks | Outside work unit | Inside work unit |
| Interpersonal contact in the job | High | Low |
| Contact with senior officials | High | Low |
| Participation in programs, conferences, meetings | High | Low |
| Participation in problem-solving task forces | High | Low |
| Advancement prospects of subordinates | High | Low |

## POSITIONS OF POWERLESSNESS

Understanding what it takes to have power and recognizing the classic behavior of the powerless can immediately help managers make sense out of a number of familiar organizational problems that are usually attributed to inadequate people:

1. The ineffectiveness of first-line supervisors.

2. The petty interest protection and conservatism of staff professionals.

3. The crises of leadership at the top.

Instead of blaming the individuals involved in organizational problems, let us look at the positions people occupy. Of course, power or powerlessness in a position may not be all of the problem. Sometimes incapable people *are* at fault and need to be retrained or replaced. (See pages 219–221 for a discussion of another special case, women.) But where patterns emerge, where the troubles associated with some units persist, organizational power failures could be the reason. Then, as Volvo president Pehr Gyllenhammar concludes, we should treat the powerless not as "villains" causing headaches for everyone else but as "victims."[3]

### First-Line Supervisors

Because an employee's most important work relationship is with his or her supervisor, when many of them talk about "the company," they mean their immediate boss. Thus, a supervisor's behavior is an important determinant of the average employee's relationship to work and is in itself a critical link in the production chain.

Yet I know of no U.S. corporate management entirely satisfied with the performance of its supervisors. Most see them as supervising too closely and not training their people. In one manufacturing company where direct laborers were asked on a survey how they learned their job, on a list of seven possibilities "from my supervisor" ranked next to last. (Only company training programs ranked worse.) Also, it is said that supervisors do not translate company policies into practice—for instance, that they do not carry out the right of every employee to frequent performance reviews or to career counseling.

In court cases charging race or sex discrimination, first-line supervisors are frequently cited as the "discriminating official."[4] And, in studies of innovative work redesign and quality of work life projects, they often appear as the implied villains; they are the ones who are said to undermine the program or interfere with its effectiveness. In short, they are often seen as "not sufficiently managerial."

## WOMEN MANAGERS
### EXPERIENCE SPECIAL POWER FAILURES

The traditional problems of women in management are illustrative of how formal and informal practices can combine to engender powerlessness. Historically, women in management have found their opportunities in more routine, low-profile jobs. In staff positions, where they serve in support capacities to line managers but have no line responsibilities of their own, or in supervisory jobs managing "stuck" subordinates, they are not in a position either to take the kinds of risks that build credibility or to develop their own team by pushing bright subordinates.

Such jobs, which have few favors to trade, tend to keep women out of the mainstream of the organization. This lack of clout, coupled with the greater difficulty anyone who is "different" has in getting into the information and support networks, has meant that merely by organizational situation women in management have been more likely than men to be rendered structurally powerless. This is one reason those women who have achieved power have often had family connections that put them in the mainstream of the organization's social circles.

A disproportionate number of women managers are found among first-line supervisors or staff professionals; and they, like men in those circumstances, are likely to be organizationally powerless. But the behavior of other managers can contribute to the powerlessness of women in management in a number of less obvious ways.

One way other managers can make a woman powerless is by patronizingly overprotecting her: putting her in "a safe job," not giving her enough to do to prove herself, and not suggesting her for high-risk, visible assignments. This protectiveness is sometimes born of "good" intentions to give her every chance to succeed (why stack the deck against her?). Out of managerial concerns, out of awareness that a woman may be up against situations that men simply do not have to face, some very well-meaning managers protect their female managers ("It's a jungle, so why send her into it?").

Overprotectiveness can also mask a manager's fear of association with a woman should she fail. One senior bank official at a level below vice president told me about his concerns with respect to a high-performing, financially experienced woman reporting to him. Despite *his* overwhelmingly positive work experiences with her, he was still afraid to recommend her for other assignments because he felt it was a personal risk. "What if other managers are not as accepting of women as I am?" he asked. "I know I'd be sticking my neck out; they would take her more because of my endorsement than her qualifications. And what if she doesn't make it? My judgment will be on the line."

Overprotection is relatively benign compared with rendering a person powerless by providing obvious signs of lack of managerial support. For example, allowing someone supposedly in authority to be bypassed easily means that no one else has to take him or her seriously. If a woman's immediate supervisor or other managers listen willingly to criticism of her and show they are concerned every time a negative comment comes up and that they assume she must be at fault, then they are helping to undercut her. If managers let other people know that they have concerns about this person or that they are testing her to see how she does, then they are inviting other people to look for signs of inadequacy or failure.

Furthermore, people assume they can afford to bypass women because they "must be uninformed" or "don't know the ropes." Even though women may be respected for their competence or expertise, they are not necessarily seen as being informed beyond the technical requirements of the job. There may be a grain of historical truth in this. Many women come to senior management positions as "outsiders" rather than up through the usual channels.

Also, because until very recently men have not felt comfortable seeing women as businesspeople (business clubs have traditionally excluded women), they have tended to seek each other out for informal socializing. Anyone, male or female, seen as organizationally naive and lacking sources of "inside dope" will find his or her own lines of information limited.

Finally, even when women are able to achieve some power on their own, they have not necessarily been able to translate such personal credibility into an organizational power base. To create a network of supporters out of individual clout requires that a person pass on and share power, that subordinates and peers be empowered by virtue of their connection with that person. Traditionally, neither men nor women have seen women as capable of sponsoring others, even though they may be capable of achieving and succeeding on their own. Women have been viewed as the *recipients* of sponsorship rather than as the sponsors themselves.

(As more women prove themselves in organizations and think more self-consciously about bringing along young people, this situation may change. However, I still hear many more questions from women managers about how they can benefit from mentors, sponsors, or peer networks than about how they themselves can start to pass on favors and make use of their own resources to benefit others.)

Viewing managers in terms of power and powerlessness helps explain two familiar stereotypes about women and leadership in organizations: that no one wants a woman boss (although studies

*220*

show that anyone who has ever had a woman boss is likely to have had a positive experience), and that the reason no one wants a woman boss is that women are "too controlling, rules-minded, and petty."

The first stereotype simply makes clear that power is important to leadership. Underneath the preference for men is the assumption that, given the current distribution of people in organizational leadership positions, men are more likely than women to be in positions to achieve power and, therefore, to share their power with others. Similarly, the "bossy woman boss" stereotype is a perfect picture of powerlessness. All of those traits are just as characteristic of men who are powerless, but women are slightly more likely, because of circumstances I have mentioned, to find themselves powerless than are men. Women with power in the organization are just as effective—and preferred—as men.

Recent interviews conducted with about 600 bank managers show that when a woman exhibits the petty traits of powerlessness, people assume that she does so "because she is a woman." A striking difference is that when a man engages in the same behavior, people assume the behavior is a matter of his own individual style and characteristics and do not conclude that it reflects on the suitability of men for management.

---

The problem affects white-collar as well as blue-collar supervisors. In one large government agency, supervisors in field offices were seen as the source of problems concerning morale and the flow of information to and from headquarters. "Their attitudes are negative," said a senior official. "They turn people against the agency; they put down senior management. They build themselves up by always complaining about headquarters, but prevent their staff from getting any information directly. We can't afford to have such attitudes communicated to field staff."

Is the problem that supervisors need more management training programs or that incompetent people are invariably attracted to the job? Neither explanation suffices. A large part of the problem lies in the position itself—one that almost universally creates powerlessness.

First-line supervisors are "people in the middle," and that has been seen as the source of many of their problems.[5] But by recognizing that first-line supervisors are caught between higher management and workers, we only begin to skim the surface of the problem. There is practically no other organizational category as subject to powerlessness.

First, these supervisors may be at a virtual dead end in their careers. Even in companies where the job used to be a stepping stone to higher-level management jobs, it is now common practice to bring in MBAs from the outside for those positions. Thus, moving from the ranks of direct labor into supervision may mean, essentially, getting "stuck" rather than moving upward. Because employees do not perceive supervisors as eventually joining the leadership circles of the organization, they may see them as lacking the high-level contacts needed to have clout. Indeed, sometimes turnover among supervisors is so high that workers feel they can outwait—and outwit—any boss.

Second, although they lack clout, with little in the way of support from above, supervisors are forced to administer programs or explain policies that they have no hand in shaping. In one company, as part of a new personnel program supervisors were required to conduct counseling interviews with employees. But supervisors were not trained to do this and were given no incentives to get involved. Counseling was just another obligation. Then managers suddenly encouraged the workers to bypass their supervisors or to put pressure on them. The personnel staff brought them together and told them to demand such interviews as a basic right. If supervisors had not felt powerless before, they did after that squeeze from below, engineered from above.

The people they supervise can also make life hard for them in numerous ways. This often happens when a supervisor has himself or herself risen up from the ranks. Peers that have not made it are resentful or derisive of their former colleague, whom they now see as trying to lord it over them. Often it is easy for workers to break rules and let a lot of things slip.

Yet first-line supervisors are frequently judged according to rules and regulations while being limited by other regulations in what disciplinary actions they can take. They often lack the resources to influence or reward people; after all, workers are guaranteed their pay and benefits by someone other than their supervisors. Supervisors cannot easily control events; rather, they must react to them.

In one factory, for instance, supervisors complained that performance of their job was out of their control: they could fill production quotas only if they had the supplies, but they had no way to influence the people controlling supplies.

The lack of support for many first-line managers, particularly in large organizations, was made dramatically clear in another company. When asked if contact with executives higher in the organization who had the potential for offering support, information, and alliances diminished their own feelings of career vulnerability and the number of headaches they experienced on the job, supervisors in five out of seven work units responded positively. For them *contact* was indeed related to a greater feeling of acceptance at work and membership in the organization.

But in the two other work units where there was greater contact, people perceived more, not less, career vulnerability. Further investigation showed that supervisors in these business units got attention only when they were in trouble. Otherwise, no one bothered to talk to them. To these particular supervisors, hearing from a higher-level manager was a sign not of recognition or potential support but of danger.

It is not suprising, then, that supervisors frequently manifest symptoms of powerlessness: overly close supervision, rules-mindedness, and a tendency to do the job themselves rather than to train their people (since job skills may be one of the few remaining things they feel good about). Perhaps this is why they sometimes stand as roadblocks between their subordinates and the higher reaches of the company.

## Staff Professionals

Also working under conditions that can lead to organizational powerlessness are the staff specialists. As advisers behind the scenes, staff people must sell their programs and bargain for resources, but unless they get themselves entrenched in organizational power networks, they have little in the way of favors to exchange. They are seen as useful adjuncts to the primary tasks of the organization but inessential in a day-to-day operating sense. This disenfranchisement occurs particularly when staff jobs consist of easily routinized administrative functions which are out of the mainstream of the currently relevant areas and involve little innovative decision making.

Furthermore, in some organizations, unless they have had previous line experience, staff people tend to be limited in the number of jobs into which they can move. Specialists' ladders are often very short, and professionals are just as likely to get "stuck" in such jobs as people are in less prestigious clerical or factory positions.

Staff people, unlike those who are being groomed for important line positions, may be hired because of a special expertise or particular background. But management rarely pays any attention to developing them into more general organizational resources. Lacking growth prospects themselves and working alone or in very small teams, they are not in a position to develop others or pass on power to them. They miss out on an important way that power can be accumulated.

Sometimes staff specialists, such as house counsel or organization development people, find their work being farmed out to consultants. Management considers them fine for the routine work, but the minute the activities involve risk or something problematic, they bring in outside experts. This treatment says something not only about their expertise but also about the status of their function. Since the company can always hire talent on a temporary basis, it is unclear that the management really needs to have or considers important its own staff for these functions.

And, because staff professionals are often seen as adjuncts to primary tasks, their effectiveness and therefore their contribution to the organization are often hard to measure. Thus visibility and recognition, as well as risk taking and relevance, may be denied to people in staff jobs.

Staff people tend to act out their powerlessness by becoming turf-minded. They create islands within the organization. They set themselves up as the only ones who can control professional standards and judge their own work. They create sometimes false distinctions between themselves as experts (no one else could possibly do what they do) and lay people, and this continues to keep them out of the mainstream.

One form such distinctions take is a combination of disdain when line managers attempt to act in areas the professionals think are their preserve and of subtle refusal to support the managers' efforts. Or staff groups battle with each other for control of new "problem areas," with the result that no one really handles the issue at all. To cope with their essential powerlessness, staff groups may try to elevate their own status and draw boundaries between themselves and others.

When staff jobs are treated as final resting places for people who have reached their level of competence in the organization—a good shelf on which to dump managers who are too old to go anywhere but too young to retire—then staff groups can also become pockets of conservatism, resistant to change. Their own exclusion from the risk-taking action may make them resist *anyone's* innovative proposals. In the past, personnel departments, for example, have sometimes been the last in their organization to know about innovations in human resource development or to be interested in applying them.

## Top Executives

Despite the great resources and responsibilities concentrated at the top of an organization, leaders can be powerless for reasons that are not very different from those that affect staff and supervisors: lack of supplies, information, and support.

We have faith in leaders because of their ability to make things happen in the larger world, to create possibilities for everyone else, and to attract resources to the organization. These are their supplies. But influence outward—source of much credibility downward—can diminish as environments change, setting terms and conditions out of the control of the leaders. Regardless of top management's grand plans for the organization, the environment presses. At the very least, things going on outside the organization can deflect a leader's attention and drain energy. And, more detrimental, decisions made elsewhere can have severe consequences for the organization and affect top management's sense of power and thus its operating style inside.

In the go-go years of the mid-1960s, for example, nearly every corporation officer or university president could look—and therefore feel—successful. Visible success gave leaders a great deal of credibility inside the organization, which in turn gave them the power to put new things in motion.

In the past few years, the environment has been strikingly different and the capacity of many organization leaders to do anything about it has been severely limited. New "players" have flexed their power muscles: the Arab oil bloc, government regulators, and congressional investigating committees. And managing economic decline is quite different from managing growth. It is no accident that when top leaders personally feel out of control, the control function in corporations grows.

As powerlessness in lower levels of organizations can manifest itself in overly routinized jobs where performance measures are oriented to rules and absence of change, so it can at upper levels as well. Routine work often drives out nonroutine work. Accomplishment becomes a question of nailing down details. Short-term results provide immediate gratifications and satisfy stockholders or other constituencies with limited interests.

It takes a powerful leader to be willing to risk short-term deprivations in order to bring about desired long-term outcomes. Much as first-line supervisors are tempted to focus on daily adherence to rules, leaders are tempted to focus on short-term fluctuations and lose sight of long-term objectives. The dynamics of such a situation are self-reinforcing. The more the long-term goals go unattended, the more a leader feels powerless and the greater the scramble to prove that he or she is in control of daily events at least. The more he is involved in the organization as a short-term Mr. Fix-it, the more out of control of long-term objectives he is, and the more ultimately powerless he is likely to be.

Credibility for top executives often comes from doing the extraordinary: exercising discretion, creating, inventing, planning, and acting in nonroutine ways. But since routine problems look easier and more manageable, require less change and consent on the part of anyone else, and lend themselves to instant solutions that can make any leader look good temporarily, leaders may avoid the risky by taking over what their subordinates should be doing. Ultimately, a leader may succeed in getting all the trivial problems dumped on his or her desk. This can establish expectations even for leaders attempting more challenging tasks. When Warren Bennis was president of the University of Cincinnati, a professor called him when the heat was down in a classroom. In writing about this incident, Bennis commented, "I suppose he expected me to grab a wrench and fix it."[6]

People at the top need to insulate themselves from the routine operations of the organization in order to develop and exercise power. But this very insulation can lead to another source of powerlessness—lack of information. In one multinational corporation, top executives who are sealed off in a large, distant office, flattered and virtually babied by aides, are frustrated by their distance from the real action.[7]

At the top, the concern for secrecy and privacy is mixed with real loneliness. In one bank, organization members were so accustomed to never seeing the top leaders that when a new senior vice president went to the branch offices to look around, they had suspicion, even fear, about his intentions.

Thus leaders who are cut out of an organization's information networks understand neither what is really going on at lower levels nor that their own isolation may be having negative effects. All too often top executives design "beneficial" new employee programs or declare a new humanitarian policy (e.g., "Participatory management is now our style") only to find the policy ignored or mistrusted because it is perceived as coming from uncaring bosses.

The information gap has more serious consequences when executives are so insulated from the rest of the organization or from other decision makers that, as Nixon so dramatically did, they fail to see their own impending downfall. Such insulation is partly a matter of organizational position and, in some cases, of executive style.

For example, leaders may create closed inner circles consisting of "doppelgängers," people just like themselves, who are their principal sources of organizational information and tell them only what they want to know. The reasons for the distortions are varied: key aides want to relieve the leader of burdens, they think just like the leader, they want to protect their own positions of power, or the familiar "kill the messenger" syndrome makes people close to the top executives reluctant to be the bearers of bad news.

Finally, just as supervisors and lower-level managers need their supporters in order to be and feel powerful, so do top executives. But for them sponsorship may not be so much a matter of individual endorsement as an issue of support by larger sources of legitimacy in the society. For top executives the problem is not to fit in among peers; rather, the question is whether the public at large and other organization members perceive a common interest which they see the executives as promoting.

If, however, public sources of support are withdrawn and leaders are open to public attack or if inside constituencies fragment and employees see their interests better aligned with pressure groups than with organizational leadership, then powerlessness begins to set in.

When common purpose is lost, the system's own politics may reduce the capacity of those at the top to act. Just as managing decline seems to create a much more passive and reactive stance than managing growth, do does mediating among conflicting interests. When what is happening outside and inside their organizations is out of their control, many people at the top turn into decline managers and dispute mediators. Neither is a particularly empowering role.

Thus when top executives lose their own lines of supply, lines of information, and lines of support, they too suffer from a kind of powerlessness. The temptation for them is to pull in every shred of power they can and to decrease the power available to other people to act. Innovation loses out in favor of control. Limits rather than targets are set. Financial goals are met by reducing "overhead" (people) rather than by giving people the tools and discretion to increase their own productive capacity. Dictatorial statements come down from the top, spreading the mentality of powerlessness farther until the whole organization becomes sluggish and people concentrate on protecting what they have rather than on producing what they can.

When everyone is playing "king of the mountain," guarding his or her turf jealously, then king of the mountain becomes the only game in town.

## TO EXPAND POWER, SHARE IT

In no case am I saying that people in the three hierarchical levels described are always powerless, but they are susceptible to common conditions that can contribute to powerlessness. Exhibit 3 summarizes the most common symptoms of powerlessness for each level and some typical sources of that behavior.

I am also distinguishing the tremendous concentration of economic and political power in large corporations themselves from the powerlessness that can beset individuals even in the highest positions in such organizations. What grows with organizational position in hierarchical levels is not necessarily the power to accomplish—productive power—but the power to punish, to prevent, to sell off, to reduce, to fire, all without appropriate concern for consequences. It is that kind of power—oppressive power—that we often say corrupts.

The absence of ways to prevent individual and social harm causes the polity to feel it must surround people in power with constraints, regulations, and laws that limit the arbitrary use of their authority. But if oppressive power corrupts, then so does the absence of productive power. In large organizations, powerlessness can be a bigger problem than power.

David C. McClelland makes a similar distinction between oppressive and productive power:

"The negative . . . face of power is characterized by the dominance-submission mode: if I win, you lose. . . . It leads to simple and direct means of feeling powerful [such as being aggressive]. It does not often lead to effective social leadership for the reason that such a person tends to treat other people as pawns. People who feel they are pawns tend to be passive

EXHIBIT 3. *Common symptoms and sources of powerlessness for three key organizational positions*

| Position | Symptoms | Sources |
|---|---|---|
| First-line supervisors | Close, rules-minded supervision | Routine, rules-minded jobs with little control over lines of supply |
| | Tendency to do things oneself, blocking of subordinates' development and information | Limited lines of information |
| | Resistant, underproducing subordinates | Limited advancement or involvement prospects for one-self/subordinates |
| Staff professionals | Turf protection, information control | Routine tasks seen as peripheral to "real tasks" of line organization |
| | Retreat into professionalism | Blocked careers |
| | Conservative resistance to change | Easy replacement by outside experts |
| Top executives | Focus on internal cutting, short-term results, "punishing" | Uncontrollable lines of supply because of environmental changes |
| | Dictatorial top-down communications | Limited or blocked lines of information about lower levels of organization |
| | Retreat to comfort of like-minded lieutenants | Diminished lines of support because of challenges to legitimacy (e.g., from the public or special interest groups) |

and useless to the leader who gets his satisfaction from dominating them. Slaves are the most inefficient form of labor ever devised by man. If a leader wants to have far-reaching influence, he must make his followers feel powerful and able to accomplish things on their own. . . . Even the most dictatorial leader does not succeed if he has not instilled in at least some of his followers a sense of power and the strength to pursue the goals he has set."[8]

Organizational power can grow, in part, by being shared. We do not yet know enough about new organizational forms to say whether productive power is infinitely expandable or where we reach the point of diminishing returns. But we do know that sharing power is different from giving or throwing it away. Delegation does not mean abdication.

Some basic lessons could be translated from the field of economics to the realm of organizations and management. Capital investment in plants and equipment is not the only key to productivity. The productive capacity of nations, like organizations, grows if the skill base is upgraded. People with the tools, information, and support to make more informed decisions and act more quickly can often accomplish more. By empowering others, a leader does not decrease his power; instead he may increase it—especially if the whole organization performs better.

This analysis leads to some counterintuitive conclusions. In a certain tautological sense, the principal problem of the powerless is that they lack power. Powerless people are usually the last ones to whom anyone wants to entrust more power, for fear of its dissipation or abuse. But those people are precisely the ones who might benefit most from an injection of power and whose behavior is likely to change as new options open up to them.

Also, if the powerless bosses could be encouraged to share some of the power they do have, their power would grow. Yet, of course, only those leaders who feel secure about their own power outward—their lines of supply, information, and support—can see empowering subordinates as a gain rather than a loss. The two sides of power (getting it and giving it) are closely connected.

There are important lessons here for both subordinates and those who want to change organizations, whether executives or change agents. Instead of resisting or criticizing a powerless boss, which only increases the boss's feeling of powerlessness and need to control, subordinates instead might concentrate on helping the boss become more powerful. Managers might make pockets of ineffectiveness in the organization more productive not by training or replacing individuals but by structural solutions such as opening supply and support lines.

Similarly, organizational change agents who want a new program or policy to succeed should make sure that the change itself does not render any other level of the organization powerless. In making changes, it is wise to make sure that the key people in the level or two directly above and in neighboring functions are sufficiently involved, informed, and taken into account, so that the program can be used to build their own sense of power also. If such involvement is impossible, then it is better to move these people out of the territory altogether than to leave behind a group from whom some power has been removed and who might resist and undercut the program.

In part, of course, spreading power means educating people to this new definition of it. But words alone will not make the difference; managers will need the real experience of a new way of managing.

Here is how the associate director of a large corporate professional department phrased the lessons that he learned in the transition to a team-oriented, participatory, power-sharing management process:

"Get in the habit of involving your own managers in decision making and approvals. But don't abdicate! Tell them what you want and where you're coming from. Don't go for a one-boss grass roots 'democracy.' Make the management hierarchy work for you in participation. . . .

229

"Hang in there, baby, and don't give up. Try not to 'revert' just because everything seems to go sour on a particular day. Open up—talk to people and tell them how you feel. They'll want to get you back on track and will do things to make that happen—because they don't really want to go back to the way it was. . . . Subordinates will push you to 'act more like a boss,' but their interest is usually more in seeing someone else brought to heel than getting bossed themselves."

Naturally, people need to have power before they can learn to share it. Exhorting managers to change their leadership styles is rarely useful by itself. In one large plant of a major electronics company, first-line production supervisors were the source of numerous complaints from managers who saw them as major roadblocks to overall plant productivity and as insufficiently skilled supervisors. So the plant personnel staff undertook two pilot programs to increase the supervisors' effectiveness. The first program was based on a traditional competency and training model aimed at teaching the specific skills of successful supervisors. The second program, in contrast, was designed to empower the supervisors by directly affecting their flexibility, access to resources, connections with higher-level officials, and control over working conditions.

After an initial gathering of data from supervisors and their subordinates, the personnel staff held meetings where all the supervisors were given tools for developing action plans for sharing the data with their people and collaborating on solutions to perceived problems. But then, in a departure from common practice in this organization, task forces of supervisors were formed to develop new systems for handling job and career issues common to them and their people. These task forces were given budgets, consultants, representation on a plantwide project steering committee alongside managers at much higher levels, and wide latitude in defining the nature and scope of the changes they wished to make. In short, lines of supply, information, and support were opened to them.

As the task forces progressed in their activities, it became clear to the plant management that the hoped-for changes in supervisory effectiveness were taking place much more rapidly through these structural changes in power than through conventional management training; so the conventional training was dropped. Not only did the pilot groups design useful new procedures for the plant, astonishing senior management in several cases with their knowledge and capabilities, but also, significantly, they learned to manage their own people better.

Several groups decided to involve shop-floor workers in their task forces; they could now see from their own experience the benefits of involving subordinates in solving job-related problems. Other supervisors began to experiment with ways to implement "participatory management" by giving subordinates more control and influence without relinquishing their own authority.

Soon the "problem supervisors" in the "most troubled plant in the company" were getting the highest possible performance ratings and were considered models for direct production management. The sharing of organizational power from the top made possible the productive use of power below.

One might wonder why more organizations do not adopt such empowering strategies. There are standard answers: that giving up control is threatening to people who have fought for every shred of it; that people do not want to share power with those they look down on; that managers fear losing their own place and special privileges in the system; that "predictability" often rates higher than "flexibility" as an organizational value; and so forth.

But I would also put skepticism about employee abilities high on the list. Many modern bureaucratic systems are designed to minimize dependence on individual intelligence by making routine as many decisions as possible. So it often comes as a genuine surprise to top executives that people doing the more routine jobs could, indeed, make sophisticated decisions or use resources entrusted to them in intelligent ways.

In the same electronics company just mentioned, at the end of a quarter the pilot supervisory task forces were asked to report results and plans to senior management in order to have their new budget requests approved. The task forces made sure they were well prepared, and the high-level executives were duly impressed. In fact, they were so impressed that they kept interrupting the presentations with compliments, remarking that the supervisors could easily be doing sophisticated personnel work.

At first the supervisors were flattered. Such praise from upper management could only be taken well. But when the first glow wore off, several of them became very angry. They saw the excessive praise as patronizing and insulting. "Didn't they think we could think? Didn't they imagine we were capable of doing this kind of work?" one asked. "They must have seen us as just a bunch of animals. No wonder they gave us such limited jobs."

As far as these supervisors were concerned, their abilities had always been there, in latent form perhaps, but still there. They as individuals had not changed—just their organizational power.

### NOTES

1. Donald C. Pelz, "Influence: A Key to Effective Leadership in the First-Line Supervisor," *Personnel*, November 1952, p. 209.

2. See my book, *Men and Women of the Corporation* (New York: Basic Books, 1977), pp. 164–205; and David Kipnis, *The Powerholders* (Chicago: University of Chicago Press, 1976).

3. Pehr G. Gyllenhammar, *People at Work* (Reading, Mass.: Addison-Wesley, 1977), p. 133.

4. William E. Fulmer, "Supervisory Selection: The Acid Test of Affirmative Action," *Personnel*, November–December 1976, p. 40.

5. See my chapter (coauthor, Barry A. Stein), "Life in the Middle: Getting In, Getting Up, and Getting Along," in *Life in Organizations*, eds. Rosabeth M. Kanter and Barry A. Stein (New York: Basic Books, 1979).

6. Warren Bennis, *The Unconscious Conspiracy: Why Leaders Can't Lead* (New York: AMACOM, 1976).

7. See my chapter, "How the Top Is Different," in *Life in Organizations*.

8. David C. McClelland, *Power: The Inner Experience* (New York: Irvington Publishers, 1975), p. 263. Quoted by permission.

# 12

## The Deadly Sins
## in
## Public Administration

◆

*Peter F. Drucker*

I

NO ONE CAN GUARANTEE the performance of a public service program, but we know how to ensure non-performance with absolute certainty. Commit any two of the following common sins of public administration, and non-performance will inevitably follow. Indeed, to commit all six, as many public service agencies do, is quite unnecessary and an exercise in overkill.

(1) The first thing to do to make sure that a program will not have results is to have a lofty objective—"health care," for instance, or "to aid the disadvantaged." Such sentiments belong in the preamble. They explain why a specific program or agency is being initiated rather than what the program or agency is meant to accomplish.[1] To use such statements as "objectives" thus makes sure that no effective work will be done. For work is always specific, always mundane, always focused. Yet without work there is non-performance.

To have a chance at performance, a program needs clear targets, the attainment of which can be measured, appraised, or at least judged. "Health care" is not even a pious intention. Indeed it is, at best, a vague slogan. Even "the best medical care for the sick," the objective of many hospitals in the British National Health Service, is not operational. Rather, it is mean-

*Reprinted from the* Public Administration Review, *volume 40, no. 2 (March/April 1980), pp. 103–106.* © *1980 by The American Society for Public Administration, 1225 Connecticut Avenue, N.W., Washington, D.C. 20036. All rights reserved.*

ingful to say: "It is our aim to make sure that no patient coming into emergency will go for more than three minutes without being seen by a qualified triage nurse." It is a proper goal to say: "Within three years, our maternity ward is going to be run on a "zero defects" basis, which means that there will be no "surprises" in the delivery room and there will not be one case of post-partum puerperal fever on maternity." Similarly, "Promoting the welfare of the American farmer" is electioneering, while "Installing electricity in at least 25 per cent of America's farms within the next three years"—the first goal of the New Deal's Rural Electrification Administration, which was, perhaps, the most successful public service agency in all our administrative history—was an objective that was specific, measurable, attainable—and attained. It immediately was converted into work, and very shortly thereafter, into performance.

(2) The second strategy guaranteed to produce non-performance is to try to do several things at once. It is to refuse to establish priorities and to stick to them. Splintering of efforts guarantees non-results. Yet without concentration on a priority, efforts will be splintered, and the more massive the program, the more the splintering effects will product non-performance. By contrast, even poorly conceived programs might have results if priorities are set and efforts concentrated.

It is popular nowadays to blame the failure of so many of the programs of Lyndon Johnson's "War on Poverty" on shaky theoretical foundations. Whether poorly conceived or not, quite a few of the Headstart schools had significant results; every one of them, without exception, was a school that decided on one overriding priority—having the children learn to read letters and numbers—despite heavy criticism from Washington and from all kinds of dogmatists.

An even more impressive example is the Tennessee Valley Authority (TVA) in the thirties. Despite tremendous opposition, the bill establishing the TVA only passed Congress because its backers promised a dozen different and mutually antagonistic constituencies: cheap power, cheap fertilizer, flood control, irrigation, navigation, community development and whatnot. TVA's first administrator, Arthur Morgan, a great engineer, then attempted to live up to these promises and to satisfy every one of his constituencies. The only result was an uncontrollably growing bureaucracy, uncontrollably growing expenditures, and a total lack of any performance. Indeed, the TVA in its early years resembled nothing as much as one of those "messes" which we now attack in Washington. Then President Roosevelt removed Morgan and put in a totally unknown young Wisconsin utilities lawyer, David Lilienthal, who immediately—against all advice from all the "pros"—announced his priority: power production. Within a year, the TVA produced results. Lilienthal, by the way, met no opposition, but was universally acclaimed as a saviour.

(3) The third deadly sin of the public administrator is to believe that "fat is beautiful," despite the obvious fact that mass does not do work; brains and muscles do. In fact, overweight inhibits work, and gross overweight totally immobilizes.

One hears a great deal today about the fallacy of "throwing money at problems," but this is not really what we have been doing. We have been throwing manpower at problems, with Vietnam, perhaps, being the worst example, and it is even worse to overstaff than to overfund. Today's administrators, whether civilian or military, tend to believe that the best way to tackle a problem is to deploy more and more people against it. The one certain result of having more bodies is greater difficulties in logistics, in personnel management, and in communications. Mass increases weight, but not necessarily competence. Competence requires direction, decision, and strategy rather than manpower.

Overstaffing is not only much harder to correct than understaffing, it makes non-performance practically certain. For overstaffing always focuses energies on the inside, on "administration" rather than on "results," on the machinery rather than its purpose. It always leads to meetings and memoranda becoming ends in themselves. It immobilizes behind a facade of furious busyness. Harold Ickes, FDR's Secretary of the Interior and one of the New Deal's most accomplished administrators, always asked: "What is the fewest number of people we need to accomplish this purpose?" It is a long time since anyone in Washington (or in the state governments) has asked that question.

(4) "Don't experiment, be dogmatic" is the next—and the next most common—of the administrator's deadly sins. "Whatever you do, do it on a grand scale at the first try. Otherwise, God forbid, you might learn how to do it differently." In technical or product innovation, we sometimes skip the pilot-plant stage, usually to our sorrow. But at least we build a model and put it through wind tunnel tests. In public service, increasingly we start out with a "position"—that is, with a totally untested theory—and go from it immediately to national, if not international, application. The most blatant example may have been the ultra-scholastic dogmatism with which we rushed into national programs in the "War on Poverty" that were based on totally speculative, totally untried social science theories, and backed by not one shred of empirical evidence.

However, even if the theories on which a program is based are themselves sound, successful application still demands adaptation, cutting, fitting, trying, balancing. It always demands testing against reality before there is final total commitment. Above all, any new program, no matter how well conceived, will run into the unexpected, whether unexpected "problems" or unexpected "successes." At that point, people are needed who have been through a similar program on a smaller scale, who know whether the unexpected problem is relevant or not, or whether the unexpected success is a fluke or genuine achievement.

Surely one of the main reasons for the success of so many of the New Deal programs was that there had been "small scale" experiments in states and cities earlier—in Wisconsin, for instance, in New York State or in New York City, or in one of the reform administrations in Chicago. The outstanding administrators of the New Deal programs—Frances Perkins at Labor, Harole Ickes at Interior, or Arthur Altmeyer at Social Security—were all alumnae of such earlier small-scale experiments. Similarly, the truly unsuccessful New Deal programs, the WPA for instance, were, without exception, programs that had not first been developed in small-scale experimentation in state or local governments but were initiated as comprehensive, national panaceas.

(5) "Make sure that you cannot learn from experience" is the next prescription for non-performance in public administration. "Do not think through in advance what you expect; do not then feed back from results to expectations so as to find out not only what you can do well, but also to find out what your weaknesses, your limitations, and your blind spots are."

Every organization, like every individual, does certain things well. They are the things that "come easy to one's hand." Nevertheless, every organization, like every individual, is also prone to typical mistakes, has typical limitations, and has its own blind spots. Unless the organization shapes its own expectations to reflect the accuracy of results, it will not find out what it does well and, thus, not learn to apply its strengths. Moreover, it will not find out what it does poorly and will, thus, have no opportunity to improve or to compensate for its weaknesses or its blind spots. Typically, for instance, certain institutions expect results much too fast and throw in the towel much too soon. A good many of the "War on Poverty" agencies did just that. Also, there are many organizations which wait much too long before they face up to the fact that a program or a policy is unsuccessful—our Vietnam policies, both civilian and military, probably belong here. One can only learn by feedback, and we know that feedback from results always improves performance capacity and effectiveness. Without it, however, the weaknesses, the limitations, the blind spots increasingly dominate. Without learning from results through feedback, any organization, like any individual, must inevitably deteriorate in its capacity to perform. Yet, in most public service institutions such feedback functions are either non-existent or viewed with casual skepticism. If the results do not conform to expectations, they are all too frequently dismissed as irrelevant, as indications of the obtuseness of clients, as the reactionary obscurantism of the public, or, worst of all, as evidence of the need to "make another study." Most public service institutions, governmental ones as well as non-governmental ones, are budget-focused, but the budgets measure efforts rather than results. For performance, the budget needs to be paralleled with a statement of expected results—and with systematic feedback from results—on expenditures and on efforts. Otherwise, the agency will, almost immediately, channel more and more of its efforts toward non-results and will become the prisoner of its own limitations, its weaknesses, and its blind spots rather than the beneficiary of its own strengths.

(6) The last of the administrator's deadly sins is the most damning and the most common: the inability to abandon. It alone guarantees non-performance, and within a fairly short time.

Traditional political theory, the theory inherited from Aristotle, holds that the tasks of government are grounded in the nature of civil society and, thus, are immutable: defense, justice, law and order. However, very few of the tasks of modern public administration, whether governmental or non-governmental public service institutions, such as the hospital, the Red Cross, the university, or the Boy Scouts, are of that nature. Almost all of them are manmade rather than grounded in the basic essentials of society, and most of them are of very recent origin to boot. They all, therefore, share a common fate: they must become pointless at some juncture in time. They may become pointless because the need to which they address themselves no longer exists or is no longer urgent. They may become pointless because the old need appears in such a new guise as to make obsolete present design, shape, concerns and policies. The great environmental problem of 1910, for instance—and it was a very real danger—was the horrendous pollution by the horse, with its stench and its liquid and solid wastes, which threatened to bury the cities of that time. It we had been as environmentally conscious then as we are now, we would have saddled ourselves with agencies which only ten years later would have become totally pointless and yet, predictably, ten years later they would have redoubled their efforts, since they would have totally lost sight of their objectives. Moreover, a program may become pointless when it fails to produce results despite all efforts, as do our present American welfare programs. Finally—and most dangerous of all—a program becomes pointless when it achieves its objectives. That we have a "welfare mess" today is, in large measure, a result of our having maintained the welfare programs of the New Deal after they had achieved their objectives around 1940 or 1941. These programs were designed to tackle the problems caused by the temporary unemployment of experienced (and almost entirely white) male heads of families—no wonder that they then malperformed when applied to the totally different problems caused in large measure by the mass movement of black females into the cities 10 or 15 years later.

The basic assumption of public service institutions, governmental or non-governmental ones alike, is immortality. It is a foolish assumption. It dooms the organization and its programs to non-performance and non-results. The only rational assumption is that every public service program will sooner or later—and usually sooner—outlive its usefulness, at least insofar as its present form, its present objectives, and its present policies are concerned. A public service program that does not conduct itself in contemplation of its own mortality will very soon become incapable of performance. In its original guise it cannot produce results any longer; the objectives have either ceased to matter, have proven unobtainable, or have been attained. Indeed, the more successful a public service agency is, the sooner will it work itself out of the job; then it can only become an impediment to performance, if not an embarrassment.

The public service administrator who wants results and performance will, thus, have to build into his own organization an organized process for abandonment. He will have to learn to ask every few years: "If we did not do this already, would we now, knowing what we know now, go into this?" And if the answer is "no," he better not say "let's make another study" or "let's ask for a bigger budget." He better ask: "How can we get out of this?" or at least: "How can we stop pouring more effort, more resources, more people into this?"

## II

Avoidance of these six "deadly sins" does not, perhaps guarantee performance and results in the public service organization, but avoiding these six deadly sins is the prerequisite for performance and results. To be sure, there is nothing very recondite about these "do's and don'ts." They are simple, elementary, indeed, obvious. Yet, as everyone in public administration knows, most administrators commit most of these "sins" all the time and, indeed, all of them most of the time.

One reason is plain cowardice. It is "risky" to spell out attainable, concrete, measurable goals—or so the popular wisdom goes. It is also mundane, pedestrian and likely to "turn off" backers or donors. "The world's best medical care" is so much more "sexy" than "every emergency patient will be seen by a qualified triage nurse within three minutes." Furthermore, to set priorities seems even more dangerous—one risks the wrath of the people who do not really care for electric power or fertilizer, but want to protect the little snail darter or the spotted lousewort. Finally, of course, you do not "rank" in the bureaucracy unless you spend a billion dollars and employ an army of clerks—"fat is beautiful."

Perhaps so, but experience does not bear out the common wisdom. The public service administrators who face up to goal-setting, to ordered priorities, and to concentrating their resources (the public service administrators who are willing to ask: "What is the smallest number of people we need to attain our objectives?") may not always be popular, but they are respected, and they rarely have any trouble at all. They may not get as far in their political careers as the ones who put popularity above perform-ance, but, in the end, they are the ones we remember.

III

But perhaps even more important than cowardice as an explanation for the tendency of so much of public administration today to commit itself to policies that can only result in non-performance is the lack of concern with performance in public administration theory.

For a century from the Civil War to 1960 or so, the performance of public service institutions and programs was taken for granted in the United States. It could be taken for granted because earlier administrators somehow knew not to commit the "deadly sins" I have outlined here. As a result, the discipline of public administration—a peculiarly American discipline, by the way—saw no reason to concern itself with performance. It was not a problem. It focused instead on the political process, on how programs come into being. *Who Gets What, When, How?*, the title of Harold Lasswell's 1936 classic on politics, neatly sums up one specific focus of American public administration, with its challenge to traditional political theory. The other focus was procedural: "The orderly conduct of the business of government" an earlier generation called it. It was a necessary concern in an America that had little or no administrative tradi-tion and experience and was suddenly projected into very large public ser-vice programs, first in World War I, then in the New Deal, and finally in World War II. We needed work on all phases of what we now call "man-agement": personnel, budgeting, organization, and so on. But these are in-side concerns. Now we need hard, systematic work on making public ser-vice institutions perform.

As I noted, for a century, from the Civil War until 1960 or so, perform-ance of public service institutions was taken for granted. For the last 20 years, however, malperformance is increasingly being taken for granted. Great programs are still being proposed, are still being debated, and, in some instances, are even still being enacted, but few people expect them to produce results. All we really expect now, whether from a new Department of Education in Washington or from a reorganization of the state govern-ment by a new governor who preaches that "small is beautiful," is more ex-penditure, a bigger budget, and a more ineffectual bureaucracy.

The malperformance of public service institutions may well be a symp-tom only. The cause may be far more basic: a crisis in the very foundations

*239*

and assumptions on which rests that proudest achievement of the Modern Age, national administrative government.[2]

But surely the malperformance of the public service institution is in itself a contributing factor to the sickness of government, and a pretty big one. Avoiding the "deadly sins" of public administration may only give symptomatic relief for whatever ails modern government, but at least we know how to do it.

## NOTES

1. On this, see my article, "What Results Should You Expect? A User's Guide to MPO," *Public Administration Review*, Vol. 36, pp. 12–19.

2. I hope eventually to finish a book on this subject, tentatively entitled "Can Government Be Saved?," on which I have been working for ten years or more.